ECONOMY'S TENSION

ECONOMY'S TENSION

The Dialectics of Community and Market

Stephen Gudeman

Berghahn Books
New York • Oxford

Published in 2008 by

Berghahn Books

www.berghahnbooks.com

©2008, 2012 Stephen Gudeman
First paperback edition published in 2012

Library of Congress Cataloging-in-Publication Data

Gudeman, Stephen.
    Economy's tension : the dialectics of community and market / Stephen
Gudeman.
      p. cm.
    Includes bibliographical references.
    ISBN 978-1-84545-514-9 (hbk.)--ISBN 978-0-85745-788-2 (pbk.)
  1. Economic anthropology. 2. Economics—Sociological aspects. I. Title.

GN448.2.G84 2008
306.3—dc22

2008008212

British Library Cataloguing in Publication Data
A catalogue record for this book is available from the British Library

Printed in the United States on acid-free paper

ISBN: 978-0-85745-788-2 (paperback)   ISBN: 978-0-85745-799-8 (ebook)

✖ CONTENTS

ॐ ACKNOWLEDGEMENTS

In the course of writing this book I have been fortunate to receive comments and ideas from numerous colleagues including James Carrier, David Graeber, J-K Gibson Graham (Julie Graham and Katherine Gibson), Chris Hann, Arjo Klamer, Frederique Appfel-Marglin, David Ruccio, Will Milberg, Ivo Strecker, and Thomas Wallgren. Over the years, Keith Hart and I have sustained a conversation on economic anthropology, and he has been a supporter and helpful critic. I thank as well the Austrian economics group at George Mason University who provided me with many comments on an earlier version of Chapter 3. Stephen Marglin and I independently reached the idea of two forms of "epistemology," and I have been fortunate to learn his thoughts on economics. Portions of the book were presented at the Max Planck Institute for Social Anthropology in Haale, and I appreciate the support of Chris Hann and his colleagues. I am especially indebted to the Swedish Collegium for Advanced Study in the Social Sciences in Uppsala, where I began this work as a fellow in 2002–03. I thank its directors, Björn Wittrock, Barbro Klein, and Göran Therborn, and my helpful colleagues there, especially Patricia Springborg. During that academic year, Steffan Löfving organized a conference on my work at the University of Uppsala and published the results as a book (Löfving 2005). I am very grateful to him for his thoughts and support, and to the book's contributors, whose responses partly stimulated this volume.

A version of some material in Chapters 2 and 4 was published in 2005 as "Community and Economy: Economy's Base," in *Handbook of Economic Anthropology*, ed. James G. Carrier (Cheltenham: Edward Elgar, pp. 94–106). An earlier version of Chapter 3 appeared in 2006 as "Trade's Reason," Max Planck Institute for Social Anthropology Working Paper no. 81, Haale/Saale. ISSN 1615-4568.

❧ 1

MODELS, MUTUALITY, AND TRADE

Why are we obsessed with calculating our selections? Why must we always make the "best" choice to feel satisfied? For many of us, rational selection is like a grammar: we use it to form acceptable statements and actions, and we invoke it to persuade others. We even value the act of choosing itself. But why does calculative reason dominate the lives of many in market economies, especially in the United States? Is it part of our genetic inheritance? Are we naturally avaricious? Have profit-seeing producers drawn us into their way of life? If so, how do we explain their calculated cravings and understand cross-cultural differences in the prominence of profit making? In this essay, I argue that calculative reason develops and expands with competitive trade.

If this answer to a complex question seems brief, it had a long birth. My puzzlement about the salience of calculated choice began during my initial fieldwork in Panama, but I did not frame it as a puzzle until I left the country and undertook more field studies. In Panama I lived with my wife in a small village where the people were shifting from the subsistence farming of rice, maize, and beans to cash cropping sugar cane. I wanted to study this transition and began by sketching decision-trees that captured their flow of choices and by soliciting their subjective probabilities for the outcomes in order to understand their crop selections. I quickly found that my questions about rational choice did not resonate with them, nor did the concept explain the social and economic conditions in which they were living. I dropped that analysis to study their material life ethnographically as well as other aspects of the culture. But I was puzzled about the gap in our reasoning.

After this work, I realized that my puzzle about the prominence of calculated choice lies at the heart of a disagreement in economic anthropology, evokes a difference between anthropology and economics, and often separates the social sciences, if not the social sciences and the humanities. In anthropology, Bronislaw Malinowski's (1961 [1922]) early critique of the concept of "rational man" had a subterranean influence on subsequent generations of anthropologists. Were the Trobriand Islanders, whom he so carefully studied, self-interested choosers, or were they acting according to other modes of reason, such as reciprocity? Two of his students burned the candle at both ends. In the style of Malinowski, Raymond Firth provided innumerable contextual studies of the Pacific island of Tikopia, but with his early training in economics

Firth emphasized how the people chose to their advantage within constraints (1951, 1964, 1965 [1939]). Edmund Leach, in a famous study of politics in Highland Burma (1954), explicitly presumed that the actors were choosing and maximizing political rewards even as he presented a cultural, structural, and contextual analysis of their polity. The issue was most clearly revealed in the internal anthropological debate during the 1960s between the "formalists," who followed a neoclassical, deductive line that centers on the supposed universality of "economic man," and the "substantivists," who were developing an institutional and inductive perspective based on Karl Polanyi's work.[1] As for the difference between anthropology and economics, the question of calculated choice surfaced in the economist Frank Knight's quarrel with the anthropologist Melville Herskovits, who then rescinded his anthropological position, to the dismay of Karl Polanyi (Herskovits 1953 [1940] 507–531; Polanyi 1968:142).[2]

These controversies reflect a larger issue in the social sciences: whether to adopt an individualistic or a relational understanding of society, a debate that might be encapsulated as the difference between Adam Smith's *The Wealth of Nations* (1976 [1776]), and Emile Durkheim's *The Division of Labor in Society* (1933 [1893]) and *The Elementary Forms of Religious Life* (1995 [1912]). Leaving aside his earlier work *The Theory of Moral Sentiments* (1976 [1759]), Smith is often seen as the founder of modern economics and is famous for his pithy statement that places self-interest with its benefits at the center of markets:

> It is not from the benevolence of the butcher, the brewer, or the baker that we expect our dinner, but from their regard to their own interest. We address ourselves, not to their humanity but to their self-love, and never talk to them of our own necessities but of their advantages. (1976 [1776]: 18)

In contrast, Durkheim claimed that society is held together not only by a general division of labor but a sharing that he often labeled the "conscience collective." To Adam Smith he might have replied, "If interest relates men, it is never for more than some few moments" (1933:203) and added, "a contract … is possible only thanks to a regulation of the contract which is originally social " (1933:215). But influenced by Rousseau (Durkheim 1960), Durkheim struggled to explain the "origin" of this collective sense. From his earlier to his later work, Durkheim suggested that it arose as the social, moral, and demographic density of society increased. (In a strange twist, I shall return to Durkheim at the end of my story to suggest that he may provide hints for contemporary economists who try to explain the social context of innovations that lead to economic growth and profits.)

One hardly finds echoes of this explanatory struggle in *standard economics*. Some economists (such as Gary Becker) use the notion of calculative reason to fashion a general explanation of market and nonmarket behavior. Other economists depart from this view by arguing that rational choice is "bounded," that information is imperfect, or that human cognitive processes sometimes lead us astray. But in these cases, the idea of calculated selection provides the lodestone or foundation for the interpretations, as if it were the gold standard. I shall even locate the "New Institutional Economics" as a form of standard economics, because it draws on the idea of the rational chooser to help explain the development of social institutions. (This part of the argument will not sit well with many economists and some anthropologists who think the New Institutional Economics is the "path" of the future, because it draws on the ideas of "path dependence" and culture.)

My view concerning the prominence of calculated selection in many Western societies grew slowly and was marked by abrupt shifts. A few years after I tried to use rational choice theory and Monte Carlo simulations in Panama, I returned to the ethnography that I had collected about material life and drew on classical economics, post-Ricardian theory, and dependency theory to understand the economic change I had witnessed, especially since I became interested in whether the subsistence crop yielded a surplus that was extracted by the unrestrained expansion or cascading of the market crop (Gudeman 1976, 1978). With this more critical perspective, I became increasingly concerned about the unrestrained effects of market economies. Competitive markets do provide goods and services in unforeseen quantities, but through them we are altering other economic formations, amplifying income disparities at home and abroad, destroying the ambient, and adopting a form of reason that increasingly shapes our identities and relations to others.

During fieldwork I recorded the people's voices about their economy with its changes, but this ethnography did not mesh well with any standard economic theory—from classical, to neoclassical, to Keynesian, to rational choice—with which I had some acquaintance. So, I asked, what would a cultural or anthropological economics look like? This question led me to explore local models and metaphors of livelihood as reported in ethnographies and reflected in some Western constructions of economy (Gudeman 1986; Gudeman and Penn 1982). Because I found that the ethnographic descriptions were sketchy, I undertook more fieldwork in the Andean highlands of Colombia, which stretch from the extreme north to the south of the country. My collaborator and I discovered that the people employ a house model of economy: they use the image or metaphor of a house to arrange, talk about, and make sense of their subsistence practices. The highland folk do trade in markets but see themselves at the periphery of the larger economy (Gudeman and Rivera 1990).

After this second field study was completed, I realized that such an *oikos* or house form of economy is one example of a communal or mutual economy, which is found around the world, and I turned to developing a comparative view of this mode of economic life (Gudeman 2001). But I knew that it, too, was only one part of economic life for which a larger model was required. And, of course, my puzzlement about the varying prominence of calculative reason across economies remained. As I worked out the larger model, however, the solution to my long-time query emerged. Economy, I find, contains both a mutual and a market realm. These two value domains are dialectically connected: they often conflict and resist each other, and their relations shift over time. I call this model *the tension in economy*, and I try to show how calculative reason emerges through repetitive transactions between suppliers and buyers to become the central force in economy's dialectic.

My view draws on ethnography, anthropology, and a range of concepts from economics and other disciplines. I shall not review all the legacies on which I draw, but a series of writers from Aristotle to Marx, Weber, Veblen, Polanyi, and Braudel, as well as neoclassical, Austrian, and "marginal" economists plus a few philosophers, have influenced me. In the process of putting the model together, I have been continually surprised at the wide divergence of perspectives between most anthropologists and most economists, not necessarily to the credit of either. I am impressed by how little each side—within anthropology and between the disciplines—understands the other: anthropologists often speak without exactly understanding what economists are saying, and the same is true of economists who rarely integrate the findings of anthropology into their work. I think both sides are right and wrong, because I find a dialectic in material life, which the discursive differences reflect.

Economy is made up of a contradiction. We live in a double, conflicting world, which is economy's tension. Shot through with practices and ideologies, with competition and mutuality, with antagonism and community, economy encompasses more than most economists and everyday dogmas allow, and it is more complex than most anthropologists realize. My aim is to provide a model for realizing this complexity, for opening a conversation about other ways of conducting our material lives that will lead to less damaging results for ourselves and the environment, and for taking greater account of what we owe to the future as part of our inheritance from the past.

Everywhere people deploy the two coping strategies of producing for themselves and trading with others. In part, individuals live from the competitive trade of goods, services, and money that are separated or alienated from enduring relationships. People exchange with others to transform or substitute what they have for something else. I term this mode *impersonal trade* or *market*.[3] I use the word trade for anonymous, competitive interchanges in which market participants exchange or barter goods, labor, money, or ideas. The term covers the notion of middlemen as well as any market consumer or producer who exchanges one thing for another in competitive conditions. But people also live from goods and services that make, mediate, and maintain social relationships. Through *mutuality* or *community* things and services are secured and allocated, by means of continuing ties, such as taxation and redistribution; through cooperation in kinship groups, households, and other groupings; by bridewealth, indenture, and reciprocity; and by self-sufficient activities, such as agriculture, gardening, or keeping house.

Trade in which goods are parted from their holders and impersonally exchanged with others occurs in all historical and ethnographic situations, though varying in importance. It may be a function of curiosity and imagination about the unknown as one tries out the life-world of another, or it may express power over the material and social environs in the attempt to reduce uncertainty. Through the force of competition, the central value in this realm comes to be efficiency in exchange and consequently in production and consumption, where rational choice is exercised to be efficient. But people also keep what they produce and transfer it through mutual relationships. Such transfers, guided by heterogeneous values and lasting social connections, offer temporal certitude but can be violated or turn oppressive. Each mode has a spectrum of appearances, for communities and markets can be large or small, and cover a varying extent of material life. Economies are shifting combinations of the two, and individuals are pulled in both directions, which they modulate, hide, disguise, and veil in practices and discourse.

The Spread of Calculative Reason

We know the act of rational choice by many labels. Sometimes it is called "being efficient" or is implied when we ask, "What's the bottom line?" and evaluate "by the numbers." We also know this practice as "calculative" or "practical reason"(Sahlins 1976): anthropologists used to term the individual who acted by its dictates *homo economicus* or "economic man."[4] Almost a century ago, Max Weber (1978 [1956]: 85–86) labeled this reason "formal rationality," which he distinguished from "substantive rationality" that refers to a value commitment. In a subsequent generation, Max Horkheimer employed the telling phrase "instrumental reason." Recognizing its centrality, the passion with which we are committed to it, and the difficulty of escaping it, he observed that "[i]t is not only the business but the essential work of reason to find means for the goals one adopts at any given time.... And ... goals once achieved ... become means to some new goal" (Horkheimer 1994:vii). Today, the concept of rational choice in its many versions provides the foundation for standard theories in economics from the neoclassical to new institutionalist versions. The calculative approach is also found in a range of sociological theories from Coleman (1994) to Bourdieu (1990), and it is central in "formalist" economic anthropology. Whatever label is used, this mode of reason has a linear form in which means and ends are linked with the means selected for the ends, or the ends chosen in light of the means, usually according to a standard of maximization or optimization.

But let us turn briefly to calculative reason's appearance in our own (US) practices, especially since the dominance of practical rationality varies even in highly developed market economies. Consider our widespread use of ratios. As the word rationality suggests, calculative reason frequently involves ratio thinking, and ratios—often combined one within another within another—usually signal means-to-ends thinking. They bring together a temporal unfolding from means to outcome, and quantify their relation. The prime example is a profit calculation. A firm begins, let us say, with $100 worth of materials, and it manufactures and sells a product for $110. Its ratio return is 110/100, which we summarize as a 10 percent profit rate. If the firm breaks even, its return is 100/100 or 0 percent profit. If the company takes in $90 for its $100 in costs, it has a 90/100 return or a 10 percent loss. Consider a literacy rate. If a teacher begins with 100 illiterate students and after a specified period 80 students can read, the literacy rate is 80 percent and the illiteracy rate is 20 percent. Consider a baseball player who comes to bat 100 times and has 38 hits. His ratio return is 38/100, which in common parlance is a 380 batting average. In each case, we start with a means, such as times at bat, and observe the result, such as the number of baseball hits. We use the ratio to judge the outcome and consider the choices, such as the batter's swing or ability to assess pitches. The ratio summarizes efficacy, and is a price: the cost of obtaining 38 hits is 100 at bats, the cost of having 80 readers is teaching 100 pupils, the cost of securing $10 in profit is a $100 investment. But a ratio is selective: we do not use it to judge the morality of the business firm, the friendliness of the teacher, or the grace of the batter, unless we think these factors influence the outcome.

The use of ratios has a special place in economic talk. We compare national economies by gross domestic product per capita, rate of growth per annum, or output per labor hour. Some assess the flow of income and holdings of assets by different strata (or ratios) of the population. Marx, highlighting the place of the laborer, argued that the rate of exploitation (in simplified form, profit divided by wages) is a key figure in capitalism, because it reflects the class struggle between capitalists and workers. At the global level ratio calculations, such as GNP per capita and growth rates, are used to judge economic success and failure.[5] The International Monetary Fund "scrutinizes" its borrowers by the numbers, such as their rate of inflation, rate of loan repayment, government expenditure in relation to national income, currency exchange rate, and export to import balance. Whether these ratios, and the structural adjustment programs that promise to produce the right numbers (also known as "getting the incentives right"), have much to do with actual practices in a national economy or with development is problematic, as Stiglitz has observed (2002).

Within an economy, industrial firms measure not only their profit rate but their return on investment, and to achieve profits most companies carefully monitor their inventory turnover per quarter or per annum. These and similar calculations, such as dividend rate and cash flow per year, are made public so that investors (and some regulators) can judge a firm's progress and monetary value. Financial markets are keenly attuned to price/earnings ratios, although in times of "fuzzy" accounting they may turn to share price divided by sales as a proxy. Of course, the price/earnings ratio itself is composed of two ratios—price per share and earnings per share. In agriculture, farmers assess their crop return per land area, and by volume of seed, but landowners are interested in the rent they can secure per hectare in relation to its market price. For individuals, we compute relative worth by comparing their yearly income, the return each produces for a money wage, or the number of fee-paying students a professor has. In all these instances an outcome, such as a harvest or salary, is measured against a means, such as a volume of labor, to assess and guide decisions, and to reward people.

The use of ratios has spread far outside the market realm. Selection among public goods may be guided by cost/benefit ratios in which prices (which are ratios) are assigned to a yearly flow of benefits that are discounted to the present (at a specified rate of interest), and then ranged against initial and subsequent costs partly figured as "opportunities foregone." The lowest or most efficient ratio is chosen. For government budgets, we debate the proportion of income to be allocated to different expenditures. The allotment for national defense, health, welfare, or fundamental research is partly figured as a ratio of a nation's gross domestic product or overall expenditures, and as a ratio of other expenditures. All budgets, from nation to state, and from charitable organizations to home, consist of ratios, and budget decisions are usually justified in the language of rational choice as "trade-offs," even when competitive bidding does not guide the selection process.

We employ this mode of reason in our reflections on social conditions and commentaries on well-being, such as calculating infant mortality and incarceration rates, and judge drugs by their rate of cure. We assess how well students perform by their scores on standardized tests relative to a state or national average.[6] These ratios embody goals or ends (low infant mortality, high rate of cures), with the suggestion that the results could have been better if the means of reaching them had been different.

Calculative reason, with its mandate to be efficient, fills a person's day in many high market societies; choosing, often rhetorically justified by the notion of individual freedom, penetrates our lives. A visit to a US drugstore, supermarket, electronics mart, or clothing store becomes an exercise in uncertainty and anxiety. We *must* choose among an array of soaps, toothpastes, perfumes, and cold medicines. Which bread, cut of beef, or can of differently seasoned tomatoes should be selected? Which telephone company should be chosen, and should one have a cell, a cordless, or a corded telephone? At what time and day of the week should one place a call, in what area code, and for how long? We feel driven to select the "best" for ourselves. With all these choices and ratios, is it a wonder that we have an industry of decision-makers or technicians of the economy—including mathematical modelers, econometricians, market analysts, financial planners, accountants, and "friendly" bankers—among whom we must choose to make decisions for us? We even employ choosers to choose the choosers. My awareness of this cultural injunction to choose, measure, and spend time in the effort was heightened by a year in Sweden. Before then I would justify my resistance to selecting by recalling one or another market narrative, such as "satisficing" instead of maximizing; my rationality was "bounded." In doing so, however, I was employing a market story to explain my behavior. In Sweden the range of market choices in most stores was smaller and the psychological stress of trying to be rational was lower. I did not need to the compare the softness, smell, or foam level of shaving creams, though I was bewildered by the array of hard breads. I felt liberated from calculative reason. A Brazilian anthropologist has recorded his culture shock on arriving in the United States and finding that he had to choose among educational programs for his children, type of bank account, and brand of pain reliever. Americans, he concluded, "have to decide all the time" (Oliven 1998:53).

Calculative reason is not only a central component of market practices, everyday ideology, and public policy; it makes up the standard definition of neoclassical economics, according to which individuals choose rationally. (For an early exposition of this formal perspective, see Robbins 1935). By placing the rational actor in heliocentric position, and attaching appropriate definitions, conditions, and constraints, many neoclassical and new institutional economists are able to derive market behavior, discuss anomalies and features of institutions and business organizations, and address market imperfections.[7] Today, this powerful explanatory model is being extended to family practices, such as marriage and divorce, as well as personal habits and tastes. These uses of the discursive representation expand and recreate the "reality" from which it is drawn.[8]

We certainly do not lack justifications and explanations for the prominence of instrumental reason. Markets do produce a cornucopia of goods, and market economies outproduce other economic forms. Many economists also claim that competitive markets yield the most efficient distribution of resources possible in conditions of scarcity. To survive in these markets, individuals and firms must fit their means to their ends, or their ends to their means, so that over time practical reason becomes their invisible but guiding hand. Even if land, labor, and capital are scarce, humans possess another unlimited resource that allows them to make the best of any situation. Of course, choosing rationally takes time, which is scarce, but that only means that we must calculate the time we wish to spend on a decision and then the time we wish to spend deciding how much time to spend on making a decision. Some people legitimate the rational selection model by claiming that calculated choice, exercised by the most able who emerge in a competition, yields an accumulation of wealth, which through a "trickle down" effect increases the welfare of everyone. By this explanation, rational choice has survival value because efficient economies, through their better provision of nutrition, happier citizens, and greater armaments, as well as their realization of the liberal ideals of freedom and choice, win in the evolutionary competition for the fittest society. In this rhetorical world, assessing a choice as rational legitimates what by a different metric might be judged as selfish and uncooperative. But since Adam Smith we have learned to accept the paradox that the exercise of self-interest leads to material benefit for all. (Even if this language seems dominant today, other voices do interject that free markets seem to produce an unequal distribution of wealth, personal distance from others, and the stunted flowering of human abilities and emotional life.)

Long before the rise of modern economics, Aristotle contrasted activities done "for the sake of" something else with activities done "for their own sake." A practice undertaken for the sake of something else is a means to ends act, whereas actions done for their own sake, such as maintaining social relationships, are complete in themselves. They are a satisfaction that embraces diverse actions and values. These practices may be pleasurable, ethical, and moral as well as parental—or bad, immoral, and ugly: for example, kinship bonds enshrine what Meyer Fortes (1969) termed the "axiom of amity" or ties of mutuality. In practice, however, the two forms of action are dialectically related: each may absorb features of the other, even while they are different. For example, means to ends actions may come to be done for their own sake, whereas social relationships may become means for the accomplishment of something else. Weber captured this confounding of the two through his encompassing and shifting use of the word "rationality" to cover both. Even if he contrasted "formal" with "substantive" rationality, he well knew that formal rationality could become a personal calling or mode of substantive rationality.

Weber not only distinguished between the two modes of rationality but also observed that the calculative one had become prominent in capitalism. He linked its emergence to the rise of ascetic Protestantism and the development of the Protestant ethic among certain sects in Europe (1958 [1904–05]). Weber's thesis was a principal forerunner of cultural interpretations and the analysis of the role of religion and ideology in historical change. To be certain, he did not claim to explain the rise of capitalism by a change in religious beliefs; however, he did try to trace a link proceeding from religious ideology to everyday practice. But even if Weber's account of the rise and spread of the Protestant ethic and the spirit of capitalism helps to illuminate the incessant call to work in industrial societies and the reinvestment of profits in order to have success as a sign of election in the afterlife, he never explained how calculative or formal reason itself became the engine of markets and modern economics as well as a core practice in other social domains.

Weber's insight about the centrality of calculative reason in modern life was addressed by some of his contemporaries, such as Simmel, and subsequently by the Frankfurt School, Habermas, and others.[9] But today, as we celebrate the continuing expansion of choice and the possibility of new combinations in global markets, the reason for practical reason and its expanding influence is seldom addressed.[10]

Suppose that we reverse Weber's ideological argument and cast aside assumptions about inherent self-interest, endless wants, and survival value. What if calculative reason arises in practices? Could the emergence of ascetic Protestantism, as Weber portrayed it, have been a response to changing conditions and not their precursor? When the pathway to grace could no longer be bought or gained through good works, the revolutionary change was that religious position could now be known through practical success. A religious quality, or certainty of the afterlife, came to be known through material accumulation or a quantity. In contrast to Weber, Albert Hirschman (1977) suggested that a rise in trade and the market economy was presaged by a shift in written discourse from a focus on the passions to praising the interests. If passions, especially in the political domain, were seen as dangerous and uncontrollable, interests—pictured as reasoned calculation in the economic realm—were tame because commerce requires polished interaction. Impelled by "gentle" or "soft" commerce (*le doux commerce*), the trader was a peaceful, inoffensive, and calm person. Thus, Hirschman concluded that prior to Adam Smith the concept of self-interest had become a realistic, safe, and principal explanation of human action, and that the subsequent diffusion of capitalist forms "owed much to [a] ... desperate search for a way of *avoiding society's ruin*" (1977: 130).[11] In his argument, a shift in political ideology accounted for the emergence of the capitalist spirit. Hirschman's account, like Weber's, starts with ideology to explain everyday acceptance.[12]

One novelty of this essay lies in my counterargument that calculative reason develops and expands through competitive, impersonal trade. In contrast to Weber, I suggest that the rise of Protestantism did not help lead to the rationalization of material behavior; instead, it represented a profound rationalization of the religious domain itself. Was the Protestant ethic a local story or narrative we told ourselves about the economic world we were transforming? The use of practical reason begins not in religion (such as the Protestant ethic), the loosening of production from traditional constraints (with the transformation of guilds), the creation of a free labor force and marketable land (with the demise of feudalism), the rise of individualism (as a result of ideological and political revolutions), or the changing human relationship to nature (with the growth of science and technology, and the expansion of the forces of production), but in trade. Competitive or asocial trade induces means to ends figuring as a personal fulfillment.

By this argument, I seemingly agree with the neoclassical economists' assumption that rational choice is the centerpiece of market activity; however, neoclassical economics does not explain and account for its presupposition that rational choice is the core of all economic and social action. The discourse simply reproduces the market's apparent reality. One might say that the use of instrumental rationality, as their explanatory tool, is the "revealed preference" of neoclassical economists. As this essay unfolds, I shall argue that while the rational actor is developed through the market experience and representations of that experience, the neoclassical account is incomplete. Phrasing it in a different language, self-interested choice is universal in the market but not universal in itself, because competitive trade depends on local specifications from which it is abstracted.[13]

Some of the recent contributions in economics revolving about bounded rationality, experimental economics, imperfect information, and the new institutionalism seem to address this issue of incompleteness. For example, it may be shown that market actors satisfice rather than maximize, that they act with imperfect or asymmetric information, that markets perform at suboptimal levels ("X-efficiency"); rational choosers may be affected by how a choice is framed, by sunken costs, by risk aversion, by the salience of information that friends offer, by buyer or seller remorse, and by constraints on the ability to calculate.[14] Some observers suggest that the standard model is not robust (or is incomplete), which may be why economics has partially shifted to a more empirical inquiry with a focus on diverse topics, such as labor markets, industrial organization, and international economics, without trying to place them within a general theory.[15] Yet most of these models presume that the economic actor is means to ends oriented and strives (more or less) to maximize, even if failing to do so. My dialectical argument is different, because I emphasize that the trading experience nurtures calculative reason: competitive, anonymous trade yields homo economicus.

But if I diverge from a neoclassical analysis, I also part from a Marxist interpretation, for I do not argue that the exploitation and appropriation of labor, as well as the class struggle, define high market society. I also depart from a classical Marxist interpretation of alienation in which the laborer, through the sale of his exchange-value, is separated from his productive powers and the product of his activity, for it is not only the laborer who is objectified and turned into a "thing" or reified.[16] Trade objectifies all market participants who become separated from their mutual relationships, from goods and services that mediate and maintain social relations, and from other subjectivities. In Collingwood's succinct characterization of market trade, "each party is using the other as means to his own ends by permitting the other to use him in the same way" (1989:65). In less bleak language, Hayek (1948:96), citing Dr. Johnson, observes that, "competition is 'the action of endeavouring to gain what another endeavours to gain at the same time.'" This unraveling of sociality through trade, however, does not result in a once-and-for-all change as suggested by phrases such as "The Great Transformation" or the "disembedding" of markets (Polanyi 1944), because everywhere impersonal trade and sociality are found in uneasy conjunction. Polanyi did not envisage this unstable condition.

I understand rationality in a broad sense. It has plural meanings that include calculated selection as well as other forms of reason. Stephen Toulmin has argued that

> The Dream of a Rational Method, that of an Exact Language, and that of a Unified Science form a single project designed to purify the operations of the Human Reason by *desituating* them: that is, divorcing them from the compromising association of their cultural contexts. (Toulmin 2001:78)[17]

By reason we sometimes mean calculative rationality, but reason can refer to deduction, induction, or dialectical reckoning. We also use figurative reason, including metaphor and synecdoche, even to formulate material practices. Pragmatic practices, or trial-and-error action, might be counted as a combination of reasoned processes, while the ability to disconnect and join, to fragment and combine, is also a form of human rationality, as Locke and Diderot, among others, observed. In an echo of Diderot's (1751) article on "art" and Locke's (1975 [1690]:119, 163) description of "simple" and "complex ideas," Simmel referred to the "connections with which, separating and connecting, we descend beneath the phenomenal side" of facts (1997:233). These analytical and combinatorial capacities facilitate creativity and innovation, and build new connections between means and ends that are used in calculated selection. The pervasive but unrecognized use of these other forms of reason suggests that calculative reason does not completely describe economy.[18]

Another reasoned practice, as I learned in fieldwork, especially marks the limits of rational choice and the realm of market exchange: thrift. Saving or economizing frames a means-to-ends act; however, it is not focused on the difference between ends and means (profitability) or on the magnitude of the ends (productivity) but on the means with the objective of preserving them for another day or having a remainder. Thrift is a form of reason that centers on keeping things as a precaution. Parsimony marks the limits of calculated choice in exchange, because it means withholding from investments in production or expenditure in consumption. Such economizing is a key practice and narrative in communal modes of economy. If dominant in competitive exchange, rational choice encounters limits in times of thriftiness that preserve relationships, which is also why its expansion into the mutual realm "debases" it. Parsimony corresponds closely to what Keynes called the "precautionary motive" that is part of the preference for liquidity and a cause of downturns in the market realm (1964 [1936]:166ff.). In my view, a precautionary motive also is found in the mutual realm as a defense against uncertainty. As Keynes observed, "[i]n the absence of an organized market, liquidity-preference due to the precautionary-motive would be greatly increased" (1964 [1936]:170). From this perspective, his theory was designed to counteract the effects of parsimony in the market.

Finally, we use the word reason to justify and explain actions. We give our reasons and tell stories to persuade others and ourselves of our projects. For example, according to Weber, the Protestant ethic provides a reason for the use of calculative reason in material practices. (We might say that Weber presents a narrative about this narrative to convince us of the connection between religious ideology and practice.) Hirschman offers another story (both his and Enlightenment thinkers') that justifies the same action on different grounds. Similarly, in our narratives about the need for environmental restoration or development aid we may draw on persuasions other than efficiency, such as the value of redressing the past or protecting future generations. These narratives or rhetorical uses of reason present value commitments and exemplify what Weber meant by substantive rationality. Likewise, when we tell ourselves that our actions were justified because they were calculated, we invoke a substantive commitment to formal rationality, and when we disparage non-instrumental reason we adhere to the same value.

The Dialectics of Trade and Mutuality

The continued persistence of people making "economic" connections outside markets provides the critical edge for this study. If, in high market society, we exalt impersonal trade and extol rational choice, we also rely on mutuality. In ethnographic contexts as well, economic practices combine mutuality with trade. I do not advocate returning to small communities as in some of the ethnographic cases, or replacing market arrangements with large communities operating by different distribution rules as in centrally planned socialism. Drawing on ethnographic reports and examples from market societies, I argue that economy is built around the dialectical relation of two value realms, mutuality and trade, and contains a tension between two ways of making material life—for the self and for others. As Rabbi Hillel observed in the Mishnah, "If I am not for myself, then who will be for me? And if I am only for myself, then what am I?"

By the word "dialectical" I refer to concepts or tendencies that, as Georgescu-Roegen (1971) suggests, both oppose and overlap one another. A dialectically defined entity may refer to one concept or tendency, the other, or both; and it is unstable. The two value realms of mutuality and market are dialectically related in many ways. For example, in markets we value efficiency, but mutual relations embody many values, such as equity, equality, age, gender, position, and merit. The realms are not comparable, but each may subsume, veil, stand off from, or absorb features of the other, and the balance between them changes, which is the dialectics of political economy. For example, impersonal trade is framed by mutuality, as Rousseau (1913 [1762]) and Hayek (1948:111–118), among others, observed. Competitive trade takes place within an arena provided by the sociality of communication and continuing with formal rules or informal protocols about it: regular trade requires shared agreements, from peace pacts to written laws enforced by commissions.[19] But trade and calculative reason often rupture or mask the very conditions that enable them. Economists sometimes ask how anthropology can contribute to *their* models, but their question precludes the dialectic. I think anthropology has more to contribute to our understanding of economy than to prescriptions about how to increase the GNP, satisfy consumers, or improve the process of development.

I am offering a shifting language of economy. The model has three transaction domains: (1) mutual sharing through allotment and apportionment as well as reciprocity, (2) market commerce or the trade of things, services, and ideas, and (3) market finance or the trade of money.[20] Across these spheres, we express different values and identities, and combine them as well.[21] The three domains usually embody a hierarchy of economic domination. Anonymous trade is a product of a base of sociality or mutuality but contains a dynamic of expansion that confronts its conditions of existence. When trade cascades into the realm of mutuality, it debases this foundation and turns into the fundamentalism of the rational actor, which reaches its purest expression in the controlling financial sphere of economy. We live in an epoch of financial globalization, institutionally supported by the International

Monetary Fund, the World Trade Organization, the World Bank, and transnational corporations, but these governing institutions are incomplete parts of economy. They may increase financial and commercial wealth, but they also debase their terms of existence in the short and long run—the environment being a primary example today—and produce resistance to lowering all national trade barriers, as well as the rise of fundamentalism, nationalism, and local and transnational action groups that seek alternative modes of economy. The financial sphere also has been historically contested through limits on or suppression of interest rates, through local controls on what may be commoditized or transformed into private property, and through the assertion of the sharing sphere of economy. To bring this dialectic to public discussion so that full economic freedom may be exercised, I use a different language for talking about economic life so that many economies combining mutuality and market, from near autarky to communes, welfare states, and beyond, may flourish.

Models

In developing this view of economy, I have expanded some of my earlier ideas about local and universal models (Gudeman and Penn 1982; Gudeman 1986). Local models are contextual formulations.[22] Diverse and found on the ground in practices and narratives, they mobilize performance. Local models have no fixed form and are unfinished as ways of constituting action within an environment that exceeds their specifications. A universal model is self-contained, derivational in form, and apparently complete. It seems to be independent of all local conditions.[23]

A universal or derivational model expresses a particular way of organizing knowledge. It has become the dominant form of knowing for some economists (and a considerable number of anthropologists). But they cling to a questionable and dated epistemology, and most are unaware of the infection. Every disease needs a name, so let us identify this epistemological malady as the search for certainty, whose most resilient form is essentialism or foundationalism. In many cases, these practitioners adopt an older "science" view of the nonhuman world. Nature consists of separate levels to be analyzed by an appropriate discipline. The layers compose a hierarchy of knowledge, such as physics, chemistry, biology, and their subdivisions. This Comtean image is projected on society, which is also seen to consist of separate self-organizing levels, such as the "individual" and "institutions," or the "symbolic" and the "material." Sometimes the levels are considered to be independent, but usually they are said to be "causally" connected. Ontological angst is banished by positing an independent bottom level (such as

the self-interested individual) from which the remaining "facts," "variables," or institutions of social life can be derived. But there are many
variations of this layer cake view. Talcott Parsons famously divided the
social world into four functions (or cells) and institutional orders, such
as behavioral organism, personality, society, and culture (Parsons 1966,
Parsons and Smelser 1956).[24] Each cell contained four more levels, and
then more in a descending and increasingly specialized order. Parsons
claimed that the different levels of society were functionally related
through input/output connections. One contemporary version presents
society and economy as consisting of discrete sectors with continuous
feedback among them (Ruttan 2003).[25] North (2005) offers a more
causal view of the relation between levels in his version of the New Institutional Economics. In these models, an epistemology becomes an
ontology.

A derivational model is both essentialist and foundationalist. In it,
some knowledge is considered to be non-inferential or self-contained;
requiring no further justification, this knowledge provides the foundation for the remainder. With its levels, the universal model has rules of
formation or derivation such as causality and deduction. (Induction
may be used to establish the premises.) Each level of economy or society is tied to the final one (foundationalism) that is self-organized or
self-sufficient (essentialism). Euclidean geometry, with its axioms and
derivations, offers a mathematical example of the consistency that makes
universal models persuasive. Coherent, consistent and replicable, it has
a bounded structure.

In economics, David Ricardo offered an early derivational model. In
his 1815 *Essay* (1951 [1815]), which was written to convince Parliament
to lift the Corn Laws, Ricardo tried to show how the laws prohibiting
entry of foreign grains benefited landowners by providing them with
increased rents, while costing the industrialists who received decreased profits due to the higher rents. His argument was derivational:
as cultivated land expanded to poorer soil, rents on better land—being
differentially determined by the last or marginal piece—rose, whereas
profits on each of these plots (being inversely related to rent) fell. The
independent or foundational variable for this derivation was land fertility, which determined rent and hence the rate of profit and the growth
of capital. Two years after, in his *Principles* (1951 [1817]), Ricardo replaced land with labor at the foundation. Only toward the end of the
nineteenth century was a more complete marginalist analysis applied
to land, labor, and capital all as scarce means; the marginalist approach
calculates the relation between the last means added to a process and
the last end received to derive a point of equilibrium where the cost of
the last input equals the revenue of the last output.[26]

Today, in most economic models, means to ends calculation provides the non-inferential basis or foundation. Making up the subjectiv-

ity of homo economicus and running through the derived domains of production, trade, and consumption, calculative reason makes and unites economy through the image of the efficient allocation of resources. For example, given the presence of homo economicus, a market is said to clear when supply equals demand. At the micro-level, partial equilibrium or stasis is achieved—nothing is left over. At the macro-level, with use of the Walrasian auctioneer, general equilibrium is attained when all markets have adjusted to one another. In conditions of equilibrium the model is complete. Rational choice theory, with its reliance on instrumental calculation, represents a refined development of a derivational model; and in the New Institutional Economics rational choice provides the foundation from which associations, rules, norms, and social relationships are derived. But as Hayek observed, "competition is by its nature a dynamic process whose essential characteristics are assumed away by the assumptions underlying static analysis" (Hayek 1948:94). This same epistemology of nomothetic-deductive reasoning is found in global financial policy. The "Washington Consensus," which guides the actions of the International Monetary Fund, the World Trade Organization, and the World Bank (to a degree), seems to be a collection of regulations that shifts over time. These norms, which include financial and commercial liberalization of trade, privatization, fiscal discipline, and exchange rate stability, broadly derive from the assumption of calculative reason, even if the steps from foundation to policy are not explicitly set forth. Despite local resistance, this model remains intensely persuasive at these institutions.[27]

Derivational models are thought to be general and objective, however the modeler situates them. For example, Marx offered a finely honed (and layered) model of capitalism that circles around the expenditure of labor: some might argue that it is positioned from the perspective of an industrial laborer for whom a revolution was justified (Gregory 2002). Physiocracy was a school of modelers, with somewhat divergent visions, who focused on the land. The Physiocrats offered a layered view of economy through their understanding that natural law, given by God, set the productive returns that accrued to landowners and should determine moral law, which framed the political order. Their model was positioned from the landowners' standpoint in pre-Revolutionary France. Neoclassical economists are positioned by their focus on choice in competitive exchanges, which is a trader's perspective. These standpoints have moral implications even if presented as objective, "God's eye" or universal views.

Local models are worlds apart. Contingent and mixed constructions, they constitute a world of relationships, objects and beings, or ways of coping with radical uncertainty. They are unfinished as ways of knowing and experiencing the world, and do not exhaust the potentiality for reinterpretation, invention, and aspirations, even as they make a necessary life world. Local models have no given structure and incorporate many forms of reason, such as similarity, analogy, contrast, identity, metaphor, and synecdoche, plus critical, dialectical, causal, and reflexive reason, as well as means-to-ends calculation. Local models are heterogeneous: malleable and without limits, in the sense of being bounded by rules of inclusion, local models are a creative mix of voices, tropes, images, and ways of doing. For example, the layered Physiocratic model combines metaphors of the human to build a picture of the functioning economy (Gudeman 1986). The Physiocrats overlapped three body metaphors—circulation, reproduction, and mind—to construct their model. The image of circulation was drawn from the blood, that of reproduction from the female body, and that of mind from Locke, according to whom external sensation precedes internal operations. The point of overlap was the land, which was considered to be uniquely productive because it was reproductive, supported the circulatory system of agricultural products, and was external to the social world (Gudeman 1986). In this respect, Physiocracy was a local model. But the Physiocrats also asserted that humans as natural beings had three material needs: to subsist, to preserve themselves, and to continue (Turgot 1898 [1770]:7; Mirabeau and Quesnay1973 [1763]:106). Material subsistence, obtained through a self-sustaining cycle that was exemplified by Quesnay's *Tableau Économique* (1972 [1758–59]), was supported by the land, which provided the foundation for their model. In *Rural Philosophy*, for example, Mirabeau and Quesnay (1973 [1763]:104–105) proclaimed:

> We must consider the common weal in terms of its essence, and humanity as a whole in terms of its root, *subsistence*. All the moral and physical parts of which society is constituted derive from this and are subordinate to it. It is upon subsistence, upon the means of subsistence, that all the branches of the political order depend. Religion, in a sense, is purely and simply spiritual, but natural law inspires us and also tells us about duties relative to our needs; the civil laws, which originally are nothing more than rules for the allocation of subsistence; virtues and vices, which are only obedience to or revolt against natural or civil law; agriculture, trade, industry – all are subordinate to the means of subsistence. This is the fundamental force.

The Physiocratic model was formed through the use of overlapping metaphors but also brought into play the notion of a self-sustaining essence, which provided the foundation for the model that had levels and derivations running from a material base to civil law, the polity, and religion.

Ethnographically, I have found local models presented in discourse, myths, and rituals. Consisting of practices and narratives, they may be sketched in the earth, written, or verbal as in the case of the rural Colombian house model that drew on local experience. I once employed a "dependency" model of economy to help illuminate ethnography from Panama, partly because that model was originally forged in the context of Latin American conditions; it uses a mélange of images, such as "poles" and "peripheries," as well as "dependency" (Gudeman 1978). Like universal models, local models are positioned, but the same people may deploy several in a context, and if they have diverse justifications or local claims to legitimacy—expressed through narratives— that range from invoking the gods or God to the ancestors and nature, their construction is a transcendent necessity.

But what is the relation between derivational and local models? Is one superior to the other, as logic supposedly stands to narrative, or prose to poetry? Is each appropriate for different contexts, or are they equal and opposite? In my view, universal models are abstractions, because they constitute relations and entities removed from any local specifications, which must be deduced from them. For example, in discourse the universal modeler abstracts levels (such as individuals and institutions), posits a self-contained foundation (such as the rational chooser), derives the levels (such as prices, institutions, or a theorem), and re-presents the result as a totality: poof, the economy is created. This culturally familiar way of arranging knowledge is persuasive; however, it creates knowledge boundaries, closes out the possibility of other experiences, and makes local models disappear. Derivational models create a breach between the actions they describe and other economic practices. They also are incomplete, because they require locally specified conditions and mutuality as their transcendent conditions of existence.

Even if the borders of a universal model and a market look firm, *cascading* continuously expands them. Cascading occurs when market participants, through the search for profit, extend their reach to non-commoditized things and services, such as forest preserves and domestic work, as anthropologists and feminist economists have observed. When markets expand, local constructions of economy are fragmented as calculated relationships replace mutuality. In discourse as well, universal modelers try to create a seamless economic totality by cascading the limits of their model. For example, *exogenous* variables not included in the model are separated from *endogenous* ones that are: social events, such as unpredicted innovations that drive change, may be excluded from the model. As one illustration, in his elegant theory of growth as an endogenous process, Solow assumes "that there is an erratic stream of innovations, each of which, when it occurs, permits a major increase in productivity.... these can be treated as exogenous" (Solow 1997:21). In market terms, exogenous variables do not respond to market incentives, whereas endogenous variables do react to market incentives.

Similarly, *externalities* are separated from *internalities*. Externalities are effects of market acts that fall outside market exchange and the calculations of profit and loss: they are not traded, as in the uncontrolled dumping of garbage in the oceans. Internalities are transacted. But events and acts categorized as externalities or as exogenous variables do not make up a local model, because they are constituted as unexplained remainders in relation to an abstracted, derivational model rather than as parts of local constructions. To encompass these leftovers, universal modelers often extend or cascade the borders of their model. For example, Solow "would invite any do-it-yourself endogenizer to add links in the other direction from the economic environment to the rate of innovation" in order to fill out his endogenous explanation (1997:21). (In the event, economists such as Lucas [2002] have tried to do so.) Likewise, as we shall see, externalities may be commensurated and commoditized to encompass a larger range of behaviors. In the process, universal modelers hide, silence, invade, or derive local models in order to be complete in discourse and to realize their formulation on the ground. I call this process *debasement*, because it converts shared benefits and social relationships to market transactions.

The concept and "reality" of the rational actor, which posits the individual as an autonomous unit who makes and orders preferences, and chooses independently of others, is an abstraction from human qualities and social relationships. As this presentation of human action is increasingly enacted and enforced through market activity, it subsumes cultural relations and often mystifies them as if they were calculated selections. For example, reciprocity and gifting may be interpreted as aggrandizement, or mutual ties may be used to cloak calculative reason. This appropriation of mutuality for instrumental purposes occurs in formal models and in practice when corporations—as one example—represent themselves as solidary groups (a family) yet lay off workers when the market environment demands. In such cases the more powerful appropriates the features of the less powerful as it dresses itself in the latter's clothes to claim legitimacy. Veblen (1914) termed this sort of appropriation "derangement," but we can also view it as a dialectical relation by which the qualities of one thing or category are mystified as those of another for material and control purposes.[28]

The dialectic of the two realms manifests itself as well in our dominant notions of freedom. Isaiah Berlin (1969) describes them as "positive" and "negative" freedom, while Amartya Sen (2002) labels them "opportunity" and "procedural" freedom. Broadly, positive or opportunity freedom refers to the individual who selects as he wishes; negative or procedural freedom, which has multiple sides, sets the space for this personal choice. If Berlin would emphasize the importance of negative freedom, Sen principally favors a commitment to opportunity freedom. I argue for a more dialectical view, because mutuality sets the negative arena within which positive freedom is exercised and on which it depends. In public discourse, however, we reduce freedom to the individual form as an expansive metaphor of market choice and we elide the need to frame it. By silencing the communal realm and the value of procedural freedom, we have reached the point where making a choice or exercising positive freedom has become a subjective compulsion or cultural necessity, which I equate to Weber's "Iron Cage" (1958 [1904–05]:181).

But now we must reassess the labels of the two models. A derivational model is actually a "local," historically situated way of arranging things or epistemology that is legitimated by stories about its universal presence and completeness. Conversely, local models are unfinished because they can never fully describe the plenum within which we live, but they are "universal" or transcendent in the sense of being necessary for experience. Even if the market dynamic, with its reverberations, cascading, and habit-forming practice, is powerful, it requires the communality that it would also contradict.

Languages

In this essay, I offer the reader a cross-cultural model of economy, an explanation for the rise of calculative reason, a way of integrating anthropology and economics, a new view about fetishism, and a theory of money. For anthropologists, I show the relevance and the limitations of standard economics. For economists, I tell what anthropology has to offer in understanding things economic. For interested parties, I provide some approaches for coping with the glaring discrepancies of income and wealth that we witness today between and within nations. To present this model, I use a different language for talking about economy. Some of the terms will be familiar to economists, others will be known to anthropologists, and some expressions I use in a new way. In Table 1, I offer a brief listing of some thematic expressions that are explained more fully in the essay; and in Table 2, I outline some of the processes with which I shall be concerned.

The Argument

I began this essay with a puzzle and a concern about the prominence of means-to-ends calculation in high market economies. The question exploded into a larger one about the meaning of economy, for one part of ours has become fragmented through the dominance of calculative reason and is hidden from view by everyday and formal discourse. Ethnography illuminates this other world that is part of us. In the remainder of this volume, I shall develop what I mean by mutuality and competitive trade, and show how their dialectical relation is revealed in standard accounts of property, modes of exchange, three spheres of

---

Table 1 | *Dialectics in Economy*

Mutual Realm—consists of heterogeneous values.	**Market Realm**—a competitive arena directed by the value of efficiency.
Base—consists of shared material and nonmaterial interests and values that mediate relationships.	**Capital**—includes financial capital and commercial capital (commodities) that is alienable.
Allocation—allotting and apportioning of the base through mutual relationships.	**Distribution**—the resources that actors bring to markets. **Allocation**—goods and services exchanged through market processes.
Reciprocity in the mutual realm—the unmeasured give-and-take over time of base.	**Reciprocity in the market realm**—the measured exchange of this for that.
Conjoint Person—identity achieved through relationships with others.	**Disjoint Person**—the self-contained or possessive individual.
Many Modes of Reason—include figurative, such as metaphor, metonym, and synecdoche, as well as calculative.	**Calculative Reason**—means-to-ends acts that minimize the means or maximize the ends.
Risk and Uncertainty—not sharply distinguished in the mutual domain but managed through social relationships.	**Risk**—random outcomes with knowable probabilities. **Uncertainty**—outcomes that cannot be quantified for lack of knowledge or information.
Local Models—incomplete, no borders, heterogeneous, constructed through various modes of reason.	**Universal Models**—complete or bounded with a foundation and levels linked by derivations.
	Endogenous Variables—fall within a model. **Exogenous Variables**—not in the model but may affect it. **Externalities**—the effects of market actions on nonmarket entities.

value, money forms, and today's problematic issues. With its effects on markets, the environment, and mutuality, we experience the growth of calculative reason and economy's tension as a subjective conflict of values that creates divided identities and alienation in economy. The argument is developed in the following chapters.

Chapter 2, Exchange as Mutuality, focuses on the communal domain of economy, describes different forms of base and its modes of allocation, which include allotment, apportionment, and reciprocity, presents

Table 2 ǀ *Economic Processes*

Prices or Exchange Rates—equilibrium in exchange established through the competitive bidding of buyers and sellers, as modeled in standard economics.

Fetishism of Prices—the abstraction of prices from things, services, and relationships.

Price Reverberations—the sequential effects of one price change on another.

Price Cascading—the expansive effect of market trades on realms outside the market.

Discourse Cascading—the colonization of local models by a universal model.

Debasement—the effect of cascading on the mutual realm.

Mystification—the presentation or dressing up of one value realm as if it were the other; one form of cascading.

Uncertainty—(1) lack of known probabilities due to faulty knowledge, (2) lack of ever knowing the probabilities of events, (3) a way of understanding the importance of culture.

Risk—probabilistic knowledge, sometimes used to cover up or mystify uncertainty.[1]

Cultural Narratives and Stories—used to justify or explain propositions, events, models.

[1]The concept of uncertainty may have different meanings for anthropologists and economists. The economist Frank Knight (1921) famously distinguished between risk and uncertainty by defining one as measurable and the other, not. Risk refers to outcomes on which we are able to place probabilities and can be subjected to calculative reason. Uncertainty refers to outcomes on which we cannot place probabilities due to lack of knowledge or information. Economists have elaborated these meanings and attempted to close the gap between them in various ways. For example, even if the objective probability of a series of events is not known, we can place subjective (Bayesian) probabilities on them to allow us to act; or, we can calculate the cost of gathering more information to reduce the uncertainty, and figure this cost against the cost of acting without it. In contrast, Stephen Marglin (2007) emphasizes the importance of uncertainty in economics and invokes Keynes's idea of "animal spirits" that lead entrepreneurs and others to act in uncertain conditions. For me, uncertainty can refer to lack of known probabilities, to lack of ever knowing the probabilities of some events, and to the role of culture in making the world more coherent. In Chapter 6 I suggest that uncertainty is often mystified or transformed into risk by assuming that the past statistically repeats itself, while contingency is effaced.

examples of this sphere of economy, and suggests how identity is constituted through its relationships.

Chapter 3, Trade's Reason, describes how calculative reason emerges through competitive trade, explores how the fetishism of prices develops, and tells how calculative reason cascades through transactions that lead to debasement of the mutual domain. The generation of prices and their cascading effects lead to the tension in economy.

Chapter 4, Property and Base, explores the substance of impersonal trade, which is private property or capital, shows how narratives differently link a base to a community and private property to individuals, and turns to a well-known discourse of economists to show how it is used to justify the expansion of capital into base.

Chapter 5, Contingency or Necessity? The Dialectic of Practices, explores the tension between mutuality and calculation in practices and institutions, and the mystification of mutuality in everyday rhetoric and formal discourse.

Chapter 6, Money, shows how money, the tool of exchange, is constructed as a shifting combination of different modes of reason and operates in the communal, commercial, and financial spheres of exchange. These spheres are dialectically related, but when money embodies only calculative reason and collects a rent, or ΔCapital/Capital, its financial use cascades into and affects the other spheres of economy.

Chapter 7, Seeking a Balance, returns to the political and moral problem of reconciling mutuality and market, and the diverging and dialectical notions of positive and negative or opportunity and procedural freedom, with a plea for an open discussion of their balance. I close with some policy implications for rethinking development and our management of the environment, for reconsidering well-being, and for enhancing our management of economy's dialectic.

Notes

1. For a recent review of this debate, see Carrier (in press).

2. In more recent times, Marshall Sahlins (1976) expresses a variation of the controversy when he contrasts culture to practical reason or utility theory.

3. For a related argument see Gregory (1997), who distinguishes between House and Market as coeval value systems, just as he differentiates between "savage" money and "domesticated" money.

4. For a discussion of "economic man," see Jacobsen (2004).

5. To assess development, the World Bank produces comparative indicators of national development that measure everything from wages to productivity, nutrition, air pollution, and tariffs—all as percentages or ratios.

6. Garrison Keillor tells us, however, that in Lake Wobegon, Minnesota "all the children are above average."

7. The literature on rational choice, its philosophical, psychological, and cultural implications, its justifications and relation to utilitarian thought, and the methodologies for its study, as well as topics such as the Prisoner's Dilemma, the Tragedy of the Commons, altruism, common property regimes, the autonomy of norms, and evolutionary biology, is enormous. The work of Elster (1986, 1989) provides one starting place for an exploration of the issues.

8. The contrast between economics and anthropology with respect to their methods and epistemologies is striking. In a recent essay, for example, Fredrik

Barth suggests that anthropologists should leave aside "a compulsive search for truth, rationality and scientific method." He urges that we attend to the processes by which knowledge is produced, and not immediately seek generalizations, consistency, and coherence—the features that characterize much of economics (Barth 2002:2, 6, 8).

9. See, for example, Adorno (1973), Habermas (1984, 1987), Horkheimer (1994), Horkheimer and Adorno (2002), and Simmel (1990, 1997).

10. In anthropology, however, Sahlins (1976)—using a structuralist approach—insightfully explored the relation between practical reason and the anthropological concept of culture, and Tambiah has provided a fine exploration of rationality in relation to anthropological issues (1990). Holmes (1989) offers a study of agrarian life in northern Italy that illustrates the Weberian concept of "disenchantment."

11. But Hirschman also concluded that *"capitalism was supposed to accomplish exactly what was soon to be denounced as its worst feature"* (1977:132).

12. Muldrew (1998), from a different perspective, also reverses the Weberian thesis by arguing that the development of commercial transactions and the extension of credit originally depended on social relationships that provided a reputation for reliability; shifting social practices furnished the vitality for the new commercial outlook.

13. Zizek (2000:225) refers to "the Hegelian logic of the retroactive reversal of contingency into necessity: of course capitalism emerged from a contingent combination of historical conditions; of course it gave birth to a series of phenomena (political democracy, concern for human rights, etc.) which can be 'resignified', rehegemonized, inscribed into a non-capitalist context. However, capitalism retroactively 'posited its own presuppositions', and reinscribed its contingent/external circumstances into an all-encompassing logic that can be generated from an elementary conceptual matrix (the 'contradiction' involved in the act of commodity exchange, etc.). In a proper dialectical analysis, the 'necessity' of a totality does not preclude its contingent origins and the heterogeneous nature of its constituents—these are, precisely, its *presuppositions* which are then posited, retroactively totalized, by the emergence of dialectical totality."

14. The literature is large. For one discussion of some of these findings, see Schwartz (2004). For implications of a behavioral approach in economics, see Kopcke, Little, and Tootell (2004).

15. I am indebted to William Milberg for these observations.

16. I follow here Kolakowski's (1978) masterful account.

17. Toulmin also contrasts a "balanced approach to the function of Reason and one in which that balance is upset.... In an unbalanced account, there is a systematic preference for the kinds of knowledge that are articulated in language, and most of all in the language of formal theory" (Toulmin 2001:177).

18. Others might expand this list to include social, emotional, spiritual and communal reason (Gardner 2004), while Markus and Kitayama (1998) argue that "rational choice" itself is socially embedded. See also Markus, Mullally, and Kitayama (1997), Hutchins (1995), and Hayek (1978:71, 1967:86–88, 90).

19. As I shall explore, this arena has many forms and scales, from a political order and laws to civic associations, family ties, ethnic identity, friendship, and fictive kinship; and it is infused with mutuality expressed as shared languages, relationships, body gestures, and ways of doing.

20. My distinction is similar to, though not the same as Braudel's (1982) division into (1) "material life" (which includes the autarkic sector), (2) markets, commerce, and the economy proper, and (3) capitalism. To picture their hierarchical power, Braudel sometimes employs the metaphor of a house with several stories, as I do from fieldwork (Gudeman and Rivera 1990).

21. For an excellent review of value in anthropology, see Graeber (2001).

22. Similarly, in speaking of models of agency, Markus and Kitayama (2003: 46) state that "these models are both forms of knowledge and social practices; they have both conceptual and material elements."

23. Some time after I formulated with a colleague the idea of local and universal or derivational models (Gudeman and Penn 1982) and used it in a book (Gudeman 1986), I discovered that Stephen Marglin had proposed a similar epistemological divide (Marglin 1990, 1996). Originally he termed these modes "techne" and "episteme." Recently he has labeled them "experiential" and algorithmic" knowledge (2007).

24. The four functions were adaptation, goal-attainment, integration, and pattern-maintenance. These social functions were principally carried out through different institutions, such as the economy, the polity, the social order, and religion.

25. Some years ago, Milton Friedman (1953:33) urged: "A fundamental hypothesis of science is that appearances are deceptive and that there is a way of looking at or interpreting or organizing the evidence that will reveal superficially disconnected and diverse phenomena to be manifestations of a more fundamental and relatively simple structure."

26. I have discussed Ricardo's model; see Gudeman (1986).

27. For descriptions of the Washington Consensus and its recent augmentations, see Baumol, Litan, and Schramm (2007), and Green (2003).

28. Veblen (1914) also referred to this process as "imputation" and "contamination."

℘ 2

Exchange as Mutuality

The dialectic of keeping to the self and exchanging with others pervades all economies. Even if the balance between these modes varies, and market trade predominates in many areas, mutual connections always help make up economy, and at several levels. Communal economies can be small or large, and market economies depend on mutuality on the small and at the large. By mutuality I mean shared language, speech codes, body gestures, rituals, and unwritten practices and processes as well as norms, laws, and other social agreements. The central components of the mutual realm alone are (1) a base, (2) local stories that justify this holding, (3) relationships that are mediated through a shared base, (4) a relational identity of the person, and (5) processes for sharing the base that are usually linked to the explanatory narrative. These features of the mutual realm are the subject of this chapter. But mutuality has a double sense, for it also provides the rules and norms for the market arena or the game of anonymous trade. This side of economy, which involves shared agreements for trade, is considered in subsequent chapters, although I observe here that the market game contradicts the mutuality on which it is based.

When the interactions of mutuality make up a collectivity of people, I term them "community." Some communities are small and visible, such as households, bands, and tribal groupings, but neighborhoods, civic groups, local governments, NGOs, and nation-states also comprise communities. Imagined or global groupings that never meet yet hold interests in common are communities (Anderson 1991). The World Social Forum, first held in Brazil in 2001 and later in India, offers a common space to any group that is opposed to neoliberal globalization. It includes communities with diverse commitments, from protecting the environment, to fostering tribal rights to promoting other social movements. As a shifting collection of interest groups, the World Social Forum aims to strengthen moral bonds between different civic communities, and is a community itself (Conway 2004).

Communities may be embedded within one another or overlap; they can differ in importance, duration, and internal structure; and their borders may be firm or permeable. For example, households may be embedded within lineages that are part of clans; their borders may be permeable, and their internal organization may be fluid. The relationships within a community also can be thick or thin constellations of ties, and the bonds may vary in strength and significance: some ties are perceived as eternal; others are short-term alliances fashioned to face a common problem, promote an issue, or confront a mutual enemy.[1] Internally, communities can be home to equality or to authoritarian leaders and inequities.

In contrast to my use of the word community, Aoki and Hayami (2001) employ a more restricted notion to refer to small, face-to-face groups, and Putnam largely confines the meaning of community to immediate relationships as well. Following Granovetter (1985), he speaks of bonding and bridging relationships, or ties within and without communities, that have different uses. Both are forms of "social capital" (Putnam 2000). (Putnam has extensively discussed the "decline" of civic engagement and social capital, or community involvement, in the United States, which he attributes to suburbanization, the rise of electronic entertainment, the pressures of money and time, and generational change; he does not explore the impact of market expansion [Putnam 2000]). Rather differently, Gibson-Graham (2006) constructs an "anticapitalocentric" language for discussing the mutual realm of economy. For them, community economy constitutes a living alternative to mainstream capitalism; it has no center or specific form. They also emphasize how much of economy takes place outside market capitalism and explore alternative ways of organizing production and consumption.[2] But I see mutuality and community as spreading through all ranges of economies. For example, in high market economies many institutions, such as corporations, cooperatives, and state enterprises, have communal aspects in addition to shared norms.

The Base

The shared materials and services of a community constitute its base. A base is a shifting, heterogeneous collection through which relationships are made. Contingent and locally specified, a base mediates relations between people and relates them to things. It is a heritage that lies outside the person as material resources, tools, and knowledge, and within as sediments from others that create an identity. Respect for the ancestors, their accomplishments and effect on contemporary life, whether manifested through lineage rituals or making a weekly visit to place flowers in a Swedish or German graveyard, expresses this social dependence.

I first encountered the word "base" or "foundation" in rural Panama, where it denotes the quality of a person's judgment in managing a household economy. Base refers to the reason and comportment that are needed to handle agriculture and the household. These personal capabilities are a product of family "breeding" in the double sense of rearing and ancestry, so that a person's base, from within and from without, reflects the relationships through which she emerges. For example, kinship is formed by sharing a genitor or blood, by living together, and by eating the same food produced from the same land. People claimed that one "looked" Panamanian from eating rice, maize, and beans that are grown in the local soil: likeness comes from imbibing the same sustenance or base. Such connections forged through the base define the person as a composite of relationships and features shared with others.

In the highlands of Colombia, as I described, a colleague and I found that the same term, base, is used more elaborately: it is part of a metaphor by which the economy is modeled as a house (Gudeman and Rivera 1990). This house economy has "doors" and "windows" through which things pass in exchange, it has "supports" that maintain it, and it can fall into "ruins" when its base is lost or becomes insufficient to support a family. The base or foundation of the house designates a collection of things or results of work, such as the farmed land, seed, crops in the ground, stored harvests, clothes, animals, equipment, and household belongings, all of which must be reasonably managed. A household's perpetuation and wealth depend on its base, which embodies "strength" or "force." Reflecting God's "power" or "might" in the world, the earth yields this strength through its products. By providing life energy, strength accumulated in the base and embodied in humans through consumption sustains the people (and animals) of a house. This strength is expended in agricultural work that through the land returns the force, which humans need to live. Because a household expends its base of accumulated strength through the work of its members that yields harvests and other sustaining returns, it possesses the results. The outcome is uncertain, however, because success depends on the fertility of the land, which may or may not "give" its products in a particular year. The size of a base, or a household's wealth, thus changes over time. Making a base is a "struggle," and everyone is concerned with "keeping" or "holding" the base as well as "advancing" it. One tries to "make" (*hacer*) a base, just as a large and successful house economy is known as a *hacienda* (Gudeman and Rivera 1990).[3] This local narrative about the base and people that unites God and man, the environment and humans, expending energy and gaining possession, revolves about cycling (or "returning") strength from humans to land to humans. Erasing the division between human and the environment, it is a model of an *oikos* economy in the original sense of uniting ecology and economy with a community of people.

More generally, a base is made, held, and used through social relationships. For example, ties may be formed around rights to a water hole, a reservoir, an irrigation system, or a fishing pond. These connections often involve a combination of neighborhood, kinship, and work bonds. But a base varies in prominence and contents across economies.

It may be very important (as in the case of lineage land), ephemeral (as in the case of shared information in an ethnic group), or relatively minimal (as in the case of a household that shares stocks of food). For example, in socialist Cuba the physical resources that make up the base are held and distributed by the state, including the education, health, and retirement systems; jobs; low-cost transport and utilities; and some food provisions. Socialism can be seen as a large community economy in which central planning determines how its base is allocated and used. With a faltering economy and shortages in Cuba, however, these supports are shrinking. Some people say that the word "base" now refers only to the personal relationships on which one relies for material assistance in times of necessity. People secure needed food, money, or an automobile part through a friend or family member.

Always in the making, a base can consist of both produced things and nonproduced parts of the environment; for example, it can be valued forests, lakes, or mountains. Some fashioned parts of a base, such as tools, monuments, or a cave drawing, emerge from intentional acts, and some are unintentional outcomes, as in the remaking of a landscape when a plant species is domesticated or in the serendipitous discovery of a drug. But a base is not the raw environment or even the "through put," as some ecological economists (Daly and Farley 2004)) would have us understand the flow of resources and energy with which economies are made, because a base is locally constituted with shifting specifications. For example, mountains or glaciers once considered a source of sacred power that links together a community and helps to nourish it may lose this value; similarly, the value of clean air or water shifts in high market societies. I thus distinguish between a base and the environs within which we live. The manifold presents the potential for a base but is not exhausted by any construction. For example, to speak of the environment as "through put" that can be measured by BTUs or some other ruler in order to display efficient or inefficient uses of the external world already represents a cultural story or "basification" of the environment for one or another community of ecologists.

Although a base consists of heterogeneous things, it may contain zones of commensuration. For example, crops, services, or implements may be separately measured or counted for different uses; it is hard to imagine a world of singularities. But the measured zones are incommensurable, such as domestic rice as opposed to game animals, or sacred land as opposed to water. Unlike capital, a base is not an integrated or systematic whole, measured by a single unit of account. For example, in Colombia, strength is not a measured quantity by which different households can be compared. It encapsulates various entities from God's might, to the environment, to goods, to human life. I thus distinguish between the concept of base and the popular terms "symbolic," "cultural," and "social" capital.[4] These words lead us to envision the realm of social relations and material things through the totalizing prism of capital. Relationships, culture, and heritage are seen as measurable resources or forms of capital that enhance or hinder trade. The expressions elide or mystify human mutuality as if it were commensurable.

Narratives of Legitimacy

In many ethnographic situations, social agreements, expressed through narratives and practices, justify a holding as a base. For example, spirits or ancestors of the living may be said to animate and offer a fertile resource, such as land or a fishing bank. This connection between the living and the dead legitimates use of the holding, and access to it may be conditioned on communal membership, with the collected goods allocated through kinship or other relationships. To create these stories that connect them to the world they use, people often employ local images, such as the experiences of touch, smell, cohabitation, a powerful event, or physical labor. The narratives usually have a phenomenological touchstone and draw on figurative projections or metaphors. For example, original connections as they appear in ethnography and other written work may be locally explained as[5]

a covenant with God,[6]
a gift of God,
a gift of the spirits,
a gift of royal authority,
a transaction between human and supernatural forces,[7]
choice of the object itself,[8]
a gift of nature,
first come, first serve,
theft,
labor embodied,
knowledge or skills deployed,[9]
a pact with the devil,
devolution from the ancestors who first arrived,
devolution from the ancestors who first emerged from the earth,[10] or
a gift from parents.

The Bemba of East Africa say that they occupy their land and have the right to use it by being descended from the ancestors who are connected to the land by having arrived there first, used it, invented agriculture, been buried there, and offered continued fertility. They created agriculture and opened the land.[11] Present-day users are matrilineal descendants of the ancestors, born in a succession of wombs, which ensures the spiritual presence of the ancestors in them. This narrative, which employs images of first come, first served, innovation, corporeal embodiment, and spirit power, legitimates the Bemba lineage holdings and is part of their economic model. For example, tribute is sent to a chief or maternal uncle because he embodies the ancestors and makes offerings to ensure their goodwill, which helps provide ample harvests. This use of the base is part of its justification as a holding. With respect to the land, Bemba act as persons-in-community and do not trade their base nor explain their connection to it as a product of calculative reason.

Selfways

Through mutual affiliations, people constitute one aspect of their identity. I have termed this relational identity of the human the "person-in-community," in contrast to the "individual" (Gudeman 1992). But Markus and Kitayama (1998, 2003) speak of "selfways" and use the telling expressions "conjoint" and "disjoint" to refer to the interdependent and independent self. In the disjoint mode, agency is rooted in desires, goals, and intentions of the independent self. In the conjoint one, identity comes through relationships with others, and—I would add—as mediated by shared social agreements. Drawing on a range of psychological studies, they show how these two selfways vary across cultures. For example, in the United States they see the disjoint self as predominant and connect this self to the compulsion to choose; in the United States, they add, choice is "taken seriously" (Markus and Kitayama 2003:22). Marilyn Strathern offers a rather similar perspective with her distinction between the "dividual" and the "individual." In Melanesia, she observes, "persons are as dividually as they are individually conceived." By "dividual," Strathern means that Melanesians are seen as divisible and porous or unbounded. She continues, "Indeed, persons are frequently constructed as the plural and composite site of the relationships that produced them," which is different from the individual person (1988:13).[12] I link these two aspects of identity to economy's breach: people are disjoint or individual selves as constituted in competitive market trade and economists' models; they are conjoint selves or persons-in-community as constituted in mutual relationships. Finally, just as we may speak of economies that are embedded and disembedded, persons may be seen as having embedded and disembedded identities. The two forms of selfhood are dialectically related and shift by context.

The Base across Cultures

Across cultures the components of a base vary widely and range from transmitted learning and shared skills to fixed resources. Often, as I discuss later, this heritage is intertwined with capital, but let us consider here some examples of its separate appearance. There is no single type of base: its significance in material life, people's attachment to it, and its recognition vary widely.

Knowledge and Skills

A base usually is a repertoire of knowledge and skills, often developed in relation to the material space a people occupy. For example, navigators in Polynesia (Gladwin 1970) may use the night sky or ocean currents to orient themselves and guide their vessels; the weather or snow may be read to find animals as among Arctic peoples. Such accumulated knowledge, transmitted through apprenticeship and explicit instruction, seemingly cannot be depleted, as in the economists' example of a shared lighthouse: one person's use does not detract from another's. The innovations of shamans, craftsmen, and herders add to their heritage, which through open access expands as one contribution builds on another. Not all knowledge and skills that make up a base are freely available to members of a community, however. Specialized knowledge may be transmitted by inheritance or apprenticeship so that only some community members become possessors and practitioners, as in the case of garden magicians in Melanesia who have learned special spells that they keep to themselves or their lineage (Fortune 1963). Others may benefit (or be harmed) by their services, which may be performed on the basis of kinship or other connections. In later chapters I return to some of the ways that such knowledge is socially shared (in the language of economics, this sharing may be the result of unintended "spillovers" from others).

Unlimited Base

A part of the material world may be used as if it were an unlimited base. This form of base may be a seemingly plentiful resource, such as air, the sky, an ocean, a sea, or a forest. But usually a community constitutes only a part of this space as a base and may share it with others. For example, a jungle may be used to hunt game, a forest may be used to lay trap lines that cross each other, or food may be freely collected from a savanna. Swidden farmers, who cut down a forest, and fishermen may use their resource as if it were unlimited.[13] In Panama, during the first half of the twentieth century, people in the central savanna would journey to salt flats on the Pacific Ocean to extract their needed salt; this base was seen as plentiful and competition for access was unknown.

Limited Base

The base may be a bounded resource, which economists identify as a limited access commons (Ostrom 1990). Possession is circumscribed and held by a community or group, with access regulated by shared rules. Clan and village land are two examples. In Latin America, a religious association or co-fraternity may hold land and allocate parcels on the basis of group membership. A base also may consist of exclusive trap lines and hunting trails, or exclusive rights to use salt flats as among the Baruya of New Guinea (Godelier 1977).

This form of holding is not private property, because it is not individually held nor is it alienable; rather, it links people to one another as part of their shared identity and is alienated only at the cost of losing mutuality. This connection of base and people is usually justified by a narrative that makes the base part of local identity. In contrast, the formation of a (limited access) commons is usually a more practical and calculated arrangement, and it is often secured through a market. (I enter now a long parenthesis to underline again the difference between a base and capital. Today, economists employ the notion of public goods and use the concepts of "rivalry" and "excludability." A good is a public good when it is "non-rival" which is to say that one person's use does not affect another's and that no one is excluded from its use. The air around us might be one example. Conversely, private goods are rival and excludable goods. And there are variations between these extremes. A common pool resource, such as wild game, is a rival but not excludable good, if everyone may hunt; other things may be nonrival but excludable from some users, such as a toll road. I would not compare the different forms of base, with their varying rules of use and allocation, to these types of capital, however. The latter all have to do with disjoint or market selves. In contrast, the base mediates and is part of social relationships.)[14]

Material Accumulations and Services

A base may include material holdings such as a stock of food, improved land, or tools and equipment. In rural Colombia, as described, a farmer considers his crops, work put into the land, house, stored food, animals, and tools as parts of his base, because it supports garnering future returns. Similarly, some national governments stockpile food, oil, gold, and other resources for emergencies and long-term use by their citizens. Cuba keeps food caches in case of natural disasters.

Prohibited Spaces

The base may define a space in which specific activities may not occur. For example, in some areas of Guatemala, communities hold higher forest lands and prohibit their exploitation in order to preserve the watershed for the lower plots on which domestic and market crops are raised. Forests or waterholes also may be preserved as sacred places inhabited or visited by ancestors or gods. These spaces—often religiously defined—are "incommensurable" zones, a term to which I return.

Base as Identity

Sometimes part of a base is epitomized as an essential good on whose existence a community relies. Whether movable or immovable, it may be exclusively held or only briefly loaned to others by its possessors (Liep 1983). These components of the base may have special significance, such as a flag, or be endowed with special powers, such as ancestral shrines. I term them *sacra*. For example, in different parts of Latin America, potatoes, maize, or rice are considered to be a basic or life necessity; raised at home, the crop is eaten daily if not at every meal and may be considered to provide strength. In East and Southeast Asia, rice is often the basic food; millet and other crops are considered necessities in parts of Africa, and among the Nuer, the milk and blood of cattle are seen as sources of vitality (Hutchinson 1996). Each household of the Iban who live in Sarawak plants a sacred strain of rice whose sustaining power grows with its perpetuation. This sacral part of the base is usually preserved and reproduced each year to protect the continuity of the living community with its ancestors and potential descendants; the sacred rice also ensures the health of the nonsacred strains and the vitality of the household that consumes it (Freeman 1958).[15] At a more figurative level, a community usually keeps emblems that stand for its presence and identity, although these symbols are often contested as to their meaning, importance, and inclusiveness. Such emblems that unite (or fractionate people) may include songs, banners, flags, monuments, totems, crowns, documents, paintings, and buildings.[16] In the United States, everyone may own and display the flag, sing patriotic songs, and celebrate Independence Day. Only the highest authority, however, may confer some markers of social standing or merit, such as the Presidential Medal of Freedom. In some countries desecration of a sacred item is a crime, such as flying the United States flag upside down, although sports fans at international competitions may paint themselves in the colors of their flag. In various European countries, when socialism disappeared, people destroyed statues of Lenin and Stalin but resurrected earlier images of czars and other leaders as part of their new identity. In the United States, especially in times of political division, leaders "wrap themselves in the flag," claiming that opposed voices are not patriotic and that they are the true leaders of the shared interests: in these cases shared emblems are appropriated for partisan purposes.

The Cree and Their Base

The James Bay Cree of Canada provide one example of a base, its link to identity and the problem of debasement. The base of the Cree was their hunting territory. Before the advent of the Quebec hydroelectric project, the Cree had a "forest-way" of life.[17] Their seasonal life was divided into winter and summer activities. In the summer they fished (and earned some wages), while in the winter they set up camps in the forest. During this time, families dispersed throughout a hunting territory where they separately trapped and pursued game, such as black bear and moose.

The land, for Cree hunters, was never individually owned: rather, stewards (known as "tallymen") managed a hunting territory. Tallymen coordinated the traplines in a territory as well as rights to hunt specific animals. They were enjoined to preserve a territory and ensure that proper hunting practices were maintained. The hunting territories were not exclusive, however; as a hunter traveled through one territory to another, he could temporarily draw on its resources to maintain himself.

According to the Cree, successful hunting and trapping depended on keeping a respectful relationship with the animals. The hunt was a spiritual relation between humans and animals who were not separate objects but part of a spiritual world in which humans were included. Animals, the Cree said, offered themselves to a hunter or remained hidden: they could be friendly or opposed to humans. During a hunt they had to be coaxed forth through ritual practices and exchanges, which meant that failure in a chase or scarcity of game was attributed to the improper behavior of the hunter. Hunters considered the animals to be in control of a hunt, so that despite good techniques, hunters' success depended on the animals making themselves available in response to the respect accorded to them. For example, a hunter should never waste animal meat or claim to have special abilities, because he did not govern the hunt. The esophagus of a goose had to be hung on a tree as a sign of respect (the windpipe was the voice of a goose). Antlers and skulls from game were suspended in trees to solicit continued offerings, and the jawbone of a bear was first tied to its skull before it was hung in respect. Black bears were considered to be the most spiritually powerful of all the animals and influenced all other hunting activities. Often, hunters sat around the carcass of a black bear and smoked a pipe in respect; a piece of the tobacco might be placed in the bear's mouth and some meat might be thrown into the cooking fire. Spiritual forces also occupied rocks, trees, and other places in a hunting territory, and running water could have spiritual power. Herbal healing as well depended on forming a connection between the herbalist who collected the medicine and the sufferer; the aid had to be reciprocated by a gift of tobacco.

The forest as base mediated social relationships and connected the Cree to animals, spirits, and inanimate things in a reciprocal relationship. Living in the forest was the principal way of maintaining calmness in the self and in social relationships. The forest offered a place of healing in which well-being, seen as physical and spiritual health in social relationships and with the environment, could be reestablished. A place of repose, recovery, and sustenance, the forest constituted the conjoint Cree identity through the sharing it established. But as the hydroelectric project invaded the area and flooded portions of the land, with its inevitable effects on rivers, the land, forests, and game, this base was decimated, and the Cree felt a sense of "irretrievable loss" (Niezen 1998:94). As one hunter explained: "Since they flooded my land, my trapline, there's not a single day that I don't think about it. I feel so sad about it. [It was] one thing I couldn't understand; I don't think I'll ever understand. One reason why I feel so bad is knowing that my land is flooded forever, that I will never see it come back [to] what it was like before they flooded it.... I am sure that I won't be able to show my grandchildren what my land was like when I was living off [it] hunting. That's the biggest change I ever saw in my life" (Niezen 1998:88). This destruction of a living local model, or a way of life built through a shared base, aptly illustrates my choice of the term "debasement."

Communal Sharing

The resources, knowledge, and equipment comprising the base are shared through communal relationships and by expansion of them. These distributions usually are directed more at maintaining persons and their welfare than at accumulating individual wealth: often the purpose is to meet socially defined needs, which allows for a degree of group independence or self-sufficiency, and to expand the circle of mutuality. Guided by written and unwritten registers of social and moral value, such as merit, age, gender, or need (including health, education, poverty, and other social conditions), these modes of distribution markedly differ from market exchange. I use the term "sharing" to cover both "allocations" and "reciprocity."

Allocations of the base may be divided into *allotment* (for assignment of a permanent fund) and *apportionment* (for allocation of a flow) (Gudeman 2001). For example, permanent parts of a base may be allotted to persons in the community for personal use, such as agricultural land, trapping areas for hunting, or an inheritance. Members of a kin group may be allotted rights to till part of the group's land; in Latin America a *cofradía* or religious brotherhood may allocate some of its forest or land holdings to its members on condition that they participate in the group's management and religious activities.

Fluid parts of the base may be apportioned, such as timber for culling and wild foods for consumption. Such flows also include payments
that help maintain the base, such as tribute, tithes, labor, and taxes.
Flows from a base may be used for productive purposes, as in the case
of fish banks or rotating water rights in parts of the Andes (Trawick
2001). Apportionment occurs on special occasions as well, when personal breaches must be rectified by payments, game is caught and killed,
domestic animals are butchered, personal services are performed, or a
wedding is held. The provider of these flows (such as the hunter of
game or the possessor of a sacrificed pig) is recognizing and activating
connections to others and their entitlements to a share of the return, because the object is not the provider's private or exclusive property. For
example, among some African groups, the success of a hunter depends
on his skills. But the hunter's skills were learned from contemporaries
or predecessors, and community amity may persuade the ancestors to
make the game available so that the catch is a product of the hunter as
a person-in-community or conjoint agent; the communal contributions
are recognized by allocating different joints of the animal in varying
amounts to social positions in the community (Marks 1976). Likewise,
tribute paid to a chief may be explained on the basis that he embodies
the ancestors and makes offerings for their goodwill, which helps provide the ample harvests on communally allotted land. Tithes may be
justified as a return for God's bounty. The narratives that enroll the
base as a holding of the community legitimate these rules of apportionment and allotment.

Many allotments and apportionments are calculated or measured.
But an overarching gage that links all the local allocations usually is not
encountered, for different measuring rods may be used to carry out the
separate allocations. The registers of division are many: a possession
may be allocated equally per person or per household; it may be divided according to need or request; it may be allocated by kinship or
social position, or by age, gender, power, and persuasion. One type of
good, such as beer or soup, may be distributed equally; another good
may flow to certain persons only, such as the hindquarters of an animal
that may be rendered to a village blacksmith or the tusks of an elephant
that may be rendered to a chief for the access he provides to the ancestors. These registers, often mixed together, changed through discussion
and contestation, and altered in relation to environmental conditions,
are mutual agreements. They are shared "preferences" that preserve
and alter mutuality through their enactment. But they are not reducible
to a single measuring rod. Usually, people mix schedules in making
allotments and apportionments. For example, in the ninth century, a
French monastery budgeted bread to different persons by weight, by
loaf, and by part loaf; other foods were divided equally according to
the number of nightly visitors; eels, cheese, and cattle were apportioned

by other stipulations. The divisions were not commensurate or matched against one another. The amount available, subsistence needs, social position, number of recipients, and equality were the guiding norms (Gudeman 2001:77).

Allotting and apportioning are everyday practices in market-dominated economies as well. In the United States we may allocate rooms in a house by age (parents and children) and by need (study space), if the holding is sufficient. Bathrooms may be equally shared on the basis of time and need, but living rooms and kitchens are common spaces, although individuals may lay informal possession to chairs within them. Food in the refrigerator or on the table may be apportioned by the principle of first come, first served. One resolution to competing television demands may be to purchase several. These and other allocations do not reflect each other, nor is an algorithm used to transform one allotment to another. They also may be modified by tactical use or reciprocity, but reciprocity does not determine the several allocations that may express social position and power.

Budgets in a household are allocated by diverse values: so much may go to the future as savings, and so much to entertainment, food, clothing, education, health services, and other valued things. In a household economy the allocations often are earmarked: in Colombia people separate potatoes into piles for seeding, eating, feeding animals, and sale (Gudeman and Rivera 1990). Today, domestic groups may earmark money by sorting it into envelopes or jars for different uses; or by maintaining different savings and checking accounts. For example, the contents of one envelope should not be used for another purpose, except at the cost of moral failure. One budget book that advocates allocating funds into fifteen categories adds that good management comes from "discipline, sacrifice, and trusting God to supply needs" (Burkett 1993: 32). In contrast, some financial advisors and universities aver that all money is fungible or that every dollar is equal: the value of educational savings can be measured against the value of a fine wine, or savings from faculty parking fees can be used to support the athletic department.

When communal allocation is politically seized, it can become a form of central planning, whether in a household or nation. But communal apportioning is not indelibly linked to central planning, as in the case of state or national taxes, which are justified by a variety of rationales and may support diverse services and goods. Socialist allotment provides a modern example of mutual transfers that are usually condemned by advocates of efficient policies. Most economists would consider mutual allotment and apportionment in small communities that often underwrite social or religious performances as ridden with frictions or transaction costs; in the process of economic development these transfer modes that connect people in relationships through their base should be eradicated in the name of efficiency. But eliminating these practices alters the meaning of the objects and services they guarantee, destroys relationships mediated by the transfer, turns the shared material interests into capital, and transforms the value registers of a community.

Since the work of Polanyi (1968) all these allocations, or allotting and apportioning, have been subsumed under the catchall term "redistribution." According to Polanyi, redistribution takes place through the principle of centricity, which is a flow from the periphery to the center and back but not in the same amounts or to the same persons. Polanyi linked redistribution to the dominance of political or religious institutions; for example, taxes and tithes are forms of redistribution. He claimed that redistribution was the dominant mode of exchange in "archaic" or historical societies. In contrast, reciprocity or the back-and-forth delayed exchange of goods and services is dominant in what he termed "primitive" (ethnographic) contexts. Implicit in Polanyi's semi-historical division is the idea that reciprocity precedes redistribution. After Polanyi, both Lévi-Strauss (1969) and Sahlins (1972) argued that reciprocity is the basic social transaction; it is the glue of society and economy. Whereas Polanyi suggested that reciprocity historically precedes redistribution, Lévi-Strauss and Sahlins urge that it is logically prior. In fact, Sahlins models redistribution as a form of reciprocity that he calls "generalized reciprocity." My view is different. Of course, the realm of mutuality entails reciprocity in that all social relationships are reciprocal. But Sahlins' application of the term to all social life and exchanges expands it beyond usefulness; for example, Sahlins sees impersonal, competitive trade as a mode of "negative reciprocity." In contrast, I argue that communal exchange is organized around allocations, which cannot be reduced to expressions of reciprocity because these forms of sharing help to constitute a collectivity, whereas reciprocity is a dyadic exchange between individuals or two groups (Gudeman 2001).

I use the term "reciprocity" to refer to nonmarket exchanges that are more a commitment than a contract. Reciprocity designates a back-and-forth movement that takes place over time; never immediate, it is based on mutual trust, which can be violated or broken. (In market contexts, reciprocity may be seen as cronyism, bad governance, or bribery, for it is viewed as a subversion of impersonal trade and undermines the free flow of information and open bidding.)

Reciprocity may accompany allotment and apportionment, but generally it connects one base to another. Whether as an exchange of favors, services, or goods, reciprocity may have significant material and social effects, for it shares identity, whether as insider information on a future buyout, as temporary help in the form of a good given to neighbors, or as the transmission of esteemed relics and symbols. Reciprocity extends parts of a base to others. For example, as I have elsewhere described (Gudeman 2001), the Jukumani of Bolivia allot village land to community members who have inherited a right to its use. These people are known as the "original ones." With population growth, a second category of people who lack usufruct has emerged. Known as "people of the margin," these late arrivals to the area secure access to plots through an original holder who allows them to use the edges of his land for seeding and grazing in return for services rendered, such as fulfilling ritual obligations or providing unpaid labor. People of the margin are neither fully in the community nor out of it; they have a conjoint and disjoint village identity founded on the reciprocity that is made up of base extension and the return of services. Similarly, the Nambicuara of Brazil apportion meat of game, which is caught by male hunters, and manioc soup, which is made by women, equally throughout the village. These are their basic foods. When newcomers arrive, they are included in the sharing before contributing, but if they violate village norms or do not apportion their game or meat, they are soon excluded. Reciprocity, a form of sharing and a mode of identity formation, is an adjunct of base making and its extension. Comprised of favors, things, and ideas, it links people and enhances (or detracts from) their well-being and material life.

Reciprocity or gift giving is a risky venture. It establishes mutuality and maintains it, but with the possibility of breaking it. This risk is very different from market risk, which can be due to economic cycles, business failures, the weather, political disruptions, contractual failure, and other events, because it is part of social relationships and cannot be quantified and condensed into a marketable derivative that measures the probability of failure (as I later describe). On the other hand, reciprocity is not a completely uncertain act, because participants usually have some knowledge about the mutual responses of others or extend it to gain that knowledge and a relationship. Reciprocity is an overture—a supplication and response—of identity and base sharing.

The Mishnah: A Model Economy

The Mishnah provides an extraordinary example of a communal economy. In Judaism, the Torah has both a written and oral form. The written Torah is the Pentateuch of the Old Testament; the oral Torah developed afterward but began to be written in the first centuries of the Common Era. The Mishnah was the first of the written forms. Composed of bits and pieces from historical practices, including ancient Greece as well as writings within and without Judaism, it was an ideal or normative model that was never fully used in practice. Jacob Neusner (1990) has provided a synthesis of this dispersed discourse. The Mishnah is not a systematic model of economy but consists of details and observations, which is the same with most ethnographic models I have encountered. In both cases, the analytical task is to make sense of the practices and verbal statements.

In the Mishnah, religion interweaves social life and economy and is partly expressed in material practices, just as the proper practices compose a religious life. As a total model of an economy the Mishnah was not complete, nor was it intended to be. Its writers assumed the presence of markets, traders, and specialists outside of which the Mishnah made up a holy economy. Through its detailed practices, however, the Mishnah set limits on the extent of competitive trade, and its prescribed practices and requirements affected markets. Describing an economy of self-maintenance, the Mishnah preserved the status quo. Because it marked a boundary between the two realms of value and did not permit penetration by markets into the sacred domain with its base, the Mishnah provides one example of the breach and tension within economy.

The Mishnah economy starts with the covenant or reciprocal relationship between heaven and earth. God is owner of the Holy Land, which is Israel, and this belief or narrative justifies the complex modes of sharing in the economy. The land that is held by a household provides its base. A male householder who is subject to the Mishnah's prescriptions heads the household, conceived as an autonomous unit in agricultural production and consumption. Other structured positions include shopkeepers, traders, and laborers, and a householder might have various dependents, including a wife, offspring, slaves, and servants. These statuses are not part of the Mishnah economy, although their presence is necessary. A householder, to be a householder in the Mishnah economy, must have dominion over land in the space that is Israel. As a community, Israel means both a land area and the Israelites who possess it. A gentile who lives in or even holds land in the area of Israel is not part of the Mishnah economy; and a Jew who lives in the demarcated area but does not possess land is not subject to the prescriptions of the Mishnah, nor is an Israelite who holds land outside it. Israel is an economic realm only in relation to the covenanted land.

As the gift of God who dwells in the land, the earth's holiness grows through Israelites living on and working it in the proper manner. A householder is like a sharecropper who owes God payments for use of the land. By keeping to the rules of producing and sharing, sufficiency and prosperity are assured, whereas breaking them leads to want. Wealth in this economy means the land as base and what it yields and supports, such as harvests, animals, laborers, and a growing population. This wealth neither increases nor decreases, but it embodies value. Thus, bartering goods produced on the land is the most appropriate way to exchange in markets, whereas money used in exchange is but a substitute for goods not on hand and has no value itself. Certainly, profits can be made in trade, but profit is not a part of the Mishnah economy, because wealth from the land does not increase. The Mishnah does contain admonitions against usury (or profit); however, their purpose is not so much to prohibit taking from others as to set aside distribution through market pricing in favor of allocation by the sanctified rules that assure God's continued blessing of the soil.

The rules of apportionment, extraordinary in their detail, are designed to preserve the status quo. They begin with tithing, which starts after the produce has been harvested, brought to the home, and claimed as personal property by the householder. (Untithed produce can only be eaten as a snack.) All the subsequent allocations are proportioned. The first of these divisions is the "heave-offering" that is given to the priest, who consumes it in conditions of cleanliness: usually, it is about one-fiftieth of the harvest. Then, the first tenth is given to a Levite, who takes from it a tenth as a heave-offering to the priest. The second tenth is sent to Jerusalem for its support. But during the third and sixth years of the sabbatical cycle, this second tithe goes to the poor. When bread is made, one twenty-fourth of the dough is given to the priest. There are other offerings as well: priests receive the shoulder, two cheeks, and the maw of an animal slaughtered for secular purposes, plus the fleece and the firstborn male offspring of livestock. They receive first fruits, too, and offerings are made to the Temple, which acts on behalf of God who owns the land. After all these tithes are paid, the householder may consume or trade the remainder (for "equal value") in markets. Goods not derived from the sacred land fall outside the tithing system.

The allocations in the Mishnah economy affect markets, because they change supplies and demand. For example, food tithed to Jerusalem lowers demand there while restricting supplies available for sale. Similarly, the entire tithing system affects what remains for sale. The Mishnah thus constructs an "enclave" economy (though in reverse of the usual meaning, according to which an enclave refers to a market within a nonmarket economy). More important, the allocations in the Mishnah economy are not agglomerated under a single measuring rod. Cattle, crops, and cooking dough are all divided differently. Each is like a "species" to be separately apportioned, just as the laws of Leviticus prohibit the commingling of various plants, animals, and fibers. All make up the incommensurable or heterogeneous parts of the base.

The Tiv: A Real Economy

In contrast to the Mishnah, the Tiv of northern Nigeria offer a practical example of the mutual domain with its many features.[18] I shall refer to this ethnography by the Bohannans in the present, although their fieldwork was undertaken from 1949 to 1953 and there have been many changes since. The Tiv do participate in local markets, but I focus on their mutual domain, because it offers a salutary example of the way a base is allotted and maintained, and how its products are apportioned through communal relationships. This mutual domain, which is guided by various values, helps determine the conjoint identity of Tiv.

For Tiv, who arrange themselves through patrilines, land is the spatial expression of lineal relationships, and social ties are mediated through the land. The territory occupied by the descendants of a patrilineal ancestor is known as a *tar*, and every male has the right to live in the tar associated with the lineage segment reckoned through his father. The tar, in my terms, is the base, for it is always associated with a social group (Bohannan and Bohannan 1968:94). For example, splitting a tar refers both to the separation of land rights with the creation of boundaries, and to a social breach, which is considered to be a moral disrupture. Lineage segments that make up a tar are composed of compound groups, which are headed by a male and contain his wives and children, who live in separate huts. The term *ya*, used for a compound group, refers to the site, huts, and shared space in the center of the compound plus the people, their relationships and their activities. The compound is a local community and base within the larger tar. In both cases, land supports and mediates relationships.

Within the compound, the head controls the magic that provides prosperity and fertility. He allots plots of land for use by each of his wives and their offspring, and he organizes the overall productive activities. All other men in the compound must obtain permission from the head before planting an area or an extra farm, but each male has the right to farm a sufficient plot and the obligation to supply each of his wives with a farm. The compound head allots these farm areas according to family need. As a family grows, so does the land it tills, and as a lineage expands, its farmland does as well. Because the Tiv practice shifting agriculture, farm locations may change rather frequently and there can be disputes within communities as these shifts occur, but the value of need always guides the allocation.

Supported by the land, the principal crop of the Tiv is the yam, which is made into porridge and is supplemented by other foods and game. The word *yiagh*, which roughly means subsistence, refers to food in the field, the granary, the cooking pot, and the stomach plus the farms, the work performed on them, and all the activities that depend on nourishment. (I might compare this term to the concept of strength or force in Colombia, for both notions erase the boundary between humans and the environs within which they work. Both concepts refer to things that are "external" and "internal" to persons, enable them to work, and connect them to others through the land.) Most of the Tiv subsistence product is consumed by its producers; very little is marketed. Even if extra portions of food do reach markets, the land cannot be sold, rented, mortgaged, or pledged; nor can Tiv buy land, because nothing—

they explain—can match it. Vending land would be like selling one's lineage position. Land, subsistence food, work, and identity belong to a value domain that is different from the market. Everything in this realm points back to the land, its proper allotment, and its promised fertility.

Apportionment of agricultural produce reflects the allotment rights. Just as a woman has rights in a farm and its products, so she has the obligation to feed her family. The man who made her farm also has the right to eat from it (and the obligation to pay taxes for it). In addition, the compound head who allots a plot to a man for his wife has rights to small portions of the produce, which he uses for hospitality and for rituals that bring prosperity. This apportioning is not done with exactitude. Tiv do not measure farm yields; even single crops are not piled up as a whole, and attempts to measure them are met with suspicion (as if the mound were to be sold). Sufficiency is the aim. People, it is said, work hard to fulfill their roles as family members and to receive help in return. The Tiv also observe that one cannot plant a large yam farm without shirking obligations to help others. If a man asks to plant a larger field in order to sell the product for money, he will usually be refused: money "spoils" the compound, say the Tiv, even if the crops that would be sold require little extra work.

Other stocks and flows are variously divided. In contrast to the land's allotment, trees, waterholes, fishing sites, and other resources are freely available. Small game was scarce at the time of the Bohannans' fieldwork, but some animals are captured. The man who initiates the hunt provides beer for drinking in the bush. Each man who catches an animal receives it but must give a foreleg to the person who issued the invitation. The meat of large animals may be sold or given to lineage mates, but it is carefully apportioned. The man whose arrow first hit the animal receives the head, the hide, and the hind legs. The heart goes to his mother. The man whose arrow next hit the animal receives a foreleg; the rest of the animal goes to the man who had the first hit, but he has to share this return with the other hunters. Different ways of apportioning apply to other yields as well. No measuring rod is used for all.

Outside the compound, a degree of sharing is also practiced through reciprocity. During lean times, Tiv "send hunger" (food) to kinsmen in other parts of the land that are suffering, and Tiv send gifts to a man on important occasions in his life. These gifts are not exactly calculated or returned but express and validate mutuality (Bohannan and Bohannan 1968:143).

Identity and Reason at the Base

Making a base and forming relationships by way of shared interests draws on a range of human capacities and forms of reason, including analytical, metaphorical, creative, reflexive, critical, and dialectical, as well as calculated choice. The mutual realm also plays home to another form of means-to-ends reasoning: being thrifty or economizing, as opposed to maximizing the relation between ends and means. Being thrifty means minimizing the use of materials. It is a way of holding what one has and preserving it for the future or as base. Ways of economizing, which can be applied to almost anything and constantly evolve, often are practiced as protection against an uncertain future. In production and consumption, parsimony, frugality, and economizing mark the limits of calculative reason, because not all means are thrown into the hopper of efficient production, as in the case of the Mishnah, or into limitless consumption. Some are held as base and stipulated as reserves for the future. (As we shall see, being thrifty in consumption also places limits on market expansion.) By relying on parsimony, a group might produce *nearly* all that it needs and consume what it produces; however, some items usually are produced for sale or exchange with others. For example, a house economy in Latin America or a compound group in Africa may attempt to be a separate entity, but it trades some goods with others. Conversely, many wage earners in market economies who exchange their returns for food and other goods also help sustain their households by cooking and gardening; by caring for the young, old, and infirm; by repairing their properties; and by building their own furniture or making their clothes. Similarly, a nation may restrict the importation of capital and goods, limit the outflow of its resources, or expropriate the investments and holdings of outsiders (such as petroleum deposits, refineries, and pipelines) in the quest to be more self-sufficient and loosen the bonds of dependency. Even if the base is but a symbolic holding (as in the case of shared sacra), to that extent a community or nation-state proclaims a self-sufficient identity. But keeping to the self is always dialectically framed in relation to the domain of trade, to which we now turn.

Notes

1. Granovetter (1973) identifies networks as having strong and weak ties, suggesting that weak ties may lead to more rapid diffusion of information.

2. Gibson and Graham's argument broadly follows their earlier work (Gibson-Graham 1996). I am indebted to them for our conversations about community economy.

3. For comparative materials, see Mayer (2005).

4. This literature is extensive, and aid agencies and policy makers often adopt the terms. For two of the important discussions, see Bourdieu (1984) and Putnam (2000).

5. Except as noted, I have discussed these connections in Gudeman (1986,

2001), and Gudeman and Rivera (1990), drawing on reported ethnography and my own.

6. As in the Mishnah described below.

7. Sneath (2004:168).

8. Among the Eveny people of Siberia, land and reindeer, both of which have spiritual force, may choose persons with whom they want to form relationships, a choice that is expressed in various ways (Vitebsky 2001). For an extended description of a base, see Vitebsky (2005).

9. Anderson (1998).

10. Malinowski (1978 [1935]:341–344).

11. I have drawn this ethnography from Audrey Richards (1939); see Gudeman (1986). For a different example in which the fertility of crops depends on the goodwill of ancestors, see Firth (1936).

12. Referring to the Siane of Papua New Guinea, M. Strathern also observes, "out of this composition of distinct elements persons emerge as hybrids of the human and non-human" (1999:123; see also M. Strathern 1988, 1993). Her interesting conceptualization of the Melanesian person partly draws on the work of Mauss (1979) and Dumont (1970). Carsten (2004), picking up on these themes, explores some ways "the person" is composed by relationships in different cultures.

13. Native North American hunters, Amazonian foragers, Eskimo hunters, and Southeast Asian farmers often exploited what was seen as an "unlimited" base.

14. Lessig (2001) distinguishes between "rivalrous" and "nonrivalrous" uses of a commons. For him, a commons is held by a community whose members have complete or partially controlled access through shared rules. Some common resources and their uses are nonrivalrous, as in the use of language, theories, ideas, and some inventions. Other commons have rivalrous uses: one person's access affects another's, as in the case of a beach, public park, or roadway. Lessig uses this distinction to explore the Internet as a commons and to argue that if its uses are nonrivalrous, innovation is increased. His distinction roughly corresponds to mine between unlimited and limited bases, but I think he leaves out the distinction between community and market uses, and the ways both types of base can be used either for community or market purposes.

15. Elsewhere I have discussed the metaphoric relation of the central rice strain and the Iban *bilek* or apartment (Gudeman 1986). The central rice is the *padi pun,* and the head of the *bilek* is the *pun bilek.* In both instances *pun* means foundation or base.

16. For a discussion of "cultural goods" that evoke more than cultural identity, see Klamer 2004.

17. For this section, I have drawn principally on Niezen (1998); I return to an earlier work on the Cree in a later chapter, and I have briefly considered the Cree in a prior book (Gudeman 1986).

18. See Bohannan and Bohannan (1968), and Bohannan (1955, 1957, 1959).

3

Trade's Reason

Trade makes the world fluid. Through it things, ideas, and even people are transformed into one another. Market trade is a dialectical process, but it occurs only when rates of exchange or prices are established between traders. And if the possibility of transforming one thing into another seems magical, the rates at which this magic takes place seem out of human control. Detached from mutual relationships and from relations between people and things, they have a life of their own. I term this seemingly independent power of exchange rates the *fetishism* of prices. We attend to prices, talk about them, and are obsessed by their influence over our lives.

The powerful, incessant fluctuations of prices impel the use of calculative reason. Instrumental rationality becomes prominent not through changes in beliefs and ideologies, growing economic scarcity, or the influence of economic theories, but through competitive exchange. Of course, anonymous trade seldom consists solely of calculated choice: it may be interlaced with social and personal ties, and affected by emotions and cognitive limits.[1] Trade also may take place under conditions of imperfect information and draw on forms of bounded rationality; for example, one party to an exchange may have greater information about market trades and values than another, which can happen in trades between high market participants and "Third World" poor. Traders also arrive with different resources, such as withholding and monopolistic power or differential capacities in language and trading skills: in financial and commodity markets, floor traders develop styles of work, and are capacitated by their local technologies (Zaloom 2003). Calculative reason has diverse local appearances. But through competitive exchange rates impersonal trade necessarily generates calculated selection.

When exchange rates shift, which they do for many reasons, market participants must respond in a calculated way if they are to continue trading in the market. Their use of calculative reason, induced by shifting terms of trade, *reverberates,* or draws a reaction in other exchanges because it changes their payoffs; the practice *cascades,* or expands into sectors of mutuality; and it turns *reflexive* as it repeats and becomes a conscious and satisfying action itself. Induced by the practices of impersonal trade, price formation, and competition, practical reason takes on a life of its own; it is *reified* or becomes an autonomous activity, although its entrenchment or subjective realization varies by market, local context, and individual. Continual market participation and success lies in the repeated use of calculative reason, which constitutes the motor, the "spirit," and the "calling" of high market economies. This dependence on calculative reason, with its endless measuring of ends against means, leads to unceasing attempts at profit making. Accumulations of wealth in money and goods signal the effective use of calculative reason, while its continual reproduction in trade reifies the rational actor, who constitutes the foundation for derivational models in economics.[2]

My use of the terms fetishism and reification differs from the traditional ones. Marx developed the concept of the "fetishism of commodities" in the first volume of *Capital* (1967 [1867]), although the basis for his argument was laid in the *Economic and Philosophic Manuscripts* (1988) and the *Grundrisse* (1973). By fetishism Marx referred to the special hold that things and money, or commodities, have on us in capitalism. We treat them as animate or lifelike. Marx explained that labor is always expended in production as humans produce and reproduce themselves and their means of existence. In capitalism the worker's objectified or embodied labor is appropriated through the exchange of a wage for work that precedes production. Following Aristotle, Marx distinguished the use-value of an object, such as the nourishment it provides or the warmth it offers, from its exchange-value, or the number of other commodities it can fetch in trade. Use-value is principally a qualitative determination, while exchange-value refers to a quantity. Marx argued that in the market, commodities are traded (more or less) in accord with the labor they embody, which is their exchange-value. Commodity trade appears to be just.

The exchange of labor for a wage is different, for the laborer trades to the capitalist his use-value, which is his potential power or ability to labor, and receives a wage, which is his exchange-value. The worker's wage (his exchange-value) pays for the labor value of the goods that sustain him and his family so that his use-value can be reproduced and once again exchanged. Through this exchange, the laborer fairly receives the value he embodies, but the capitalist obtains something different. By payment of the wage (or the exchange-value of the laborer) he secures use of the worker's labor, and labor in action can be made to yield more value than is required to sustain it. Through the exercise or expenditure of his use-value, the laborer reproduces both the labor value of his wage and a surplus of labor that is embodied in commodities, which the capitalist seizes. The surplus falls into the capitalist's hands because he has purchased and owns the worker's labor capacity or use-value, and the capitalist receives this surplus as money profit when the commodities are sold. But this extractive process, by which profits arise and are appropriated in production, remains hidden in exchange, because in trade all commodities—including labor—are exchanged at their values. The underlying reality that commodities are congealed labor is veiled in the market, with the result that commodities seem to have an independent, objective, and active life of their own. For Marx, this *animation* of commodities in exchange constitutes their fetishism: it is but the other side of the draining of labor in production. The fetishism of commodities is a symbolic re-presentation of the human labor they embody, while their real life remains hidden.

After Marx, Georg Lukács (1971 [1922]) extended the notion of fetishism and reformulated it as reification. Broadly, reification means to make something into a thing or to "thingify" a concept that denotes a process, relationship, or object. The two notions of fetishism and reification are related to what Alfred North Whitehead called "the fallacy of misplaced concreteness" in which the abstract is mistaken for the concrete (Whitehead 1925:52). But Lukács's reformulation takes it some distance from Marx's original idea, for Marx had distinguished objectification and thingification from fetishism. For Marx, in all economies (from slavery to communism), humans objectify themselves by laboring and producing objects. Only in capitalism is this objectification systematically exploited: commodity fetishism is specific to capitalism. In contrast, Lukács equated reification with the objectification of labor and then expanded the idea to cover all of capitalist thought, as well as philosophical issues and the consciousness of the proletariat, who must finally "see through the reified objectivity of the given world" (1971 [1922]:193) if they are to liberate themselves. By this interpretation all of bourgeois civilization and culture may be seen as a reification, which may be why the subsequent Frankfurt School could never overcome its pessimistic view of society. In recent years, the use and meaning of the terms fetishism and reification have grown even more convoluted as anthropologists, particularly those examining native monies and transgressive objects, have adopted and employed the word fetishism to designate the ambivalent and tangled relationships in which these entities are embedded.[3]

In contrast to Lukács I distinguish reification from fetishism; and unlike Marx and many others, I shall not refer to the fetishism of commodities but argue that prices are the fetishes of the market. The construction of prices in impersonal trade brings together different qualities and transforms them into a quantitative equivalence, so inscribing calculative reason as the subjectivity of traders.[4] This reified notion expands its hold as individuals increasingly live by trade. At the extreme, as one bond trader said, "Whatever money you make is what you're worth" (Abolafia 1996:30), meaning that his identity was defined by the cumulative efficacy of his calculative reasoning. He priced his "worth," which was a reification of his diverse qualities.

Commensuration in Theories

Trading revolves about commensuration, which means to compare by use of a common measure.[5] Shared measures are found in all economies. But is making things commensurate a pragmatic act, an inherent function of the human, a product of comparative work, or an outcome of trade? Why does commensuration arise in market trade, and where does the measuring rod come from?

In many nontrade settings the assessment of quantity is useful, such as calculating the volume of a harvest to know how long it will last, figuring the food required to nourish a family for a week, or estimating the amount of labor needed to finish a job. Measurement scales, used for different purposes, often are locally formulated. In rural Panama, body parts—fingertips to elbow, fingertips to nose, hands outstretched across the body—were used to size a work area or measure space for building a house; different-sized gourds and baskets measured harvests of maize, beans, and small crops; plates and cooking pots measured the food needed each day. People create domains of comparability and devise scales to grade items within these domains. These are registers of value, which are used for many purposes. Numbers are used not only because they are "objective" and distant from individual interests, which allows for trust in them (Porter 1995), but also because they are helpful in everyday life.

Applying a common measure permits comparison. A thermometer records the heat of human bodies, air, and water; it can be used to compare one human body to another, to itself at different times, or to a different entity, such as a body of water. A yardstick measures linear space, and can be used to compare the length of a room with that of a pencil. A weight scale measures the mass of an object, and a speedometer measures velocity: two cars can be compared by weight or speed. Similarly, different tasks can be compared by the time needed to complete them, and a genealogical tree can be used to compare kinship distance. These measures are quantitative abstractions from the diverse qualities of entities that otherwise are not similar: for example, two days with the same heat at a specific time may differ in rate of air flow, humidity, hours of daylight, and duration of the heat; a human and a day that share the same temperature are otherwise different, just as speed is only one feature of a car, the earth's rotation, or a walking person. The measuring rod keeps the category of comparison constant across a range of objects and captures one dimension of an entity's qualities, each of which may be multiply determined.

Sometimes we link different registers experimentally or intuitively. For example, a day's heat or hours of light might be compared to the growth rate of plants or the activity level of animals. Sometimes we combine incomparable measures to make an intuitive judgment. A person's temperature, weight, body fat, blood pressure, and cholesterol count may be used to assess her health; drawing these measures together, health workers may reach different conclusions about her overall state, depending on their confidence in the scales, the meaning and importance they attach to them, and their experience in using them. Medical researchers, of course, may gather large samples to correlate the measures and make diagnostic predictions. But scales, whether linked by intuition or experiment, by definition are not translatable. Each scale, being a convention, covers a designated realm.

Given the many measuring rods in a society, how is commensuration established in trade? I distinguish three spaces of value and commensuration in relation to trade and mutuality: (1) the incommensurable, (2) the incommensurate, and (3) the commensurate. Incommensurable things are mutual holdings that never reach the market. They are not measured against or exchanged for other things, and pertain to noncomparable registers of value. Stipulating an act or item as incommensurable keeps it within the realm of mutuality and communal management.[6] For example, do we trade Notre Dame, the Taj Mahal, or Luxor? Designating a place as a "world heritage site" is an act of a global community that places an object in the incommensurable domain and marks its status within a specific culture as well as all cultures.[7] (Designating a place as a world heritage site may have market implications, for the site may draw tourists who want to participate in its "community"; spending money, they support and expand local commerce that in turn may help maintain the site.) Art, architecture, and space are not the only components of the incommensurable.[8] The Islamic prohibition of collecting interest (*riba*) on a monetary loan stipulates an incommensurable act.[9] Allah prohibits gathering an effortless profit or securing an increase from a borrower who is obliged to return more than was lent. This gain cannot be part of Islamic financial markets.

Within the arena of trade lie the incommensurate things that can be brought to the bar of exchange and made commensurate. Through pricing, the incommensurate, or qualitatively different things, become commensurate. But here I depart from the two generally known approaches in economics. I do not ask what is the nature or source of the common measuring rod (as if it had a content). I do not assume that a common metric, such as energy units or labor value, exists before trade and "makes" items commensurate, and I do not assume that humans independently order or commensurate their preferences before trading. I take the more anthropological position that things are incommensurate (or incommensurable) until we establish a relationship among them, and that market commensuration emerges in trade where we use a conventional scale to mark their relation. Market commensuration is an after-the-fact register.

Commensuration by labor is key in Marx's theory of capitalism. He argued that labor is both the source and the measure of value (Meek 1973). Market prices reflect (and vary) from the labor value of commodities or the traded things and services, but ultimately, the value of every item can be reduced to the socially necessary labor time required to produce it. Consider a shirt and pair of pants made by a tailor. He spends a number of hours making them, and eventually will have an average labor time for making an outfit. From this average time of numerous tailors, the average labor time required to make a shirt and pair of pants in a society can be figured. Incorporating this required time with other forms of clothes making, the average time needed in all of tailoring and ultimately the labor time required to produce all the necessary goods and services of a society may be calculated. This sum of labor, which is required for social reproduction, represents the value of all the commodities in a society; each good or service embodies a percentage of this total value. Thus, when two commodities are traded, socially formed labor is actually being exchanged, and, Marx continues, because labor is the value-creating agent in production, labor time provides the measuring rod for the trade. Market prices do diverge from labor values, but for reasons such as monopolistic pricing and superexploitation.[10] Regardless, the measure of labor value exists in advance of exchange; the commensuration of commodities—reached through the prior social division of labor and expended labor time in production—precedes trade. Labor value provides the foundation for his model.

The neoclassical approach is different. By this argument, and there are many variations, trade reveals preferences. Each individual has preferences that are independently formed: they are exogenously determined or set outside the realm of pricing.[11] But individuals order their preferences. The order can be cardinal or ordinal, or even follow a meta-preference scale (Sen 1977); however, the ordering must be transitive. If A is preferred to B, and B is preferred to C, then A must be preferred to C as well. If C is preferred to A, the order is not rational. In addition to being transitive, preferences are rational when they are complete (or all the options can be compared), and when they are continuous, meaning that small changes in prices lead to small changes in demand (Hausman 1992; Helgesson 2002, 2005).

Rational choice itself is sometimes distinguished from rational preference. Selection is rational when the preferences underlying it are rational (as described) and a person does not prefer any option other than the one selected (Hausman 1992; Sen 2002). Rationality has a double aspect: ordered preferences and optimal choice. Other qualifications are sometimes added. For example, rational choice is usually seen to be context-independent: the preferences and choices of market actors are assumed to be independent of one another, except when they have an impact by way of pricing. (Other assumptions in this account often include that people are free of emotional behavior in their choices.)

From an anthropological perspective, two assumptions of the standard theory are questionable. First, people are presumed to arrive at the moment of trade with a "preference" for rational scaling. The contents of the scale and the magnitude of the differences on it vary, but people order, arrange, and measure in advance of trading. According to the standard wisdom, we can be certain of this disposition through the preferences that are revealed in exchange. Scaling and measuring are not part of the act of trade; they are a prior propensity. This assumption obviates value incommensurability, for it is assumed that every individual always brings his tastes to an overall, totalizing benchmark or has a complete utility function: according to the standard account, values are not disparate. The presumption implies that people are naturally rational and so enshrines rational choice at the foundation of the model. (Of course, if people do not commensurate their tastes, they are not rational and fall outside the model.)

The standard account of preferences also elides conditions of uncertainty, which may be distinguished from risk. In situations of risk, probabilities can be attached to known outcomes. In conditions of uncertainty the likelihoods of outcomes are unknown. The problem is that rational choice cannot operate in conditions of uncertainty, because outcomes cannot be fully defined. (To reduce uncertainty to risk, the idea of subjective probabilities is sometimes adduced: even if we do not have hard data about the likelihood of outcomes, subjective assessments of their probabilities can be attached.) To be sure, not all our choices are made in conditions of uncertainty, but many have contingencies: their outcomes and implications are not fully predictable. Furthermore, how can we know our preferences unless we experience them? After their satisfaction, preferences also may change, just as they may change in the experience of trade. Claiming that real preferences are revealed in trade simply says the trade is done; it tells nothing about them as a process, it leaves out learning-by-doing in trade and consumption, and it omits human reflexivity or action as an emergent process. As Helgesson (2002:193) remarks about revealed preferences, "]t]he theory's explanatory power … is limited to post-event explanations."

Commensuration in Practice

In contrast to the Marxist and neoclassical assumptions about commensuration, my view is more pragmatic: the act of trade creates the *necessity* of comparing, even if we tell soothing stories about prior preferences or embodied labor. Scaling is induced by context, which in the case of markets is the trading relationship. The measure is made by the exchange.

What are the implications for the way prices are understood? Exchange rates, marked on a money scale, represent the commensuration of incommensurate things. Displaying an equivalence between different entities, and combining unlike things in a single number, prices are an abstraction through which things become alike as if a base metal could be transformed to gold, which can happen if the quantities are "right." But we are never certain of the consequences of a trade or its desirability. An exchange projects people from what they are and know to what they may be and will have. How do we know that an exchange will be right for us or even fair? Prices dance out of control but affect our sense of well-being. In market economies, we talk about prices as if they had independent efficacy, such as the shifting prices of gasoline, electricity, and heating oil, or the ever-escalating compensation packages of top managers. When prices rise while income lags, one feels impoverished; when they fall when income grows, one feels empowered. We may be told that exchange rates form a negotiated system in an overall market of supply and demand, but prices confront us individually as the power to transform our personal worlds through the interchanges they effect. Trade has a transgressive quality—dangerous, attractive, perplexing—because it alters a context by conjoining and equilibrating socially separate things. Like alchemy, trade transforms one thing into another: two objects or services become substitutable. But are they?

Surrounded by a degree of uncertainty, every sale and purchase fills us with a degree of tension about what we are giving up for what we are gaining. However, this frisson of making things commensurate varies, and we might distinguish degrees of the shudder in exchange. At one extreme, incommensurable items—as locally defined—occasionally are traded; and the border between incommensurable things that cannot be traded, and items that can be exchanged shifts over time, especially as the market realm expands. Ethnographic cases graphically reveal the tensions that emerge when social identity, relationships, and shared holdings are priced and sold. The Luo of Africa sometimes use inalienable lineage land (their base) to gain money by selling it, using it to mine gold, or planting it with tobacco or cannabis. The money gained from this diversionary use of lineage land is said to be "bitter." Cattle and brides obtained with this money die, because ancestral spirits pursue them (Shipton 1989). Some rural farmers in Colombia believe that illicitly baptized money has the power to multiply (Taussig 1980). Likewise, rural Panamanians report that if a godfather holds money under his godchild's head and has it blessed instead of the baby, the money will multiply. Eventually it is lost, however, because the godfather's sacred tie to his godchild cannot be measured, renounced, and changed to money. In Bolivia, if a member of the Juku-mani community sold a part of its shared land he supposedly was put to death (Godoy 1990). These exchanges exemplify attempted trans-actions between incommensurable value realms, and according to the local stories, they never reach successful completion because they vio-late moral borders or the disjunction between the communal and mar-ket realms.[12]

In reverse, many groups consider the practice of autarky, or keeping to the self, to be a moral obligation that preserves community. In the Lawonda community of Indonesia, people do not sell the rice they grow and consume, nor do they buy rice from others or desire to receive it as a gift in times of need, because doing so would indicate their inability to achieve self-sufficiency by using their own base as well as their de-pendence on the work and land of others (Vel 1994). But the line be-tween the incommensurable and the incommensurate may be porous and breached by the powerful. Bohannan (1955) observed that in Tiv society transfers usually occur within three spheres: bride for bride, a special cloth for metal bars, and subsistence foods for subsistence foods. Exchanges within a sphere are morally neutral; however, trans-fers between them, such as metal bars for a bride, or subsistence goods for the cloth, bring prestige to one and moral failure to the other: a man who accomplishes the feat of trading upward is said to have a "strong heart." Closer to home, many question selling body parts and sperm, paying for designer children, or renting wombs, for they embody as-pects of identity, although they can be explained as a way of sharing (Hewitson 2001; Radin 1996). We do advance monies, however, to uproot coal miners from their long-established communities when the underlying veins are exhausted. When incommensurable things are exchanged—one Hollywood film features selling a wife for a night—we expand the arena of the market, or the range of the incommensu-rate, and find ourselves without precedents for pricing the transaction.

Even when the seam between the incommensurable and the incom-mensurate, or between mutuality and market, is not breached, pricing arouses tension, for trading goods or labor is a shock, a rupture, be-cause it means making incommensurate things commensurate and substituting one for another. Of course, many trades become routine: we buy salt as needed without too much attention given to its price. Small and regular trades arouse little tension; pens for pencils, paper-clips for staples, "bread" for bread are exchanges so ordinary that the frisson is not noticeable. For many of these trades, set prices provide predictability for the manufacturer, save time for the retailer, and relieve the customer of bargaining and engaging in an antagonistic interchange with the seller. Finding signs at a store proclaiming "no bargaining" can be a pleasure. But buying a "big ticket" item such as a home, car, or household appliance is different. Their purchase leads most people to seek more information about the good, the seller, and related prices (all at a cost); yet the information does not quell the tension, because we cannot predict the impact of the trade on our welfare. We continually ask: Is it worth it? Was the purchase a good one? And we feel better when the salesperson assures us it is an excellent buy or the dress looks good, for then we feel more assured about the commensuration. Making our labor, leisure, relationships, or aspects of our environment commensurate is even more disquieting. Do people ever feel satisfied that they have been properly compensated for their work? "Wage grumbles" are encountered among the grossly underpaid as well as the blatantly overpaid, such as business leaders and sports stars who may seek even higher compensation to assure themselves of an identity in a world of uncertain prices.

Experts on development may claim that when economies are modernizing or when socialism is shifting to capitalism, participants must learn how to bargain, and to price goods and services. But the change to a market economy transcends the imparting of technical skills. Consider the medieval and early modern concern with establishing a "just price" (Baldwin 1959). In part, the disquiet focused on the use of fair physical weights and measures, but underlying the discussion was the question of commensuration as people began to bring more and more goods from different places to a common bar of exchange. How should the objects be joined?[13] In rural Panama and Colombia people would talk about a just trade, but often without conclusion: did it mean exchanging a sack of maize for a sack of tubers, trading different crops by equal weights or their cost of production, or using accurate weight scales? Did it mean trading a day of work for a day of different work, or did it refer to trading work in the same task? On the island of Sumba (Indonesia) people say that market thinking is new and that formerly "no one calculated the value of what they gave" (Keane 2001:72). Different goods were exchanged in equal quantity; one sack of low-priced rice was exchanged for an equal volume of more expensive coffee. In Latin American marketplaces, when a transaction is completed, a seller often offers a little bit more (a lagniappe) as if to help bridge the incommensurate and relieve the tension. The practice is not unlike offering a baker's dozen.

As humans increasingly submit to the mechanics of the market and learn to evaluate by price, the trade-off ratios or prices that we achieve become our indices of well-being, as quantity itself becomes a quality: a nation's health is indicated by its productivity or its gross domestic product per capita; a company's value is measured by its profit and growth rates, as well as the percentage of profit it distributes in dividends; a charitable organization's effectiveness is known by its benefit/expense ratio; and individual "worth" often means assets owned by a single individual, because it summarizes a person's effectiveness in trade. Austrian and neoclassical economists emphasize that prices are a form of "information," because they convey signals about supply and demand. But we also interpret and imbue prices with deeper meanings: the better the trade-off or purchase price, the happier we are. We exalt in and are disappointed by prices, and we watch these ratios that discipline and compel us to see the world in terms of means-to-ends connections. Sales attract us, regardless of the good on offer, by the feeling of instrumental success they provide, although—in a dialectical reversal of quantity and quality—one beer in Sweden proclaimed it must be good because it cost so much.

Veblen captured this increasing dominance of the price mentality when he distinguished between the "captains of industry" and the "captains of finance." The former, he argued, provide leadership in making things, refining processes, and selling products. In contrast, the captains of finance use the measuring rod of money, and they produce and trade property with an eye to the bottom line. The division, Veblen thought, was growing, with the captains of finance not only achieving supremacy in the economy but also securing the honor and prestige (or qualities) that rightfully belong to the captains of industry. He termed this dialectical transformation a "derangement," which is the mystification of quantity as a quality. One of the most honored and successful companies in the United States, General Electric, has long operated by the numbers: if a division does not meet its standard for return on investment, regardless of product and absolute profitability, it may be sold to achieve efficiency; in fact, General Electric is primarily a financial corporation. A few years ago, Merrill Lynch went through "bloodletting," replacing top executives who possessed people skills and expertise in relationship banking with "quants," or numbers-oriented managers (*New York Times*, 5 January 2003).

Reification, Cascading, and Debasement

Trade leads not only to the fetishism of prices but also to the reification of the rational actor. Market trade takes place between people who do not share mutuality. The exchange disconnects people from relationships with others and from themselves. Each market trader, from the perspective of his counterpart, is an other who is empty of communal and historical characteristics, and has no subjective qualities except the desire to trade and the ability to calculate.[14] Each uses the other as a means. But in objectifying the other and suppressing a social relationship, the trader objectifies herself. Each becomes an other, for the self and the other. The asocial trade "thingifies" the trader by emptying him of social qualities and personal characteristics. His social personhood and force, his animating connections, are eliminated.

The trade of object for object, realized and abstracted in their exchange rate, replaces sociality with calculative reason as a trader's subjectivity. A price, whether calculated in money or goods, is actually a four-part analogy: three apples for two oranges can be read as

3 : 2 :: apples : oranges,
or as
3 : apples :: 2 : oranges.[15]

The price can be read in either direction, corresponding to the trader's position: three apples are gained for two oranges given, or two oranges are gained for three apples submitted. For each transactor, price is the same ratio but inversely seen; and for each, price creates a means-to-ends relationship by comparing his return to his offer. One submits three apples to secure two oranges—the apples are his means, the oranges are his end. The other trader submits two oranges, as means, to secure three apples that are his ends. Because one trader's offering is the end for the other, just as the other's offering is the goal for the first, the trade comprises a threefold exchange. Each trader exchanges his means for an end, and he does so by exchanging with the other.

As ratios, prices constitute means-to-ends activity and instrumental reason in the person, because the trader—to be able to continue in the market, especially in conditions of competition—must act in an instrumental fashion. Because traders have no communal ties, each persuades others to trade through competitive pricing. Trade produces the ratio, and the ratio constitutes means-to-ends activity or practical reason. (Conversely, the nontrader, such as the self-sufficient producer or the welfare recipient, may be said to lack rationality and deemed to be unworthy.)

The ratio formed through market exchange has *reverberating, cascading,* and *reflexive* effects on other traders, the self, and communities, so that calculative reason continually expands and reinforces its domain of practice. With population expansion, increased density, shifting political and environmental conditions, technological change or innovation, heightened mobility, improved transportation, or an increase in traders and competition, rates of exchange alter. As rates change, so do the means-to-ends relationships of every trader. For example, for reasons of demand or the weather, the rate of three apples offered for two oranges may shift against the apple seller so that she must offer four apples for the two oranges. To continue trading, she must (1) reduce her consumption of oranges, (2) produce more apples with the same means as before, or (3) produce more enticing apples with the same means. To remain in the market, the trader must minimize her means or maximize the ends she offers. The trader must increasingly become a calculator. But as the apple seller adjusts, her new means-to-ends relationships reverberate on other traders through the alterations she makes, such as buying fewer consumables elsewhere, hiring more laborers, or purchasing more fertilizer. Through its reverberations across exchange rates, trade is the continuing impulse for the use of rational choice. [16]

Trade also has a cascading effect on mutuality and communal modes of transfer. The oranges and the apples that serve as means in a trade are themselves prior ends that had to be secured or produced by earlier means. When rates of exchange shift, these "pretrade" acts are affected. Reducing or enlarging the means or ends in one trade both reverberates on "prior" and "subsequent" ones, and cascades from ends to means to earlier means until the process finally reaches into the mutual realm affecting the materials and labor that connect people in relationships. For example, if the apple seller devotes more of her own labor (by working longer hours) to producing four apples for two oranges, she must draw from efforts previously committed to sociality or to self-sustenance, such as repairing her house or participating in a neighborhood group. Alternatively, she may dedicate her house garden to raising apples for sale, so diminishing that part of her base. Ultimately, competitively determined exchange rates increasingly diminish mutuality or the shared base of community exactly as anthropological studies have shown. For example, when a cash crop, such as sugar cane, is added to subsistence farming, such as raising rice and maize for consumption, it increasingly draws on the labor and land devoted to the latter, and usually leads to the extinction of the original crops (Gudeman 1978; Gudeman and Rivera 1990). I term this cascading process from markets to community—by which the expansion of markets and calculative reason subsume mutual relations, increase commoditization and draw the incommensurable into trade—"debasement." But we might also employ Habermas's term, "colonization" of the lifeworld, for its resonance with the situations in which anthropologists often undertake research (Habermas 1987 [1981]:318).

The cascading process is a general one, and its occurrence in the Third World provides a mirror from the margin of the dynamics of high market societies, because cascading is within our economy. For example, when prices rise and wages remain constant, many people work longer hours, overtime, or at two jobs; wear socks longer and darn them; keep a car for an extra year or two; sell an heirloom; downsize a house; take in boarders; or impinge on the earth's potential. As they do, the range of other possible modes of mutuality shrinks. Even when wages remain constant or rise as the economy grows, people may—as in the United States—work even more to participate in the expanding market and to display to themselves and others their effectiveness in doing so (Linder 1970). Cascading affects both female and male labor in households, resources devoted to mutuality, and expectations about tradable holdings. Sometimes the trade process may lead to strengthening mutuality through use of the wealth it generates, but the repetitive effects of calculative reason lead to its expansion, with consequent communal fragmentation.

As calculative reason, repeated through reverberation and cascading, and refined by learning-by-doing, becomes habitual, it is ever more reified. When it becomes an end or something done for its own sake, calculative reason turns reflexive and the trader becomes the embodiment of rational choice. As we increasingly and reflexively survey ourselves as means to trade labor, ideas, ingenuity, and body parts, our singular and constant component of identity becomes the ability to fashion and calculate means-to-ends relations. Always searching for better means or ends, we encapsulate profit making within ourselves. This reification develops not in the Marxist sense that labor, which creates and measures value, is alienated from the worker and embodied in commodities, but because humans are drained of identity built through mutuality. The calling to trade leads to divided subjectivities, because humans have both conjoint and disjoint identities; they have mixed "selfways" (Markus, Mullally, and Kitayama 1997), which is economy's tension. But as we turn others and ourselves into things and as competitive trading expands—by its reverberating, cascading and reflexive effects with the rational actor serving as the processor of exchange rates—calculative practices enlarge, penetrate new realms of life, and expand the market arena.

Neoclassical economics and rational choice theory do help explicate this market reality. The first theorem of neoclassical economics is known as Pareto optimality, which is a collective condition in which no one can achieve a better means-to-ends ratio through a further trade without someone else moving to a worse one.[17] Some neoclassical economists emphasize that preferences or tastes *are* exogenous to the market actor, and so they may be. But this model also fortifies and legitimates the world of the market by turning the practices of trade into a theory of the rational actor, and then re-presenting this market reification as his original subjectivity and mode of being.[18] Ultimately, this representation of the actor can be used to justify the expansion of the market in order to increase "welfare." Re-presented in the discourse of economics and market participants, the rational calculator—that measurer of means and ends—increasingly becomes the subjectivity by which we live. Formal rationality is dialectically transformed to substantive rationality, becoming the only expression of its opposite.

Theory, Pits, and Experiments

My model of impersonal, competitive trade and the production of calculative reason was presaged a century ago by Simmel, who observed that the

Modern mind has become more and more calculating. The calculative exactness of practical life which the money economy has brought about corresponds to the ideal of natural science: to transform the world into an arithmetic problem, to fix every part of the world by mathematical formulas. Only money economy has filled the days of so many people with weighing, calculating, with numerical determinations, with a reduction of qualitative values to quantitative ones (Simmel 1997:177).

In recent years a number of ethnographic and experimental studies have been filling out Simmel's observations and describing how the competitive market process leads to the reification of calculative reason. For example, Zaloom (2006) shows how economic man—that aggressive, competitive, and antagonistic person—is brought to life in the pit of the Chicago Board of Trade (CBOT).[19] The physical actions and language of traders in the pits are as boisterous and impolite as they are competitive and individualistic: in their daily face-to-face interactions, floor traders become self-interested and present themselves and address others as atomistic persons, as if they had no other subjectivity. Their raw character, observes Zaloom, is not "natural" or given but emerges through the trading experience. The pit itself was not only architecturally designed by some of Chicago's famous architects; it is a socially made arena, governed by rules, such as properly recording every trade and fulfilling each contract. These mutual agreements compel traders to become embodiments of calculative reason. But traders share the mystification that trust in others arises from their individualistic behavior, for they tell themselves that only the market expresses a universal human instinct. Just as this narrative frees them from experiencing ties to other traders (much as standard economists view social bonds as frictions on trade or as transaction costs), it allows them to reflect on, experiment with, and cascade their behavior outside the pit. Through financial trade the disjoint and reflective calculator emerges. Homo economicus, as Zaloom remarks, is an "emergent figure" (2006: 197, fn. 8).

In recent years, some forms of experimental economics also have demonstrated how calculative reason is brought forth by context. To be certain, one part of experimental and observational economics shows how people are not always perfect calculators. For example, sometimes we focus more on losses than gains (people can be risk averse); do not treat money as fungible (by keeping separate mental accounts and failing to calculate our marginal preferences in consumption); and keep in mind sunken costs while failing to consider current opportunity costs. Similarly, as Taleb (2005) observes, we may think we find patterns in small sequences of numbers that are random and base our stock market selections on these improbable events.[20] Undoubtedly, we all may fail in our attempts to be calculators, but much of this work seems designed to show that we fail against the standard of rational choice. It subtly adopts the market image as the baseline.

A different genre of experimental economics, however, suggests how calculative reason is circumstantially produced. For example, some studies show that in anonymous games or situations people become less socially minded; market competition fosters opportunistic behavior, lowers "other-regardedness," and reduces preferences for mutuality (Carpenter 2005). Conversely, reducing anonymity makes people more social and diminishes their ability to engage in opportunistic acts. In one set of controlled experiments, researchers showed that people primed with reminders of money (by use of pictures, symbolic tokens, and language) acted more self-sufficiently. Participants with money on the mind preferred to work alone, to separate themselves physically from others, and even to play alone. Money, these observers concluded, "enhanced individualism but diminished communal motivations" (Vohs et al. 2006). Other empirical studies suggest that students majoring in economics tend to act in a more self-interested and less cooperative fashion as their knowledge of the subject grows (Frank, Gilovitch, and Regan 1993).

Price Fetishism

Prices bring together different qualities and contradictory persons: each wants what the other has, and each has what the other wants. Prices transform their positions through bargaining or calculation, and they signal the transformability of things. I use the expression "price fetishism" for this improbable joining of opposites in a movement that seemingly has an independent dynamic. As the joining of opposite intentions, however, prices are unstable, unpredictable, and filled with tension. Like a rushing current, prices continuously seem out of control, with no predictable channel or end point. Just as oil gushes from the ground, its price at the pump jumps this way and that. For traders, prices have no grounding. To provide an anchor, we invent stories that legitimate prices—by narratives, such as fair trades, just prices, fair exchange, labor value, supply and demand, and free choice—but market prices elude control (except by monopolies). With a force of their own, they are a mystery that profoundly affects daily lives and relationships.

In the market arena, every traded entity or commodity, including goods, labor, resources, and money has no referent other than its shifting price, which is its transformability to other goods, labor, or money. In the market realm, prices define the identity of a thing. I draw a contrast, then, between my fetishism of prices and the Marxist fetishism of commodities. The latter refers to the abstraction and alienation of a commodity from its conditions of production, specifically from the labor that produced it, so that commodities are things that seem to have an objective, independent existence. These things are fetishes. In contrast, price fetishism refers not to things but to relations between entities, whether they are labor, resources, or money, and it pertains to the realm of exchange. In a broad sense, commodity fetishism can be traced to the idea of the disjoint individual acting in production; price fetishism refers to the relation between disjoint individuals who exchange. If commodity fetishism has a putative grounding in labor, price fetishism has no grounding except in shifting relationships. I refer back to my initial observations about our overwhelming use of ratios. Exchange rates or ratios have become a principled way of knowing, of understanding, and of acting in the world. We know commodities or property by their prices: work by its wage, land by its rent, capital by its return, the interest rate by its price (as I shall explain), and thousands of other phenomena, such as mortality, births, and marriages by their rates. The fetish has cascaded from the market to become an everyday obsession outside it.

There is another aspect to the fetishism of prices: prices refer only to themselves. Empty of substantive content, they leave a space for local interpretation of labor, goods, resources, and money. Here the world of narratives in economic theory (such as supply and demand) and advertising for consumers opens. Items traded mean their price, but the price can mean anything, and that anything is open to advertising or rhetoric. Objects may symbolize new worlds. Jameson finely captures part of this process when he observes,

> But this in no way means that we cannot consume the product in question, "derive enjoyment" from it, become addicted to it, etc. Indeed, consumption in the social sense is very specifically the word for what we in fact do to reified products of this kind, that occupy our minds and float above that deeper nihilistic void left in our being by the inability to control our own destiny. (Jameson 1991:317)

Even if Jameson is more concerned with the way commodities are delinked from their history and conditions of production (in a Marxist sense) as opposed to exchange rates that make this separation possible, he is pointing to their reification, to their emptiness of meaning in exchange, and to their "openness" to new rhetorics of meaning, which is advertising. Elsewhere he remarks,

> [In] the tendential identification of the commodity with its image (or brand name or logo), another, more intimate, symbiosis between the market and the media is effectuated, in which boundaries are washed over … and an indifferentiation of levels gradually takes the place of an older separation between thing and concept (or indeed, economics and culture, base and superstructure).… The products sold on the market become the very content of the media image. (Jameson 1991:175)

Again, I depart from Jameson's more production oriented, Marxist analysis, which invokes base and superstructure, as if the former were an anchor for his critique. But his emphasis on media is telling.

In this space of meaning produced by the abstraction of exchange rates, advertisers prowl, drawing on images that convince their audience. Traditionally, one world of images has been the inanimate and animal world. Prudential Insurance stands like a rock (of Gibraltar); Merrill Lynch runs with the bulls; the Ford Mustang runs quickly and the Ford Thunderbird flies, whereas the Volkswagen Rabbit bounds ahead. Sometimes an object refers to another object that has features it metaphorically conveys: the Nissan NX 2000 car is like a late-issue airplane that connotes speed and human domination of machines with their continuous improvement. Sometimes brands refer to the qualities of an object—whether wet, cold, or flying, as do the Whirlpool washing machine, the Coldspot refrigerator, and the Nike Air series of athletic shoes that includes the Air Zoom, the Air Force, the Air Jordan, and the Air Max. We become what we buy, with multiple identities so that choice becomes ever more important, if we "buy" the rhetoric. In a later chapter, when I examine the dialectic of mutuality and market, I return to the semantic space created by price fetishism to show how images of mutuality also are used in advertising to create a social relationship between the buyer who consumes a product and the worker who helps make it. In those cases, especially, the rhetoric of community mystifies the contractual relation.

Simultaneously, as Naomi Klein observes, this vacant space leaves open the possibility of resistance in the form of effacing billboards, running countercampaigns, mocking the images, revealing what lies hidden behind them, and more (Klein 2002). So, the space produced by price fetishism does not yield a lack of meaning but a superfluity of shifting images.

Price fetishism removes moral and social constraints between buyers and sellers. Producers have no responsibility for their conditions of production (such as pollution and sweatshops), and no responsibility to their consumers. Consumers have no responsibility for the production conditions of the products they buy or for the negative externalities of their use—unless outside restraints are imposed. This is a profound problem. Again, compare this fetishism to Marx's. He proposed to "solve" the problem of fetishism by a revolution that would overthrow capitalism, which had alienated workers from their products and the value they produced. But his solution concerns only a special form of price fetishism that arises in the exchange of work for a wage. Price fetishism has to do with the nullification of all mutuality, and its externalities and cascading effects affect all social relationships and subjectivities.

Crossing all domains, from human interactions, to production, to consumption, to bodies, and to subjectivities, price fetishism can only be contested by local actions that resist anonymous, competitive trade by limiting markets and relinking buyers and sellers. For example, fair trade movements can have many purposes, including alleviating poverty, promoting sustainable development, offering "fair prices" to producers, enhancing working conditions, and supporting gender equity. Fair trade does not necessarily lead to market efficiency; it promotes a transparent relationship between consumers and ultimate producers. In this case transparency means that the buyer (who usually is far removed from the small-scale producers) knows what she is buying in the sense of a commodity's total conditions of production, which can affect her choice. Fair trade movements expand the notion of product information from price signals to include market externalities. If I buy an Air Jordan, I may feel like Superman given the advertising, but in the broader context of transparency, I also may feel like Fagin.

Products come with negative externalities, the unpriced effects that are imposed on consumers or the public. Advertising focuses on the "internalities" of a product or its apparent qualities and image. Some drug advertisements today must explain their negative externalities or side effects. But should this not be the case for all products? Some cereals may be "good" for us because they contain fiber, fruits, and vitamins, but do they also make some children hyperactive? Truth in labeling might not be limited to the contents of food, medicines, and other goods (with their externalities) but should be about where the good comes from (such as a fragile rain forest), where it is made and by whom, and what it does (such as carry a nondegradable plastic to the environment). We can fill the space created by price fetishism with a plurality of meanings. One objective could be to strengthen mutuality as part of our economic practices and well-being.

A Historical Speculation

If—as I argue—the use of calculative reason expands with the practice of competitive trade, and is reproduced in the discourse of standard economics as an understanding of that practice, what is the evolving historical connection between the two? Can we speculate about a shift from market practice to formal theory and universal models that in turn affect a cultural ideology and national policies? To fill out my story, let me offer a conjecture about this relation between practice and theory—one that reverses the accepted narrative. I surmise that the presumption of instrumental rationality as a human universal spread in European culture with the uncertainty produced by the expansion of market trade. Practiced first in bits and pieces in material life, it was attributed to others as to the self in the market, then conceptualized, partly on a philosophical basis, and finally inserted into the center of the discipline of economics. Throughout this evolution, practical ways of doing things were abstracted and voiced, and these formalizations influenced what people did in a continuing cycle. But again, this is my narrative, which begins with practices and possibly local voices, as I have argued in a previous work (Gudeman and Rivera 1990).

This Western story could start with early household life, and with writings about it by Aristotle, Xenophon, and Roman authors who emphasized economizing. It might continue with the late-1200s estate tracts from England, such as that of Walter of Henley, who developed a system of audits for manors and a partial theory of profit.[21] Certainly, the development of double entry accounting in Italy during the 1300s was a significant moment, as Weber (1961) and Sombart (1967 [1915]) have observed, because in double-entry accounting assets represent ends and liabilities represent means (the shareholders' equity listed as a liability is accumulated profit kept for investment). Double-entry accounting encodes the joint stockholding unit (or the corporation) as a means-to-ends entity. This part of the historical account might also include the many rational tools of the market that developed in subsequent centuries, from bills of exchange, to letters of credit, to derivatives.[22] But I want to make the case for the development of another, more profound sense of rationality as it is used in economics. Economics is not simply a logical, derivational, or rational discipline that focuses on means-to-ends relations; rather, rationality has become the grounding or anchor for its view of market life.

The neoclassical or late nineteenth-century revolution in economics did not simply extend marginalist principles from Ricardo's theory of land rent to all factors of production; it was not simply a use of the calculus to describe the marginal distribution of resources and the allocation of product; nor did it only signify the application of sophisticated forms of mathematics to material life. The revolution of the late nineteenth century was broader, for it lay in the insertion of calculative reason into the models of the market actor, who gradually emerged as an individual separated from his societal context. For example, Ricardo—writing in the early decades of the nineteenth century—was surely the first exponent of the use of a derivational model in economics. By showing how the land margin determined rents that determined profits (land was later amended to labor), he attempted to provide a logical model of the economy. But Ricardo did not establish calculative reason as the rationale for economic action, even if that was implicit in his portrayal (the emphasis on marginal productivity and its reward). The decisive turning came with the late nineteenth-century neoclassical revolution, after which von Mises (1976 [1933]) and Robbins (1969 [1935]) made the centrality of calculative reason explicit. Instrumental rationality in the actor provides the certitude on which much of modern economics, and now market practice, is based. Now, instead of "rationality" referring to an attribute that an observer may use to construct a model or assign to a pattern of thought, rationality is understood as an innate form of thought (or competence) that we deploy more or less adequately in material life.

But how was this notion of rationality culturally justified? What made it rhetorically legitimate or persuasive? Or, what was the context to which it was a response? Modern notions of individual reason, though owing to many sources, are often traced at least to Descartes (1596–1650). I want to suggest how this philosophical grounding could have arisen from the starting point of Descartes. With a radical skepticism, he first brought into doubt all knowledge, all convictions, and all philosophy. But this act of doubt allowed him to find an absolute foundation for knowledge because universal doubt had to be carried out by an ego, and this self had to be excluded from such doubt. Absolute doubt, in this sense, led Descartes to the conviction that the one clear grounding for knowledge was provided by the thinking ego, which because it was above doubt could bring into doubt the experienced world. Descartes, through his radical skepticism, came to the conclusion that the foundation for knowledge was the indubitable certainty of self; by excluding this ground for doubt from doubt itself, Descartes was able to provide a foundation for universal knowledge, judgment, and reason within the thinking being.

As Husserl (1970 [1954]) explains, this new way of knowing the world led to the modern mode of philosophizing and penetrated ever more fully into the European spirit. The divisions between mind and body as well as subject and object—dualisms that are embedded in the modern discourse on economics, with its bodiless agents and passionless calculators—are built on the Cartesian construction. The mind of economic man, external to feeling, sentiment, values, and relationships, can observe them to determine and order preferences for which it selects the means most appropriate for their satisfaction. By means of the Cartesian assumption it becomes possible to postulate an ideal, rational individual who, acting outside history and society, performs rational calculations.

Husserl, however, questioned Descartes' dualism and assertion by showing that they took for granted the Galilean-Newtonian view of the physical world as a separate, enclosed system of interacting physical bodies, and that the concept of the thinking ego was a result of this formulation, which disconnected objects from subjects. The alleged clear and certain grounding afforded by the Cartesian mind and soul was a deduction and abstraction given the mathematical construction of nature established by the Galilean revolution.

Husserl, by placing the Cartesian revolution within the context of Galileo's ideas, drew attention to its rooting in a world where science was growing and religious certainties were being questioned. But even if he provides a contextual, perhaps phenomenological account, it is still based heavily on the idea of an epistemological shift. Recently, Toulmin (1992 [1990])—tracing the turn to modernity and to essentialism in Western thought—provided a new account of the rise and wide acceptance of Cartesian epistemology. He argued that Descartes' search for certainty was a response to the unstable political and religious conditions, epitomized by the assassination of Henry of Navarre, in which Descartes found himself. Toulmin's even more contextual argument for the rise of Cartesianism is persuasive, but he omits consideration of the rapidly changing material life of the time and the reasons for the eventual, widespread Western acceptance of the Cartesian view as a depiction of everyday life. Political events, which provide the context for Toulmin's argument, have varied over time and by governmental form, but Cartesianism as an aspect of Western modernity spread widely, which remains unexplained by Toulmin.

I surmise that the Cartesian revolution may be seen not only as a response to the growth of scientific thinking, to the increasing independence of philosophy from theology, or to the rapidly changing political climate, but also as a response to the increased presence of the "other" created by the growth of markets in early modern Europe. It is far beyond my brief to trace these real-life changes in Europe during the seventeenth and eighteenth centuries—Braudel's historical work (1982) is magisterial—but I do suggest that the acceptance and spread of Cartesian thinking was tied to the expansion of market life.

In this lengthy development, the interaction of practice, reflection, and written discourse involved acts of modeling and metaphoric projection. As markets expanded within nations and across their boundaries, trade more and more took place between people who spoke different languages, held different social matrices, and had incommensurable values. Material life grew increasingly dependent on unknown and unpredictable others who provided and traded the goods that met one's needs and growing wants. The realm of the conjoint self as defined through community diminished, while the opposition between the disjoint self and the disjoint other, emerging from the market experience, provided the image of the knowable and of the uncertain.

In the trading context, each encounters the other as a means to attain something else. When this dialectic is projected on the self, the mind becomes the calculable self, and the body becomes the uncontrollable other. The first can be known, the second cannot. Then, reprojecting this self-image on others in the market, one may assume that they are calculators also, who use one as one uses them. This image of the disjoint person, drawn from the growing trading experience, became an expectation of others in the market. In scope and detail, the construction process was Vichean: "The human mind, because of its indefinite nature, wherever it is lost in ignorance makes itself the rule of the universe in respect of everything it does not know" (Vico 1970 [1744]:28).

From this combination of market experience with its uncertainty and a cultural image drawn from at-hand experience, the rational actor was crystallized as a local model. The image of the rational actor is an outcome of cycling from practices, to reflection, to formal theory, with its blowback on experience, as a way of understanding market transactions. Neither "default theory" nor natural touchstone, the rational actor is the consoling tool when community seems to disappear. Market competitors are disjoint but knowable beings who calculate means in relation to ends, because they are rational beings in the market community.

Two centuries and more after Descartes, his epistemology was fully realized in the discipline of economics. Beginning with Bentham's utilitarianism—his "felicity calculus" or account-book image of the human— in the late 1700s, continuing with the deductive models of Ricardo in the second decade of the 1800s, and culminating with the rise of marginalist economics toward the end of the nineteenth century, models in economics witnessed a radical transformation. The nineteenth-century neoclassical or marginalist revolution represents the full and final realization of Cartesian economics. According to the modelers, the economy is made up of bodiless and timeless minds—without substance, affect, life, or death—that calculate similarly. This commensurability of disjoint minds explains apparently uncertain free exchange: environments, resource endowments, and personal preferences may differ, but as reasoning selves (without matter or extension), humans are the same. This "base" promises rationality in the economy, especially as the participants, through practices as well as formal and informal modes of transmission, come to share the view of the modelers.

The rationality assumption provides clear insight into the motives of others. It affords the "in-sight" of a Benthamite prison or panopticon by which a single prison guard, located in the hub of a circle of cells, can observe all the inmates because the light that passes from one end of a cell to the other reveals their movements even if they are in shadow (Foucault 1979). Similarly, the market participant, able to see into the behavior of others through the assumption of calculative reason, can control their behavior "by getting the incentives right." And when the incentives are right, the market achieves clarity, that is, it clears—or so say standard economists.

The assumption of universal calculative reason provides a way of controlling vagaries, such as emotions and passions, and of banishing their disruptive effects in the theory of economy and to a lesser degree in practical life (recall the pit traders who even model life outside the pit in this way). Emptied of all passions but the desire to optimize, devoid of "animal spirits," lacking in the confidence of an entrepreneur, the human is constructed and conceived as pure homo economicus. Love, desire, and human sociality do not matter, for they are not required in this experience and explanation of behavior and would disrupt its predictability; hence they are banished to the position of preferences.

As a part of market activity, the rational actor model permits the formation of stable expectations, converting what otherwise might be unpredictability in others to measurable probability on which calculations can be based. And on this assumption that the market is a realm of calculable risk (as opposed to uncertainty), the regnant values of efficiency and optimality must stand.

The search for certainty, which starts perhaps with Aristotle's model of community economy and continues—with the rise of market experiences—through the mercantilists, the physiocrats, Ricardo, and Marx, culminates with the assumption of means-to-ends, calculative reasoning, though not without costs, such as excluding ties of mutuality, encountering disturbing paradoxes like the Prisoner's Dilemma, and inscribing a gendered dualism (Jaggar 1983).[23] This modernist assumption that the market realm is invested with rational action is a local, experiential model of the market, yet it describes a decultured individual. Instrument of last resort when community seems to disappear, the universal model founded on the rational actor asserts the presence of a timeless human core while denying its local fabrication by humans.

Notes

1. Lane (1991) discusses the limits of the rationality assumption for economic behavior by focusing primarily on the psychology of feeling, thinking, and behaving in the market.

2. For a recent treatment of capitalism as an abstraction and "virtual" economy, see Carrier and Miller (1998) and Carrier (1998); our views overlap but do not coincide.

3. From this perspective, the many studies today that trace the social history of commodities are one way of "de-fetishizing" them by revealing their qualitatively different contexts of production (see, for example, Appadurai 1986, Boisard 2003, Mintz 1985, and Roseberry 1996).

4. Pietz emphasizes that a fetish brings together heterogeneous elements or "incommensurable social values" (1985:16).

5. For some recent discussions of commensuration see Espel and Stevens (1998) and Povinelli (2001).

6. Raz (1986:346) might term such incommensurable items "constitutive incommensurabilities."

7. For an anthropological consideration of world heritage sites, see Nas (2002).

8. For an extended discussion of non reducible cultural values, see Klamer (2004).

9. For an anthropological account of Islamic finance and accounting, see Maurer (2002).

10. One problem, long explored, revolves about the fact that labor values of commodities cannot be transformed to market prices, for various reasons, especially because the organic composition of capital or the ratio of labor to equipment varies across industries. An alternative approach would be to say that Marx provides a critical perspective on what ought to be rather than what is. The metric of labor time and labor value provides a moral analysis, against which actual markets can be measured. From a different perspective yet, Marx is highlighting labor productivity and how it varies with the accumulation of capital.

11. But see Becker (1996), who argues that preferences may be endogenously determined in the market itself.

12. For an example from the community realm alone, consider the world discussion when the Taliban destroyed the giant Buddha statues in Bamian.

13. The concern was much earlier voiced by Aristotle in the *Ethics* (1984).

14. A neoclassical economist might claim that the subjectivity of a trader is "exogenous" to the act of trade; only if *it* is traded, and priced, does it affect, and is it a value in, trade. Or, it might be claimed that the trader's subjectivity is a transaction cost that one trader levies on another, and so should or can be incorporated in the price. Conversely, if the trader's subjectivity is calculative reason, there is no transaction cost.

15. As price ratios the formulation can be rewritten as $2/3 = $ apples/oranges, or 3 apples $=$ 2 oranges.

16. My account of markets with competitive pricing thus moves away from an equilibrium view according to which prices represent moments of stasis, when the supply and demand crowds settle, to seeing prices and markets as ongoing processes; to a degree, my approach accords with an Austrian view of competitive markets (Boettke 1989).

17. For an excellent discussion of Pareto efficiency and the two welfare theorems of economics, see Marglin 2007.

18. Fine (1998) offers an excellent discussion of the reification of the actor in the work of Becker, but he does not suggest that reification is first produced in the market itself nor that this "reality" is then reproduced in the discourse of economics.

19. See especially Zaloom 2006:111–114, footnotes 5, 7. The Chicago Board of Trade was literally an arena or pit reserved for traders (and their assistants) who through open-outcry trading exchanged corn futures by shouting and hand signals. It may now merge with the Chicago Mercantile Exchange: both are converting to electronic trading.

20. For a few discussions of these examples of bounded rationality, see Coyle (2007) and Kopcke, Little, and Tootell (2004).

21. Henley, with others, used the concept of a return beyond what was needed for the next cycle on an estate. Known as the "commodum" or "verus valor," it was rather like the rural Latin American household concept of the "remainder" or what remains after deductions for the next cycle. Oschinsky (1971) sometimes translates the expressions as "profit."

22. For one account of the development of financial innovations, see Goetz-mann and Rouwenhorst (2005), who trace the use of calculations to Babylonian times.

23. The Cartesian division between subject and object, mind and body, inner and outer, discipline and passion has provided one way of constructing Western patriarchy by linking mind and discipline to those who participate in the market. Passions and the body, as inferior and uncertain sources of knowledge, must be brought under control of the rational market ego, who usually is a male. Rigged to the market, the duality of mind and body often has been projected on gender to produce and justify an asymmetric power relation between male and female.

4

PROPERTY AND BASE

Private property and mutual holdings are dramatically different types of possession, even if we confound them in theory and conflate them in practice. Private property is the substance of market trade; it is partible, alienable, and held by individuals or disjoint persons. In contrast, conjoint persons share access to a base in the mutual realm. The two forms of possession are distinctly justified. Local narratives, drawing on rhetorical devices and figurative forms of reason, usually legitimate a base and connect it to daily life. These persuasions are linked to the way a base is used and allotted. Private property has its stories, too, but seems to persist without their everyday evocation or recognition. Participants in a market, for example, arrive with legal rights to resources, such as land, labor, goods, money, or ideas; these rights are transferred through bidding, regardless of their earlier acquisition by trade, inheritance, robbery, purchase, or the remaking of materials.[1] The history or memory of a property is irrelevant, because anonymous trade involves quitclaims: after a good is sold, the seller has no legal or ideological connection to a property unless by contract, such as a warranty. But the question remains: How is private property explained? What makes these holdings legitimate?

Justifying market possessions has become increasingly challenging because new forms of property are continually being devised, such as books, phrases, goods, technologies, medicines, and derivatives, which do not fit within a single category. Property rights also are divisible in continually new ways as proportional claims to the same thing or as claims to different features of it: for example, a building's owner may lease space to a corporation that is owned by shareholders and rents its equipment from still others. Rights to the building may be held by the owner but also by the person who gave the owner a personal loan secured by secondary rights to the building, by a bank that provided his mortgage, and by others to whom parts of the mortgage are sold and then resold until ultimate ownership with its credits and liabilities spreads through markets, shifts by the day, and becomes nearly untraceable. Yet, the formation of a transparent system of property rights and markets in which they can be traded, it is said, hastens economic development. Because it clarifies incentives that lead to the efficient allocation of resources, creating and enforcing a property rights system has become common sense among policy institutions, such as the International Monetary Fund and the World Bank, neoliberal market advocates (de Soto 1989), new institutional economists (North 2005), and other standard economists.

Legitimating or explaining the presence of property rights, however, remains a point of discussion in Western philosophical and political thought. For example, Hobbes, Locke, and Rousseau all recognized the need to justify a state or sovereign order before individual property rights could be established. Rousseau observed that "[t]he right of the first occupier, though more real than the right of the strongest, becomes a real right only when the right of property has already been established" (Rousseau 1913 [1762]:17). But how is a system of property rights and their arena of trade justified, and what is the relation between the shared framework that is created by persons-in-community and the individualized or disjoint holdings it supports? If local stories provide a relatively seamless connection among a base, allocations from it, and the conjoint person, do market narratives encounter a breach between the shared system and the private holdings it supports?

Market Narratives

In economics, the problem of justifying private property has been variously handled. Broadly, classical economists, such as Smith and Ricardo, when building their models of economy, assumed a prior class structure of property holders, such as rentiers, capitalists, and laborers; neoclassical economists omit this social and historical datum and start with market trade; new institutional economists, who accept the assumption of homo economicus, try to show how a property rights system evolves. Macpherson (1979) has usefully distinguished two ways of justifying property in economic and philosophical writing. He argues that from Aristotle through Aquinas, Hegel, Rousseau, and Marx, private property was justified as a means for achieving human welfare and well-being. But after the writings of Bentham, the development of utilitarian thought, and the rise of capitalism, the accumulation of property was validated as an end of activity (see also Macpherson 1962). In one case, we might say, holding property serves social purposes; in the other, private accretion becomes the goal.

Marx offered one of the memorable and persuasive narratives about market property. Proudhon, said Marx (1995 [1865]:195–196]), had claimed that property is theft, to which Marx wryly responded: From whom was it taken, except another property holder? Marx himself drew on the arguments of John Locke in the *Two Treatises* (1960 [1690]). Locke had proposed a kind of imprinting, annexation view of property. His account was based on the misguided idea that the Americas were open territories, ready for taking through individual labor, because the existing inhabitants had not improved the land by applying their labor. (By some estimates, there were over 100 million inhabitants when the Europeans arrived, and the land was certainly used and transformed by their activities.) According to Locke, a person projected or extended himself to land and materials through his labor; by mixing this self property (the possessive individual) with an object in the world and by improving it, the entity became his property.

> Every Man has a *Property* in his own *Person*. This no Body has any Right to but himself. The *Labour* of his Body, and the *Work* of his Hands, we may say, are properly his. Whatsoever then he removes out of the State that Nature hath provided, and left it in, he hath mixed his *Labour* with, and joyned to it something that is his own, and thereby makes it his *Property*. It being by him removed from the common state Nature placed it in, it hath by this *labour* something annexed to it, that excludes the common right of other Men. For this *Labour* being the unquestionable Property of the Labourer, no Man but he can have a right to what this is once joyned to, at least where there is enough, and as good left in common for others. (Locke 1960:287–289)

Locke's narrative employed synecdoche, or part for all (labor for human), as well as metaphor (the projection of the human on objects); and he presumed the presence of separated or self-possessed individuals rather than persons constituted in community. His assertion, that the means-to-ends or calculated act of laboring creates property, was successively elaborated by Adam Smith (1776) and David Ricardo (1951 [1817]). But Marx provided the most complete labor value story, beginning in the *Manuscripts of 1844* (1988), where he set forth the idea that property is objectified labor: through the activity of work, labor is congealed in objects and so confronts the human as an estranged part of the self. This thingification of labor in objects is a consequence of human work, but it leads to alienation when capitalists appropriate the objectified labor and separate the worker from the product of his activity.[2] Following Marx, profit is an extraction from the laborer.

Some people might reply that Marx was describing property rights not as they are but as they should be. Marx certainly used his narrative to offer a critique of market distribution. But why not—if property accounts are stories with moral messages? More pointedly, Marx assumed, along with Locke, that an individual has rights to his own labor prior to working and trading with others. But property in the self is a social entitlement; and the individual laborer is locally skilled or capacitated through a base of language, know-how, and habits (which many now reduce to "human" or "social capital"). Still, the labor right story, devolving from Locke and his successors, provides a justification today for claiming many forms of property. It legitimates rights to intellectual property such as a song, dance, or book; it encompasses claims to material or nonmaterial discoveries; it covers rights to an innovation such as a product, the reorganization of a production system, or the re-fashioning of a managerial structure; and it can be used to justify the appropriation of property held mutually by others, from oil, to land, to traditional medicines. More broadly, according to this individualistic story, property rights protect the labor and capital an individual invests and provide the incentive to improve the holdings: one works harder on personal property than on common holdings due to the certainty of claiming the product and its betterments.

Preferences

Recently, Carol Rose explored the issue of property justification to argue that it represents a "glitch" (1994:27) in the neoclassical conception of economic behavior, because people must cooperate to set up a system of rights before the self-interested actor can enter the scene and trade property rights. "There is a gap," she observes, "between the kind of self-interested individual who needs exclusive property to induce him to labor and the kind of individual who has to be there to create, maintain, and protect a property regime" (Rose 1994:38). (I might refer to her distinction as the gap between the disjoint and the conjoint person.) Rose concludes that classic theorists of property had to employ stories to explicate the beginnings of property regimes: "their narrative stories allowed them to slide smoothly over the cooperative gap in their systematic analyses of self-interest" (1994:32). In my terms, property theorists invented local models, but the difference between the two realms of mutuality and market remains.

Some economists might deny the existence of a gap between initial mutuality and current self-interest on the grounds that shared property systems emerge to avoid a war of all against all that could lead to the destruction of a resource, as in the "tragedy of the commons" (Hardin 1968). This explanation of property law as derived from self-interest requires that cooperation or mutuality be an effective preference within individuals, a theme that has been developed by Gary Becker, who claims that his economic approach does not assume self-interest. Instead, Becker claims to offer a "*method* of analysis [and] not an assumption about motivation." He wants to shift the emphasis away from "narrow assumptions about self-interest" (Becker 1993:385). Becker urges that in their separate utility functions, "[i]ndividuals maximize welfare as *they conceive it,* whether they be selfish, altruistic, loyal, spiteful, or masochistic" (Becker 1993:386). He argues that preferences may include benevolence (1976:5) and sees both altruism in the family and selfishness in the market as means-to-ends behaviors (1981:194). Becker thus claims that self-interest—like the taste for altruism, cooperation, or music—is a preference and separates self-interest as a motivation from its embodiment in the human calculator who maximizes preferences. But the idea that self-interest is only a preference, which the utility-maximizing individual may or may not entertain, seems like a fudge, for Becker concedes that there are wants in an individual's utility function that always remain unsatisfied. Can self-interest be seen as an optional preference that is separate and different from an individual's ever-present desire to maximize his personal welfare? Is not individual welfare maximization the same as self-interest? Becker isolates the maximizing actor from his enabling social context and fills him with the preferences needed to explain his social choices. Ben Fine (1998) also argues that Becker turns both accumulated personal and social capital into things by including them within a person's extended utility function, which allows Becker to keep to his methodological individualism while denying the existence of moral commitments. In my terms, Becker abstracts several levels—preferences plus a utility function plus an outcome—to create a derivational model with the rational actor at its foundation. He then cascades his model by explaining all social commitments as individual preferences. In effect, Becker turns mutuality into a private property of the self. By his neoclassical account, the presence of a mutual context that uniquely constitutes the self-possessed, self-interested individual remains unexplained. A breach remains between the cultural agreements that a property paradigm first requires, and the rational choices within it.

Cascading in Theory and Practice

New institutionalists offer a differ explanation for the emergence of property rights. Broadly, they agree that economics is a theory of choice given the problem of scarcity. They add that the structure of constraints (or nonconstraints) determines the way the competitive game is played. This structure can lead to (Pareto) efficiency as in the standard account, to stagnation, or to a position in between, given the "path dependence" (or cultural history) of institutions (North 2005). In order that the competitive structure lead to efficiency, a clear and enforceable property rights system is needed. For the New Institutional Economics (NIE) a principal empirical and theoretical concern is to show how a property rights system develops in different ways. In a later chapter I return to an example of the NIE paradigm; here I want to focus only on property rights and an explanation for them by turning to an early and almost canonical account that is cited by NIE and others. This story is especially relevant because it is one of the few occasions in which an economist used ethnography to justify his claims. I think it displays the breach between derivational and local models, or between market and mutuality—but let us turn first to the economist's account.

In a frequently cited article that was written two score years ago, Harold Demsetz drew on a market model to explain the beginning or "emergence" of property rights (1967). They "arise," he argued, by matching benefits against costs.[3] Using the rhetoric of a universal model with its foundation and derivations, Demsetz claimed that property rights emerge to internalize externalities. Demsetz tried to lend realism to his model by applying it to the origin of private property among the "aboriginal" Montagnais-Naskapi of Labrador. But with his turn to ethnography, Demsetz encountered the breach between universal and local models; in fact, Demsetz did not provide an origin account but showed how the market realm of private property cascades into and debases mutuality. He assumed that the Montagnais-Naskapi were imbued with calculative reason prior to constructing a system of private property, which emerged in response to their innate reasoning, although the Montagnais had long held a shared story about their base, its productivity and how it was to be used. Demsetz's narrative did not close the gap between how a mutual system of rights arises and the way a market arena is expanded, except to say that the market players make the market that constitutes them. Being designed to explain what it presumed, his tale turned solipsistic, while his suggestion that ethnographic realism provided his narrative's proof was a sham, because he silenced the extant Naskapi economy. So go anthropology's lessons.

Actors, Rights, Morality, and Externalities

Demsetz's story revolves about market actors who compete, aggrandize, and achieve economic efficiency. He imagines a world of socially unconnected individuals who nonetheless are endowed with language, expectations, and preferences. To justify this position, he refers to another tale often cited by neoclassical economists to charter their model: "In the world of Robinson Crusoe," says Demsetz, "property rights play no role" (1967:347). This anchor, thrown to the realm of literature and a Victorian story about shipwrecks, race, power, class, virtue, and capitalist discipline, provides an image of origins if not autochthony and a tone of realism. In the Crusoe world, property rights do not exist because there are no "others" competing for scarce goods; nor does mutuality exist—but rational man does. According to Demsetz, property rights concern the extent to which one person can act in benefiting or harming himself or others. They specify the realm an individual controls. Demsetz allows that these "expectations" are expressed through custom and mores as well as law (1967: 347), but homo economicus precedes and impels their construction.

To this plot line based on the calculating actor, Demsetz adds the subplot of externalities and internalities, which have to do with the interactions of market actors, and the extent to which their products and services are commoditized. Externalities, to recall, occur when one person's actions have a beneficial or harmful effect on another. For example, farmers who are upslope may unintentionally waste or lose some of their irrigation water, which becomes a benefit to farmers who are downslope for whom the extra water is a free resource or positive externality (also known as a spillover). Conversely, the sediment and waste from upslope farmers that may fall on crops downslope is an unwanted harm or negative externality. An externality is neither bought nor sold but can be measured against (or commensurated with) other goods and services, and assigned a price. In contrast, internalities are transacted or bought and sold in the market.

The dividing line between externalities and internalities changes in accord with "transaction" costs. Transaction cost refers to all the expenses of trading, such as contract and set-up costs, insurance, and the risk of exchange failure. For example, if the upslope farmer can sell his extra water for more than the cost of channeling it, he will do so. But if his transaction cost is more than the gain, the spillover remains an externality. Demsetz expands this conception to argue that a "primary function of property rights is that of guiding incentives to achieve a greater internalization of externalities" (1967:348). He adds, "property rights develop to internalize externalities when the gains of internalization become larger than the cost of internalization" (1967:350).[4] The relation between externalities and internalities alters with technological change (Demsetz 1967:350), but the dynamic in the internalization of externalities and the growth of markets is the search for profit, which is property itself and a means to ends calculation. The spatial expansion of property rights need not be consciously achieved, so long as the teleology of efficiency pulls the development. "Legal and moral experiments [with property rights] may be hit-and-miss procedures to some extent but in a society that weights the achievement of efficiency heavily their viability in the long run will depend on how well they modify behavior to accommodate to the externalities associated with important changes in technology or market values" (1967:350). Demsetz's actors exist in a world of teleological Darwinism in which efficiency defines fitness, and the fittest property systems survive.

Enter Ethnography

Demsetz draws on Eleanor Leacock's (1954) study of the Montagnais-Naskapi to cloak his tale in ethnographic realism.[5] Leacock's account, based on fieldwork in 1950 and the use of earlier studies, revolves about the transition from production for use to production for exchange. Originally, groups in Labrador trapped animals for domestic consumption of meat, hunting and fishing as well. But with colonization by Europeans, spatial encroachment, and the arrival of French and British traders, fur trading (principally in beaver) increased. As groups in Labrador shifted from hunting for meat to hunting for salable fur, exclusive rights to trapping territories developed (Leacock 1954:2, 6); command of a hunting territory gave control over its animal population and exclusive rights to the furs that could be secured.

Before the fur trade, people had cooperative patterns of use: "Formerly the Montagnais hunted co-operatively and shared their game" (Leacock 1954:7). Evidence for individual territories shows up in the 1700s, when people began to blaze trees as markers of separate areas (Leacock 1954:15, 16). But even after the advent of the fur trade, individuals could enter the territory of others to gather berries and bark, to fish or to hunt game; and in cases of need, Montagnais could take what was needed within the area of another without payment or permission, because these products were communally possessed (Leacock 1954:2). Among some groups, game caught for consumption was also communally shared, and even fur-bearing animals shot with a gun were divided on the basis of need and a person's debt at the store. The fur of muskrats that were trapped was shared as well (this fur had a low market value), and when a beaver dam was collectively raided, the fur was shared (Leacock 1954:33, 34). Leacock observes that the Montagnais showed "considerable resistance to giving up communal for individualized patterns of living ... there was a *conflict* [italics added] between their desire to increase their incomes ... and their resistance to changing basic patterns of everyday existence" (1954:9).

Demsetz's recounting of the changes follows Leacock, but his Montagnais have market motivations from the outset, even if they lack property rights. Before the fur trade, says Demsetz, hunting was carried out to secure food; however, "the externality was clearly present" (Demsetz 1967:351), meaning that one person's hunt affected another's, although it was not cost efficient to establish property rights. Demsetz does not recognize the existence of a prior economy based on mutuality with local leaders and fails to see the later tension or conflict between the two, because *the presence of an earlier sharing economy provides evidence of other than market motivations.* For Demsetz, the inception of the fur trade changed only the cost/benefit ratio of trapping, making it "economic to encourage the husbanding of fur-bearing animals" and to establish property rights (Demsetz 1967:352).

When rights are open or under communal ownership, says Demsetz, animals will be overhunted, because the effect will be borne by others. The community could meet and negotiate rights, but the transaction costs of doing so are high. Thus, "the effects of a person's activities on his neighbors and on subsequent generations will not be taken into account fully. Communal property results in great externalities" (Demsetz 1967:355). In contrast, the owner of private property takes the future into account because it affects the present value of his holding:

the cost of overhunting is imposed on the hunter alone. As Demsetz moralizes, "We all know that this means that he will attempt to take into account the supply and demand conditions that he thinks will exist after his death" (1967:355). The owner of private property also can count on others not to invade his holding, so making his efforts at husbanding effective. "Forest animals confine their territories to relatively small areas, so that the cost of internalizing the effects of husbanding these animals is considerably reduced [as compared to plains hunting]. This reduced cost, together with the higher commercial value of fur-bearing forest animals, made it productive to establish private hunting lands" (Demsetz 1967:353). Finally, because the cost of negotiating externalities is lower when done one-to-one between Montaignais, more externalities can be internalized, with the result that resources are even more efficiently utilized.

But What Did Leacock Argue?

Demsetz stays reasonably close to Leacock's account as a series of historical events, but a very different perspective emerges if one includes the ethnohistorical material and local voices that she adduces. Leacock observes, for example, that colonization, European expansion, and the placing of trading posts, as well as the arrival of new traps that could be purchased, all had an effect on the Montagnais. She emphasizes the impact of trade and consumption.

Leacock observes that even as early as the 1670s, with their desire for goods, the Indians had become partly dependent on traders' supplies and had learned to play the traders one against another (1954:12). Later, in the 1800s, the Hudson Bay Company tried to induce the Indians to hunt fur by creating artificial wants. According to one trader cited by Leacock, "[a]s trading posts, however, are now established on their lands, I doubt not but artificial wants will, in time, be created. They may become as indispensable to their comfort as their present real wants. All the arts of the trader are exercised to produce such a result, and those arts never fail of ultimate success. Even during the last two years of my management, the demand for certain articles of European manufacture has greatly increased" (McLean 1932:262). Leacock adds that the more furs a person collected, the more material comforts he could obtain. In contrast to the aboriginal situation in which sufficiency was the aim, material wants had become possibly limitless (1954:7). As she observes, the relatively early displacement of native equipment by tools secured from the traders indicates the importance of trade for the Montagnais (Leacock 1954:11). And there was a close connection between this dependence on fur-trading and individualized hunting (Leacock 1954:17). Leacock even begins her story by saying, "Private ownership of specific resources as exists has developed in response to the introduction of sale and exchange into Indian economy which accompanied the fur trade" (1954:2).

Leacock presents ample evidence, as I mentioned, that the pattern of individual holdings did not develop smoothly and that the Indians showed "considerable resistance" to giving up their communal mode of existence. Aware of this conflict between the desire to augment income to acquire goods, and changing their mode of existence, they resisted full-time trapping (1954:9). With trade, selfways also changed: "the individual's most important ties, economically speaking, were transferred from within the band to without, and his objective relation to other band members changed from the co-operative to the competitive" (1954:7). According to Bailey, whom she cites, "[t]he French were always desirous of dealing with individuals rather than with groups, the members of which were not thought by them to be responsible for each other's actions. Moreover, the actual pelts were owned by individuals. Thus personal ownership might by easy transference have been extended to the hunting lands" (Bailey 1937:88). In other words, consumption desires and the art of trading, which demanded the use of calculative reason, were the origins of this dramatic change. Through them market reason and practices cascaded into and colonized the Montagnais economy just as I explained in the prior chapter.

Derivations and Local Models

This is not the end of my counterargument, because Demsetz's account is actually circular or solipsistic. He started with the purpose of showing how private property rights arise, which he says occurs through the internalization of externalities. For Demsetz, externalities exist in advance of private property; they existed in Labrador before the fur trade and exist whenever a resource is held mutually or in commons. For externalities to exist, however, *they must be measured and made commensurate or matched against other benefits and costs,* which means that there are market exchanges. And if there are market exchanges, then private property also exists, because it is the substance of anonymous trade. In contrast to Leacock's description of the prior economy, Demsetz assumes a world in which actors compete for wealth and private property, because if externalities are to be internalized, rational actors, markets, and property rights must be on the stage. The outcome is presumed at the start. Demsetz diverts attention from the solipsism of his derivational model, however, by his rhetoric of realism and beginnings, as if the Montagnais represented an original moment before economy.

I might contrast our arguments in shorthand. For Demsetz, given the universality of homo economicus, then

Scarcity (the economic problem) → Competition → Private Property.

For me, given norms of exchange, then

Trade → Competition → Scarcity → Calculative Reason
(homo economicus) → Private Property.

Demsetz has no account for how people come together to constitute
shared rules for the trade of private property. Stable property rights for
use in trade presume shared rules for trade, which involves property.
Property institutions embody more than the use, winnowing and refining of existing calculative reason—they embody mutuality, which in
Demsetz's account is missing.

Thus, Demsetz is not describing the origins of private property
rights but how they cascade into or colonize the realm of mutuality. He
tells a story about the extension of private property and the expansion
of commoditization but not about their inception. By metaphorically
projecting inception on expansion, Demsetz implies that the causes of
expansion are the same as the causes of origin; in doing so, he elides
the local situation as well as the shifting conditions of conquest, mili-
tary power, and the state that helped bring the traders. The persuasive-
ness of his argument depends on the reader's belief in a foundational
model with levels, derivations, and a self-sustaining essence.

So What?

We might confine this argument between anthropologist and economist to the dustbin of their other peevish disagreements, except that it
emblemizes a theoretical difference, for the Montagnais experience has
been replicated countless times around the globe. In fact, it is very similar to what I observed in my Panama fieldwork, where I witnessed the
shift from subsistence farming to cash cropping sugar cane. Precisely as
this change occurred, calculative reason was spreading and claims to
private property were being made.

My initial field attempts to elicit choices and trade-offs concerned
only the subsistence crops, such as rice, maize and beans. This decision
tree analysis did not work because the people knew what they needed
to feed a family for a year, and by rule of thumb they cut down sufficient forest to plant that amount. The forest was not conceived to be
scarce. Traditionally, the people were squatters on land held by a set of
absentee siblings who used the territory for grazing cattle. (The family
had inherited their possession from a general who fought in the 1840
war of independence and seized the land afterward.) The siblings and
earlier owners permitted the people to live and work on the land because their swidden (slash-and-burn) farming created pasture in a rotating cycle: after two years of use the land was left to regenerate for ten
to fifteen years while the cattle grazed in the cleared areas. Then, after

the Cuban revolution, the Panama sugar cane quota was increased, and two relatively nearby sugar cane mills began to augment their production. At roughly the same time, the aging absentee owners sold their land, and after a series of events it ended up in the hands of the agrarian reform agency, which did little for many years. Shortly before my arrival, this world began to change. Enticed by the possibility of trading for cash, the people began to raise sugar cane, especially because they thought they could raise it in the off-time from their subsistence work. Increasingly, they supplied sugar cane to the mills and with the receipts became dependent on market goods, from radios and batteries, to kerosene lamps, and finally to rice, the subsistence food. Two changes followed. First, midway through my fieldwork, as I was trying simply to grasp the work flows and subsistence returns, I was struck by a difference in the use of measuring rods, or more exactly the use and absence of a measuring rod. The subsistence crops were "measured" in a variety of traditional units, from irregular gourds that held quantities of seed, to different ways of measuring work in a field, to how many days a harvest would last. But in the same conversation, when I switched to discussion of the cash crop, money was the unique measure. (The mills would walk a field, determine the production volume it would support, and then advance a sum to pay for seed and labor. At the harvest, a mill would pay the supplier for the weight and purity of his sugar cane, less the advances.) When I asked a person about his sugar cane harvest he would tell me about its weight and the money it provided. I also learned about all sorts of calculated ways the people could enhance their returns at the expense of the mills. For this crop, calculative reason was used.

The second change was equally dramatic. During the time of the absentee owners, the people had constructed temporary wooden fences around their plots, not to mark them as private property but to protect the crops from cattle. When the sugar cane arrived, the people began to fence the land with barbed wire aiming to hang onto it as a possession and keep out other croppers. The opportunity to trade for cash and goods produced competition for land to raise sugar cane, which led to fencing. The rural folk tried to maintain their subsistence cycle of raising rice and maize by integrating it with the sugar cane that was raised in the same field. But sugar cane is a perennial, which wears out the soil, and as the domestic harvests diminished, the people began to ask whether the inception of the cash crop helped or hurt their existence. The sugar cane helped us and ruined us, they would explain, especially since the cash earnings never covered subsistence costs. As in the case of the Montagnais, trade produced self-interested calculation that led to property claims and debasement. Once again, the sequence ran

Trade → Competition → Scarcity → Claims to property for trade → Debasement.

But so what? That's modernization. In the absence of compelling market narratives that justify private property, however, and in the semantic breach left by price fetishism and the effacement of mutuality, the local stories that people have about connections among themselves and to their world cannot always be silenced. These narratives have continuous hold, as today's events in countries shifting from socialism to markets illustrate.[6] For example, who has legitimate claims to a state's former possessions? Is it global capitalists who have purchasing power, national capitalists who offer a lower purchase price but keep local control, former government administrators who have managerial experience, party officials who have the social connections to make the acquisition, or workers who previously used the property? In Israel, where there are long-held, conflicting claims to the same land, who has rights to it? And which rights should be recognized—those based on the Bible as described in the Mishnah, on historical use, on colonial occupation, or on present power? This allocation problem cannot be resolved by replacing local stories of justification with the narrative of market efficiency and Pareto improvements, for it erases the problem. With persuasions about property, the derivational model reaches one of its limits: it does not describe a total economy, while calculated trade contradicts the shared system by which individual possessions are constituted.

Property and the Base

Today, with the widening influence of global markets, the relation between property and base takes many forms. Base becomes property, property becomes base; each may support the other, one may be seen as the other, and their intersection may become a point of conflict. For example, a house, supported by the market returns of its members, makes up a sharing community. A family usually does not rent its bedrooms or bathrooms to its members but apportions their use. Market calculations, however, may not stop at the doors of a house, which may be colonized by calculative reason when the relative financial contributions of members are used to apportion allowances, chores, or use of the family car. Establishing a communal identity also may affect the way a house is built. In Dalarna, Sweden, the successful artists Carl Larsson and Anders Zorn used their financial earnings to build their family homes as working, living, and display spaces as expressions of their identities: these houses now serve as exemplars of community and cultural well-being, even if they were built using market returns.[7] On a smaller scale, a bimonthly eating club that pools some funds to share a meal, an alumni group that charges dues to share memories once a year, a monthly play-reading group that buys texts for sharing, and participants in a costly ritual performance, that takes place once every ten years compose attenuated communities that none the less transform financial property to mutuality.

The dialectic can be more complex. Supported by contributions and state grants, a university's base may include its library, laboratories, offices, common rooms, and communication systems, although today these bases are being transformed back to capital by accounting systems designed to determine their financial returns: labs that bring in outside grants usually grow in size, though not always in correlation with their intellectual contributions. Today, a base may be so closely mixed with private property that it becomes colonized by market practices and language. Components of a base were outlined in chapter 2; let us revisit them as they are conjoined with capital.

Knowledge and Skills

A nation, through taxes on market activities, may support a base. For example, government-sponsored research, made freely available, increases the knowledge of a country or the world, as does information transmitted through a public library, a free university, or at a public vocational or agricultural school. This stock of knowledge, ideas, and technologies can aid well-being and economic growth, as in the case of a peasant household that builds on a legacy of practices. In economics, as I shall later consider, one theory of growth posited that exogenous knowledge outside the market helped create growth; a newer theory foresees knowledge as accumulating through the market and spillovers, but it relies on the enabling condition of mutuality. By either theory, mutuality and a base are needed for market growth.

Knowledge and skills also may be directly intertwined with capital. For example, guilds and trade unions, in which apprentices gain knowledge in hierarchical circumstances, build and pass on accumulated skills. The transmission of this property is limited to members, who may pay a fee or perform services in return for their access to a heritage that capacitates them to gain a market return, although originally this knowledge may have been built from an unpaid heritage. Professional organizations, supported by dues on the earnings of their members, may accumulate and share knowledge that capacitates both their lives and their monetary returns.

Base practices and knowledge also may be colonized by market actors and turned to capital advantage. Folk medical knowledge, accreted over time and spread among a population, may be discovered and "mined" by pharmaceutical companies for hints to new remedies or folk medicines may be analyzed to extract agents for new drugs. This base is not lost to its holders but is used for profit by others, often without recompense: it becomes both a shared base and technological capital. In different terms it may be said to be a "nonrival" good: one person's use does not detract from another's, except when it is privatized. When a university professor offers a lecture to colleagues and students, she adds to the base of knowledge and scholarship; when she gives the same lecture to a corporation (often without recompense), the knowledge may be turned to private profit. Likewise, government-sponsored medical research at a university, which adds to a nation's heritage, may be freely disseminated, and then turned to private profit. The Linux operating system, whose source code is freely available, is a shared base that expands with applications. Microsoft's privatization of an alternative system forecloses this sharing and the potential for contributions and innovations from outside the corporation. Lessig (2001) has compared the internet to a commons and software codes to private property in order to argue that an open commons can lead to greater and more rapid innovations. But recently some cable providers have argued for the right to charge for access to internet sites, which would convert it from a global base to private property.

Often the presence of knowledge and skills may be so accepted that their contribution passes unrecognized: for example, traditional tunes are used in commercials to make them persuasive. To suggest that its cars are sprightly and energetic, one automobile manufacturer shows its cars on television cavorting and acting like children, which is one common image of youngsters in certain cultures. As we observed, price fetishism leaves a semantic space for advertising. Here, and in the subsequent chapter, I suggest that this space is often filled with images of community. This use of mutuality provides a different level of meaning to the concepts of debasement and mystification: if cars are childlike, do children become more carlike through this metaphoric transfer? Market activity often draws without cost on a heritage of knowledge, skills, and performances.

Unlimited Base

A part of the material world may be used as if it were unlimited. Economists term this type of holding an "open access" commons (Ostrom 1990). Windmills that power electric generators for a market return exemplify this form of base, provided that one user does not impinge on the wind, the noise level, or the sightlines of another. Using the ocean and the atmosphere as free spaces for dumping pollutants implies they are unlimited bases, although some nations and transnational communities contest these actions.

When population increases and the market realm expands, an unlimited base usually does not endure. In Sweden by the law of "everyman's right" (*allemansrätt*), anyone may cross or enter the private property of another to enjoy nature, gather wild berries and mushrooms, or even camp overnight while taking care not to bother the owners or harm the domesticated plants. This open base exists "on top of" private property and limits the owner's rights. Traditionally, citizens carefully exercised the right and respected the property. But today, *allemansrätt* is being severely strained in popular tourist areas of Sweden (and Norway, which has a similar right), because many non-national tourists, who are unfamiliar with the legal and tactical rules of use, overcrowd and damage the base by passing diseases such as tapeworm to livestock, and by polluting watersheds. Their monetary power to travel and lack of mutuality allows them to colonize it. What was an unlimited base, respected by a community as large as Sweden, is becoming an open access commons in market terms. It is being debased or subjected to the negative externalities of market actors who are destroying one of their reasons for visiting. By negating ties of community and converting a base to capital, they provide one example of what is meant by the "tragedy of the commons."

Limited Base

The base may become a closed resource. In modern economies an extraordinarily large number of limited bases, and bases mixed with capital, are variously allocated, such as museums, hunting areas, freshwater streams, forest preserves, or rights to fish.[8] Use may be restricted to members of a taxpaying community who pay a (usually small) fee for access, such as fishing a river. A city or university library, to which one gains access as a taxpayer or student, is a base made through capital financing as well.

But the resources in a public, limited base may be controlled through leasing, often at a low rate, or opened to bidders who secure access for their market purposes. A government may assign or auction wave bands to private radio stations, or rent national range lands for pasturage, forests for exploitation, or mineral deposits for extraction, often for a small fee that subsidizes the private use and profitmaking.[9] Airplanes with advertising banners freely use the sky, but to help defray its costs a Russian space rocket agency rented signage to private enterprises (Bollier 2002a:159). In Sweden many municipalities possess garden land that is rented for a nominal fee to nearby residents. The allotment rule is first come, first served, with the distribution overseen by a local committee consisting of community members who share an interest in working the soil and the values of solitude, silence, and closeness to nature. In some areas, people from ethnically diverse backgrounds now use these plots, and their plantings transform the traditional conception of this communal holding by using it for market activities. In one municipal garden of Stockholm, "Swedes" (Europeans) raise flowers and garden for relaxation and quiet as they have long done. However, "Turks" (Middle Easterners) plant kitchen vegetables, such as garlic and leeks. Their products help defray the cost of household food. "Chinese" (East Asian) women plant greens and are able to harvest up to five times a year by using pesticides and fertilizers; they supply restaurants with their products. Each group, with rightful access to the land, uses it differently: for local pleasure or for its own sake; for local support or for the sake of saving money; and for the market or for the sake of making money. Within this common space, members of the three groups resent and often quarrel with one another, for they are using the land differently: as a base that makes mutuality, as a mix of base and capital, and as subsidized capital. The culturally diverse groups, with differing positions in the larger economy, build disparate communities in relation to the same base (Klein 1993).[10]

When a community expands its base that is supported by taxes on market returns, the capital value of neighboring private property may change and lead to conflict between the interests of the community and the property holders. When airport noise increases due to runway expansion or when a road is widened, adjacent property is affected. Sometimes the owners are recompensed. But at what price should a small business be moved? (The opportunities for chicanery, or use of advance knowledge about base expansion, often are exploited for private advantage.) But does the price paid for this "basification" of private property ever fall to the level of the reverse flow that is the price paid for "debasement," such as the market use of a shared forest or the destruction of wildlife in the interests of seeking oil? The shifting dialectic of base and capital affects the mutuality of a community, the subjectivity of its members, and their well-being; and it is a continual source of political discussion.

Material Accumulations and Services

In many cases, a community—drawing on taxes levied on market returns—provides material support and services for its members. National governments stockpile food, oil, gold, and other resources for emergencies and long-term use and sale by their citizens. The United States holds armaments (Cuba keeps food caches in case of natural disasters). Some nations provide retirement payments for workers, milk for children, and welfare stamps for the impoverished. The recipients, as members of the national or local community, share these bases according to set and contested rules. In the United States the range of recipients and shared holdings are shrinking as the commitment to a national obligation declines and a neoliberal discourse urges that the impoverished turn to the market for jobs and provisioning. In contrast, Sweden retains relatively strong welfare programs, such as social services, and has a zero poverty level as part of its commitment to national well-being.

This dialectic of base and market has other forms as well. For example, a government may offer support for social services and welfare, but the services or goods may be produced and provided through private enterprise. Local communities also provide services, from universal education to health care and job training, although these programs are being curtailed and privatized in many countries. At an even more local level, almost everywhere, households as communities keep stocks of food and clothing in varying amounts. Poverty, from this perspective, means having no base. For example, squatters on the margins of a city may together demand access to water and electricity as well as proper sewage as an initial step in making their local world. Conversely, waste products and spillovers from market activities may become part of a base, as in the case of shantytowns made from cardboard. Charitable organizations that receive and provide secondhand market goods, such as Goodwill in the United States, may help provision the bases of the less affluent. Even a soup kitchen offers a temporary base and community; though the recipients may not know one another, they may be required to receive temporary instruction in a religious faith, so experiencing a temporary commonality in food and religion. But the problem of lacking a base afflicts a very large number of people in the world, from urban squatters to landless agriculturalists.

Prohibited Spaces

A base may set boundaries on market activities. Regulations about automobile emissions and car safety that enhance welfare define spaces in which private property cannot encroach. Rules about workplace harassment and safety, limits on the use of child labor and hours of work, zoning laws, and restrictions on the use of pesticides on crops and food additives also define shared spaces that cannot be used in the market, or sometimes, in community. Regulations on logging in a national forest stipulate both legitimate and prohibited uses, and limit the degree to which this base may be used in the market. These stipulations that limit debasement and contribute to well-being are often contested.

Identity

Symbolic goods may interweave base and property. In the United States a basic (and masculine) meal used to consist of meat and potatoes; this purchased "home" meal is still consumed but now takes the form of hamburgers and fries purchased in fast food outlets. Other market foods in the United States that vitalize communal affiliation include hot dogs, mother's chicken soup, Easter ham, and Passover lamb depending on the community and occasion. Some capital items are symbolic of the market as an arena of trade, such as Wall Street, the New

York Stock Exchange, the Merchandise Mart, and the former World Trade Center. Entrepreneurs sometimes name office buildings after themselves, such as Trump Tower, or companies place their names on a building. These purchased expressions of market success differ from more social sacra, such as totemic names and symbols, for they combine the two realms. But in both cases, destruction or debasement of the symbol, as in the case of the World Trade Center, can have devastating effects.

The Commons Model

The word *commons* is variously used. Some interpret a commons as property that is owned by a people or nation rather than individuals or corporations. For example, Bollier claims that "[a] reckoning of what belongs to the American people is a first step to recovering control of common assets and protecting them for public purposes" (Bollier 2002b:8). He advocates forming stakeholder trusts containing common property that can return rents to all citizens. Other writers have been using the idea of a "civil commons." This concept is more encompassing, for it addresses real property and the provision of "life goods" as well. For example, by one definition the civil commons offers "all members of a community [access] to life goods" (McMurtry 2001:820). The civil commons underwrites life-needs, while any tradition or law that hinders this access is not part of it, nor are "life-disabling" customs such as mutilation ceremonies or a "natural" rate of unemployment (McMurtry 2001:820). Although this morally defined commons is not based on local narratives to justify its presence and connection to its users, it is somewhat like a base.

The term commons, as now employed, is usually a form of private property within a market system. The principal difference from individual private property is that a commons is a unit, such as land or fishing rights, within which distribution to individuals or families takes place through allocation rules rather than market bidding. In this sense, a commons can be both capital and base. For example, the village of Ramosierra (Spain) holds a commons of trees. Given by King Juan II in the 1400s, it has been held and inherited outside markets. Each year culling rights are allocated to male citizens who are above twenty-five, married, and residents of the village for more than six months in the year. The rights are apportioned by a lottery (known as the Pine Luck). The forest is the property of the village; the rights to a stand of trees become the temporary private property of the individual who wins them. Private property obtains as the village right to the commons and as temporal rights to lots of timber, but the allocation to individuals does not take place through competitive bidding. In this sense, the forest is a base that unites or is shared by the community, and it helps make what it means to be a qualified citizen with a conjoint identity, but its produce can be alienated or sold. In contrast, as we have seen, the land held by a Tiv lineage is not precisely demarcated and its borders change; neither it nor its products are sold, except at the loss of Tiv identity, for the ancestors dwell in the land, and it mediates relationships.

Often the commons refers to a bounded zone of "natural resources" with the argument that collective action can best manage scarce resources such as irrigation water, fishing banks, forests, and agricultural plots that otherwise would be depleted through competition over the limited good (McCay and Acheson 1987; Ostrom 1990). Various economists, political scientists, and environmentalists urge that holding property in common can lead to its careful use. They see a commons through the perspective of markets with self-interested actors; it is a means for profit rather than a way of connecting people. Usually, this type of commons is private property that was purchased by a group, inherited by a community, or allocated by the state; emphasis is placed on efficient management and the control of free riders. This type of commons sets an arena in which calculated practices take place.

For example, in Oregon a group of trawl fishermen possesses rights to fishing quotas as a communal property. According to one study of them by economists, the fishermen, with their separate quotas and operations, are disjoint persons who are maximizing individual utility functions, although their preferences are broader than making money and include being independent, working outdoors, competing, and being in contact with nature. Establishing social relationships is not a preference, nor does participation in the group produce mutuality; in fact, boat captains reported they had "poor communication between themselves," which hindered the creation of new forms of association (Feeny, Hanna, and McEvoy 1996:7). The economists conclude that the fishermen are calculating actors with ordered preferences—and so they may be, because their commons is private property or a collection of quota rights within a market. In this case both the actors and economists use the language of a commons, but this commons provides the justifying framework or arena for establishing and holding private property, which may be why offshore fishermen often are governed by state regulation and not by mutuality. These types of commons are not a base, although sometimes, through cascading and the mystifying of calculative reason as if it were mutuality, the necessary and the contingent exchange positions—a process to which we now turn.

Notes

1. I consider property to be a "bundle of rights" or social entitlements among people, as do most anthropologists (Hann 1995). But other definitions are used.

Humphrey and Verdery (2004:1) observe that property has been considered to be a thing, a relation between person and thing, and person-to-person relations mediated by things, as well as a bundle of rights.

2. The argument is developed in many of Marx's other writings, for example the *Grundrisse* (1973) and *Capital*, vol. 1 (1967).

3. Alchian and Demsetz (1973) subsequently expanded the argument.

4. Demsetz states and restates his central theme: "The emergence of property rights can be understood best by their association with the emergence of new or different beneficial and harmful effects" (1967:350). "The emergence of new property rights takes place in response to the desires of the interacting persons for adjustment to new benefit-cost possibilities" (1967:350).

5. See also Speck (1926).

6. Verdery offers a detailed account from Transylvania (Romania). She notes that land reform involved the contradictory issues of historical justice, political expediency, distributive effects, ethnic empowerment, economic efficiency, paying off the losers, equality, and accumulating political capital (Verdery 2003:80), Even historical justice was ambiguous: did it mean restoring land to its owners before socialism or to the laborers who farmed it collectively (Verdery 2003:158)?

7. Carl Larsson, like Norman Rockwell in the United States, grew up in urban poverty. Both artists achieved market success by creating idyllic pictures of thriving, rural community life that for their compatriots became one meaning of the essence of "Sweden" and "America." Both created nostalgic visions.

8. See, for example, Bollier 2002b.

9. Bollier (2002a) provides a number of examples. Sometimes government rent-seekers use their office to allocate these base resources for payments under the table, thus doubly privatizing and selling the shared base.

10. Ten years after this study was undertaken, a sign posted outside the commons announced: "Twentieth Anniversary 1998: A Multicultural Gardening Association." Earlier the aim had been to reach unity in styles and appearance; by 1998 diversity in use of the base was accepted (personal communication, Barbro Klein. See also Becker and Klein 2003).

CONTINGENCY OR NECESSITY?
THE DIALECTIC OF PRACTICES

Karl Polanyi bequeathed to anthropology the concept of the embedded economy. First developed in his book *The Great Transformation* (1944) to describe the transition from "pre-industrial" to industrial life, Polanyi subsequently used the idea of embeddedness to understand ethnographic ("primitive") and historical ("archaic") economies In the ethnographic cases, reciprocity is the predominant transaction mode; in the historical contexts, redistribution primarily governs the transaction types. In modern societies, disembedded markets dominate transactions. Despite his earlier historical presentation, Polanyi offered a static typology of economies that has usually been set within a binary opposition: either material life is embedded within social relationships or it is disembedded as anonymous exchanges. For Polanyi, the historical reversal of the necessary (society) and the contingent (the market), which occurred with the emergence of industrial society, was a one-time event that was accomplished at great human cost. Granovetter (1985) modified the stark opposition by observing that many economies are more embedded than economists perceive, whereas material life is more disembedded than anthropologists allow. But neither he nor Polanyi developed the theme that the embedded/disembedded pair, or mutuality and market, make up the dialectic in economy.

I argue that neither realm persists without the other. But my view diverges from most of standard economics (including both neoclassical and New Institutional Economics) as well as most of anthropology. For example, in contrast to Polanyi, a neoclassical economist might argue that real markets sometimes do include communal attachments, but these ties are imperfections in an ideal model. To the extent that personal relationships, misperceptions, emotions, and imperfect information influence price setting, markets are less efficient than they might be, and mutuality ought to be elided. Becker, as we have seen, surmounts this problem by including mutuality as a preference or taste of the rational actor. For him, mutuality is a contingent variable that he "endogenizes" by including it in a utility function. Closely related to the neoclassical perspective is the older "formalist" view in economic anthropology by which culture and social obligations are sometimes seen as constraints on optimal production.

New institutional economists offer a different perspective. Drawing in part on the work of Coase (1988) concerning transaction costs, the new institutionalism has developed in recent years and expanded its reach to the realm of public choice, history, and governance, among other topics. As we shall see, the new institutionalism revolves about the idea of calculative reason (and scarcity) but employs it to explain the changing forms of economic institutions. New institutionalists insert another level into a universal model: institutions. Social bonds, in their view, are not always frictions or inefficiencies to be eliminated in modernization, because these ties can be efficient in a historical context. Instead of calling social bonds *altruism,* and inscribing them as one among other preferences of the self-interested actor as does Becker, new institutionalists argue that social relationships are conscious or unconscious selections in the drive to be efficient given scarcity. Institutions can stabilize markets (sometimes as oligopolies), reduce risks, lower transaction costs, and make specific markets more efficient. But there is an elision in their model, because new institutionalists are explaining the uses, predications, or spillovers of existent mutuality. By presuming that individuals are self-interested, which leads to contextually efficient organizations, new institutionalists fail to account for the prior, necessary presence of relationships that constitute disjoint individuals (as we have seen in the work of Demsetz).

Unlike these perspectives, I hold that all economies are dialectical combinations. In this chapter, I explore the dialectic within cultures and in theories, for it is encountered in high market economies, in ethnographic cases, and in models. This story involves practices and discourses, and entails cascading, debasement, and the appropriation of materials and labor, as well as veiling and mystification. In some theories the tension is denied by seeing the shift from mutuality to trade as a progressive historical process; in others, it is negated by using standard economics to encompass both sides and mystifying or veiling mutuality; in still other cases, the tension is denied by seeing the two as mutually embedded. On the ground, these same processes emerge along with resistance. To highlight the issue, I shall begin with an ethnographic example in which the dialectics are not fully recognized. Subsequently, I suggest how an arena for trade is assured by mutuality before considering the ambiguities of establishing market trust. I then turn to some of the ways mutuality is inside markets and how markets cascade into mutuality. I close this account of economy's dialectic with a new institutionalist's mystification of anthropology's most renowned illustration of mutuality

What's Contingent? What's Necessary?

What does embeddedness mean for a contemporary ethnographer? Is it one part of a shifting relation between markets and mutuality, or is it a static concept in which mutuality evaporates and becomes a means for trade? I begin with an example in which economy's dialectic is not fully recognized.

Thomas Bestor has provided a fine, well-rounded ethnography of the Tsukiji market in Tokyo. Tsukiji is the world's largest marketplace for fresh and frozen seafood; during 1996 nearly six billion dollars worth of seafood changed hands in this one locale. From a trade perspective Tsukiji is a spot market in which goods are exchanged between anonymous actors for short-term advantage and profit maximization. Supplies come from local fishermen and from around the world, so pricing reflects global trends as well as Japanese tastes or demands. But Tsukiji trade, says Bestor, is embedded in the relationships, beliefs, and values of Japanese life, and he demonstrates that social patterns enable and constrain the competitive exchanges: history, customs, and physical layout all affect price setting. For example, seven auction houses lie at the center of the market. Although most specialize in specific products, they compete with one another and with other markets. All seven, however, have semipermanent relationships upstream with suppliers and downstream with purchasers. In addition the market is permeated by *keiretsu*, which are vertically integrated combines that link fisheries, trading companies, and supermarket chains. Market embedding extends further, for small retail firms that purchase fish for sale and keep stalls at the marketplace are often organized around family ties.

Bestor interprets this thick mix of mutuality and trade by drawing on the New Institutional Economics to claim that the various social ties lower transaction costs (Bestor 2004:192). According to Bestor, the upstream and downstream bonds modulate market swings through the transmission of information that reduces search costs. Similarly, the combines stabilize the market through their spread of ties, and so it may be. But when Bestor asks what "the glue" is for these longer-term bonds, he answers that it is "the flow of information" that they assure (2004:206–207). In contrast to his initial claims that trade as well as economic institutions are embedded in the cultural and social life of Japan (2004:12–15), Bestor eventually says that the cultural and social bonds consist only of economic information that lowers costs and increases profits. Here then is the problem: Are mutual ties in Tsukiji different from trade, do they consist of calculated trade, are they being mystified as trade, or do the two realms persist in tension?

The Arena: Framing Markets and the Necessity of Mutuality

Mutuality establishes markets by specifying the arena in which trade takes place. Referring to market agreements, Hayek states, "It is the acceptance of such common principles that makes a collection of people a community" (1960:106). The ways of defining a space for trade include formal and informal laws, norms, and rules. Markets are contained within social agreements, such as a peace pact, threatening fetish, or legal organization through which expectations about the conduct of others can be assured. Ethnographic studies reveal that people may inherit trade partners or project kinship bonds to stabilize an exchange and create a zone of peace. When trades take place in a local marketplace, the norms may be customary, with an agreement sealed by a handshake. When markets are large with anonymous participants, the rules usually are explicit and the agreements specified or written; shunning and personal sanctions work in a small market but not a large one. Markets also may be thickly or thinly regulated, ranging from the minimal specification of a peaceful space for interaction to a tightly controlled drug or food market. The varying agreements may be assured by a government, by kinship, by the participants, or by cultural expectations, and they are reformulated over time and contested; even if "silent trade" between noncommunicating strangers, outside any social framework, might occasionally have occurred, it soon developed a set of market agreements.[1]

Market agreements also specify who may enter and what can and cannot be brought to the bar of exchange. In many exchanges, a trader may be required to purchase a license or a seat, as on the New York Stock Exchange. But informal markets arise without legal permission, although their marginal space is usually limited to an alley or sidewalk. A market may have rules about the order of entry for buyers and sellers (through rationing and quotas), and about its physical layout (Gell 1982). Mutual accords frame rules of exchange and the obligations of traders, such as agreements to use fair weights and measures. Such concords include laws of ownership and contract, rules about product quality and disclosure, and controls on oligopolies and the modes of trade (such as one-to-one bargaining, set prices with add-ons and discounts, or auctions). Markets also have rules about what can and cannot be made commensurate, as in the case of automobile emissions and regulations on the use of a natural resource. But entry stipulations that enhance communal well-being via exclusions are often contested and subverted: there are black markets in babies, drugs, and many other "goods."

Consider an ethnographic example of the way mutuality and reciprocity determine the contents, participants, and space of a market. In Arnhem Land (Australia) the Gunwinggu held a "ceremonial exchange" (called *dzamalag*) with neighboring groups.[2] In one exchange, which took place on a dancing ground or designated space, the mutual festivities included music making, singing, dancing, joking, and sharing food. The two groups also circulated tobacco, beads, and sexual favors between their opposite moieties that regulated marriage. These shared and reciprocal transactions created and expressed communality between the groups, and they provided the frame for trade, for as these forms of sharing took place, cloth and blankets were offered by the Gunwinggu to the other group; upon completion of this exchange, the visitors presented spears, although in a threatening manner. As a result, spears were traded for cloth and blankets; however, all the other goods and services went in a circle from a moiety in one group to its opposite moiety in the other and then back! The ethnographic report provides no information about the trade rate of the blankets plus cloth for spears, but we may suppose that it could vary even if "prices" were sticky in the short term. In this exchange, mutuality between groups provided a structure for market trade by specifying the locale, rules of exchange, and contents of the trade. Communal bonds of reciprocity within a group were extended or projected to the other group so that trade could occur.

Making Markets: The Precariousness of Trust

In recent years, trust as mutuality has drawn the attention of various scholars, because being able to rely on another person's words or actions is a necessary part of market relations.[3] Ties of trust play several roles in markets, such as insuring that information provided between traders is reliable, that debts will be paid, or that open-ended contracts may be formed so adjustments can be made over time. But trust can be an ambiguous relation, for it would seem to deny the exclusive presence of the self-interested actor in the market. Does trust provide a framework of mutuality in which competitive trade and calculative reason may be exercised, or is trust a calculated bond that reflects self-interest? If trust is a calculation, it cannot be a shared commitment and offers an unstable framework for traders; conversely, if trust is a commitment, can it be insulated from the expression of self-interest that it nourishes? A leading economist, Kenneth Arrow (1990:137), states the problem for standard economics and in effect observes that mutuality must precede trade:

> In a rational type of analysis it will be said that it is profitable to be trustworthy. So I will be trustworthy because it is profitable to me. But you can't very easily establish trust on a basis like that. If your basis is rational decision and your underlying motive is self-interest, then you can betray your trust at any point when it is profitable and in your interest to do so. Therefore other people can't trust you. For there to be trust, there has to be a social structure which is based on motives different from immediate opportunism. Or perhaps based on something for which your social status is a guarantee and which functions as a kind of commitment. How all this works is not explainable in Becker-type terms.

How is trust within a market first formed? The Frafra migrants from northeastern Ghana who moved to a shantytown in Accra provide one example of the way trust bonds can emerge in an informal market. Lacking resources, Keith Hart (2000) reports, the Frafra became very small traders who engaged in both licit and illicit activities. Because they had little access to currency, traders often relied on loans and the extension of credit among themselves, but default was an ever-present reality. The shantytown traders existed at the margins of state control and enforcement, so legal contracts to ensure trade could not be used, while resort to violence or public shaming could not be long-term solutions to the enforcement problem. In the rural area, the Frafra traders had belonged to large kinship groups, but this traditional ethic of sharing did not fit with the self-interested exchanges in which the traders engaged: "separate interests" could not be expressed through the idiom of kinship (Hart 2000:190). Also, most of these ties dissolved when people from different clans mixed together in the urban context: kinship morality that connoted identity, sameness, and a collective self no longer had a strong claim. How did the migrants solve the risk problem? Eventually, through trial and error, and at the cost of time and monetary losses, individual trust relationships began to emerge, and credit was offered only to these partners. Loans were never provided to strangers, with whom transactions were always immediate. Ultimately, within the large, ill-defined market, a loosely structured arena consisting of personal networks of debits and credits emerged. The relationships were instigated by the need and desire to have market trade, and they could be broken. In this and other cases, I suggest, market trust is a projection from prior experiences of mutuality; however, this commonality is tenuous because it is caught between calculation and commitment. With their slowly emerging trust bonds and failures, the Frafra migrants exemplify the unstable seam between the mutual and moral basis that trade requires and the calculated transactions that it sustains.

Establishing trust within a larger market arena is even more fraught with tension, as illustrated by the changes in Eastern Europe from a socialist to a market orientation. Caroline Humphrey, a long-time observer of Soviet and Russian life, reveals the conflict between the intent to form a market economy and local pressures to keep trusted groups together, such as extractive plants or collective farms. Enterprises that were state-managed during the Soviet regime have become legally independent entities in markets, but they are directed not so much at securing profits as at ensuring their survival and the protection of their members. In many cases they aim for self-sufficiency: an enterprise may provide houses, food, or heating for its members, or it may offer small plots so that people can help provision themselves (Humphrey 2002a:75). Humphrey observes that "defensive territoriality now exists in incoherent confrontation with the simultaneous realization of globalized desires and demands," and economic units erect "palisades" around themselves (Humphrey 2002a:72, 20). She remarks that an agricultural or provincial enterprise often "sees itself as a productive unit concerned with reproducing itself as a kollektiv.... What the corporations are reproducing is not a monetary fund or an economic capacity to supply a product but a social community that is specific in its localization at a certain place and in its occupational characteristics" (2002a:80).

These communal enterprises engage in barter and monetary exchanges with traders, but independent traders often symbolize a threat, and enterprises are reluctant to search for optimal offers. Traders, people add, extract local property while bringing goods with little moral value; they produce nothing. As a result, regional exchange flourishes, whereas trade that crosses social boundaries is avoided. Yet the use of currency and consumption of international goods provide a sense of participating in the global arena. Russians, Humphrey concludes, "cherish concepts of production collectives to which they are attached, and they feel loss if the kollektiv itself disintegrates, but on the other hand, it is they themselves who stand at the warehouse doors ready to make a deal" (2002a:96). This dramatic shift from an embedded economy of immediate trust to a disembedded economy requiring trust in the larger arena reveals the participants' ambivalence about the change and the dialectics of mutuality and anonymous trade.[4]

Mutuality Inside Markets: Communities, House-Businesses, and Houses

Communal agreements not only set a space for trade, they may be inside the market arena. Market traders themselves often incorporate the dialectics of mutuality and market. A house-business and even a house combine the two projects, because they place communal commitments on their market participants and their returns. For example, one Sunday, I saw a range of house-business combinations in a town market held high in the Southern Andes of Colombia.[5] At one extreme, an older man, who lived a few blocks from the marketplace, sat on a stool next to a wheelbarrow filled with blocks of partially refined brown sugar. His sales were minimal and earnings negligible, but he had no house commitments: he came to visit with people who browsed, and he used the proceeds to replace his stock so he could return the next week. He was trading to create mutuality in the market. Near him, two adults with three young children were selling a small range of agricultural goods, which they had grown and had purchased for cash. Their goal was to maintain their household. On the one hand, they were trading some homegrown goods for cash to buy other necessities. On the other, with the purchased items they had bought for resale, the couple tried to recover their monetary costs and to have some goods left over, which they could take home for consumption during the week. Neither transaction was directed toward making money (which would have been difficult to calculate since their own productive labor was unpaid and not measured). By contrast, a number of transporters sold food from the backs of their trucks. They were buying and selling to make a profit but were assisted by their offspring and other young kin who were learning the skills of trading and transporting. These youngsters earned a small wage and were provided with cooked food. Finally, in a different area of the plaza, a woman was selling small hardware items (knives, locks, and nails) that she purchased from wholesalers. She sold in three different markets each week and rented space for her inventories in each market town so she would have no cartage costs. Her aim was to make a money profit, which she used to purchase food and clothes for her children. She was trading, but for domestic maintenance. Overall, these market participants displayed shifting combinations of mutuality and trade.

A house-business that draws on family labor can be filled with disagreement about the allocation of the returns. Do family laborers deserve a market wage or are they providing communal support that is returned in disparate ways? Who deserves what, when offspring are expected to perform chores such as washing dishes or working in the fields? I once recorded the suicide of a young man in rural Panama who thought he was being denied the monetary returns that his brother received for driving a truck for their father, which is an extreme example of the dialectic as played out in everyday life.

When individual traders participate in a market as representatives of a community, mutual obligations link their trading resources and returns to others. These traders exchange with commitments on what they offer and receive, for the purpose of the trade is to maintain the community on which they and others depend. Because these trades are impersonal, calculated, and bargained, the traders continuously shift between the contradictory roles of being a person-in-community and an individual. For example, in the interior of Panama, agriculturalists bartered their homegrown rice and maize for salt that was needed at home, and the exchange rates shifted over the years. But agriculturalists were not empowered to barter chickens or other household belongings for salt; their trade was limited to agricultural products, and they were trading to meet the needs of the house. Their offerings and takings were structured by domestic mutuality, although this communality was partly maintained by competitive exchange.

This transformation of the conjoint person-in-community into the disjoint, individual trader sometimes leads to tension between the two identities, For example, in Guanajuato, Mexico, miners collect their pay on Saturday afternoon. Sometimes they spend a part or even all of their returns meeting other men and drinking, with the result that their wives accuse them of seeing prostitutes and being worthless (Ferry 2005:130, 134). One man justified his actions by explaining, "I deserve a little 'motherlessness'" (Ferry 2005:44): he was denying his mutual commitments. Elsewhere in rural Latin America when men sell a household animal or crop, they may use part of the return for private use. In Panama, the private sugar mills paid their cane suppliers on Saturdays. The cash return was gained in place of using the land for subsistence farming; however, men often spent a portion of the money on drink and amusements, In contrast, some of the women sewed clothes or wove straw hats for sale; they used this return to buy food for the house This gender difference between the strength of communal commitments often led to quarrels within a household,

Mutuality inside Markets: Oligopolies

Mutual ties within markets often burst the expectations of perfect competition. These relations seem to be like the communal agreements that set a market arena. But there is a difference: they are used by a community within a market often to the detriment of other market participants. In these cases, calculative reason cascades into and appropriates mutuality to become a means of individual profit making and accumulation.

At times mutual relationships create cooperation among competitors and help frame production arrangements. Cooperatives (sometimes as expressions of market resistance) can unite competitors to bolster their individual purchasing or selling power (or to serve social welfare purposes), as in the case of the Mondragan cooperatives in Spain.[6] Social ties also may structure trade through longer-term exchanges between production firms that adjust their output and techniques in relation to one another, as in the case of the Tsukiji market combines. Harrison White shows how upstream and downstream commitments between firms help frame production markets and reduce uncertainty for individual firms. Networks of intermediate products and services, he argues, belie simplistic views of markets as containing isolated firms that form spot contracts with each other (White 2002). Likewise, a number of studies, from areas such as northern Italy, France, and Germany, show how cooperation among small-scale producers and some larger firms emerges to form industrial districts.[7]

Mutual ties also occlude competition when information is withheld from others to be circulated only among a few, as in attempts to rig the initial public offering of a stock; also, they can be used to send false information. Diasporic traders, who are linked by kinship or ethnicity, may pass information across large distances, provide special prices and unsecured loans to each other, offer spaces for private trade, or reach agreements informally (Greif 1993, 1994; Middleton 2003). The Roth-

schild brothers used family ties to send secret information between national markets and thus accumulate profits. Today, antique furniture
dealers or rare book sellers sometimes buy and sell among themselves
to keep up their listed prices, share information, and have temporary
control and use of the circulating goods: they project similarity of interests on otherwise competitive ties. Similarly, barter clubs that include
competitors and buyers and sellers help members to sustain a business
in lean times, to evade taxes on financial profits, and to form new connections. In a competitive market as well, individual buyers and sellers
may form a semipermanent tie that promises better product information, assures favors when trading, or modulates risk (Mintz 1961).

On a larger scale, market collusion, cronyism, and cooperation among
competitors and friends are especially frowned on and variously prohibited by governing authorities that set the market arena. A scandal
emerged in 2000 when it was discovered that the two oldest and largest
auction houses—Christie's and Sotheby's—were colluding on their commissions. The FBI investigated, but Christie's gained immunity from
prosecution when an employee confessed and cooperated with the inquiry. The main owner of Sotheby's and the chief executive officer were
convicted and sentenced. Other senior managers were dismissed from
the company in this high-profile case, which affected other wealthy individuals who had participated in this "high" market. The open market was once again freed of mutuality and an insider's network. The
same problem occurs on an international scale. The World Bank, under
its former president Wolfowitz and others, has been trying to eradicate
cronyism, collusion, and corruption in borrowing countries, which is a
strict application of the neoliberal agenda. In contrast, the online auction space eBay, which has millions of loyal customers, rigorously controls collusion among participants. It acts to minimize risk and prohibit
price manipulation, false advertising, and pyramid schemes, and it has
a host of other regulations. It promotes eBay as a community that has
many and ever-changing facets.

Market agreements about proper comportment also may be quasi-
formal or tacit, such as providing "transparent" accounting, and new
and shared regulations are sometimes needed to limit new illegal or
unacceptable practices. The Enron Corporation and the Arthur Anderson accounting firm took part of the corporation's debt off its balance
sheet and out of footnotes in order to increase Enron's profit and credit
rating, and when these techniques were shown to be used by others as
well, investors were shocked.[8] The two participants composed an inside community that shared alternative accounting practices. Enron
investors lost money, but the larger market tremors had to do with the
broken trust and the revelation that a nontransparent community was
secreted within the market. As a result, the larger community insisted
that some accounting practices be made more explicit and enforceable,

and oversight was formalized and shifted, to a degree, from market participants to a governing board. New laws also were passed, and principals were convicted. The Enron case offers a different example of the ever-present dialectic: a small community within a larger shared arena may subvert it, or a market made possible by a community may be debased by a smaller community of calculating actors within it.

On the consumer side as well, information gained through mutuality may influence market choices. Individuals seeking work, whether in industrial markets or on plantations, may find jobs through social connections.[9] People often select lawyers, doctors, dentists, mental health professionals, insurance agents, accountants, restaurants, college professors, and car dealers using information gathered through social relationships. Stock tips, too, often pass between acquaintances. Economists may argue that such social connections lower the cost of securing market information, but often this knowledge arrives serendipitously through relationships maintained for other purposes. In these cases, community provides a costless "spillover" of information for trading purposes. But how is this "free gift" reciprocated? Or is it? Economists claim there is no free lunch, and anthropologists say there is no free gift. But is this spillover a gift from mutuality to market, a case of debasement, or a strengthening of communal ties? Should one offer a friend payment for advice? If so, what does that say about the friendship and open-ended reciprocity that is suddenly measured? In one case a businessman offered his cousin valuable market information and was repaid with an expensive piece of art. Was the object a repayment or a gift that represented strengthening of their kinship bond? Was profit making being mystified under the cover of mutuality?

From Mutuality to Market: Cascading, Subsidies, and Debasement

The transformation of base to capital, which is driven by the cascading power of calculative reason and capital, is found in many spaces of economy, from the national to the local level. One example of this dialectic at the national level comes from a study of the inception of fishing quotas in Iceland (Helgason and Pálsson 1998). What had been a shared base individually apportioned for market trade became private property under the influence of competition and seeking a return to capital. The story partly replays the Naskapi encounter with the fur market and my Panama example, but it occurred at the national scale and displays the dialectic today.

Traditionally, fishing provided a supplement to farming in Iceland, and from earliest times, the ocean was viewed as a shared resource to which all Icelanders had equal access. During Iceland's struggle for

independence from Denmark (which was achieved in 1944), this resource came to be seen as the economic base for the new nation. In 1948
the Icelandic government declared that it held exclusive fishing rights
in coastal waters. By 1976 the territorial claim was extended to 200 miles
off shore, partly in response to increased foreign fishing. Then, as local
fishing intensified, Icelanders recognized the need to exercise restrictions on their fishing, and in 1984 a quota system was started. The government apportioned costless quotas to existing boat owners on the basis
of their historical catches. Originally seen as a temporary measure, the
quota system was continued over time. Then, in 1991 quota rights were
separated from boats with permission to trade them for cash. This new
privatization produced a reaction: in a national survey, 87 percent of re-
spondents said it was unfair to let boat owners profit from the earlier,
free allocation, while 95 percent wanted the fisheries to remain as a
shared holding. A birthright or legacy had been transformed to pri-
vately held capital. Soon, the change was accentuated when owners of
large boats, who had access to banks and loans, acquired the quota
rights of small owners who could not withstand downturns or invest
in new equipment. In 1991, sixteen "giants" controlled 25 percent of the
quota rights, but six years later the number of quota holders had decreased by one half, and twenty-two giants controlled 50 percent of the
rights. The situation became even more asymmetric when small boat
owners, who lacked quota rights, entered share arrangements with the
giants, who also controlled processing plants: their catch was split 50/50,
and the fisherman's portion was delivered to the quota owner cum
processor at below-market prices.

Eventually, large holders became known as "quota-kings" and "lords
of the sea," while small-scale operators were likened to tenants and
serfs who labored on the estate of the medieval lord. Boats lacking quota
rights were termed "eunuchs." Today the system "horrifies" many fish-
ers, and one stated, "I think that [un-caught] fish can never be counted
as property. They can't do that. I don't believe that boat owners can
appropriate animals that are not yet born as their property, like calves
that have not yet been conceived" (Helgason and Pálsson 1998:129).
The tension between the value of capital returns and the value of mutual holdings persists in the voiced protest against the conversion of
the necessary to the contingent.[10]

This same dialectic by which base is slowly transformed to capital
can be seen even more graphically in my ethnography from Colombia,
which also shows how the mutual realm may subsidize the market. In
the Colombian Andes, as I have observed, material practices are organized around house economies, which are located on the margins of productive land. As I explained, according to the people the land, which is
their base, provides strength to their crops. The earth receives this
strength from the elements, such as rain, wind, and sun, which ema-

nate from God's might. In raising crops, humans "compose" the land by using the strength they previously received from their foods that came from the land. In good years the land "gives" enough strength for working in the subsequent one and provides "remainders" or "leftovers" that augment the base. But the remainder is a shifting category that depends on household apportioning. When a harvest is brought to the house, it is allocated to various uses. First, an amount is set aside for seeding in the following year. Then, a quantity is saved for household consumption. After this amount, some may be held for feeding animals. Finally, part of a harvest may be put to one side for sale in order to obtain necessities the household does not produce. At each stage, the extra amount is termed the leftover, which is not a surplus or profit but what remains after the prior sequence of needs are met. A leftover represents the unmeasured strength of the earth and work (or parts of the base) that were expended in producing it.

When a household trades a remainder, its project usually is to replace the base, just as one replaces the base by keeping part of the harvest for seed. Many households, however, also raise some crops for direct sale, and this project can draw on what otherwise would be remainders that are part of the base. The process works as follows. Suppose a base crop, such as potatoes or maize, is being raised. Given the marginal land, a market crop, such as tomatoes or onions, could not be profitably grown if all its costs (seed, fertilizer, pesticides, and labor) were calculated and paid in money. Instead, a house may feed itself and outside laborers on its harvested potatoes, and sell some of the potatoes to purchase the other inputs for the cash crop. It substitutes house potatoes for market costs, or uses base remainders to subsidize the market return. In the local language, it converts what would be market "costs" in money to household "expenditures" in order to make a gain. But this return is not a profit in market terms (for it is a loss) or in the people's language. It is a return for the unpriced subsidy they must pay to enter the market. This debasement process is usually irreversible (Gudeman 1978; Gudeman and Rivera 1990).

More generally, small-scale farmers often subsidize the larger economy by providing "subsidized" foods and other commodities that would not otherwise be available (Mayer 2002). This communal subsidy is very different from the one a national government may provide to its capitalized farmers. Precisely because it comes from the mutual domain outside the market, this subsidy has no market cost, although it lowers the cost of industrial laborers. In Panama, I once explored how sugar cane as a cash crop could be raised only by using the surplus time that was generated by the workers' subsistence production. For example, the field laborers received a small money wage, as did the field "owner," who took his cut. But the amounts they received were used up in daily food. No one could have worked or provided for a family without his own subsistence supplement that supported the "free" time for the cash work. I have sometimes termed this reverse subsidy a "negative rent" in recognition of what people located on submarginal land must pay to sell on the market. But even that expression, like "unequal exchange," reduces the dialectic to market terms and fails to capture the debasement. Whatever expression is used, the same dialectic can be found in market economies, too.

Resistance

Market cascading and debasement are also resisted by communal action. An example, provided by Guyer (2004) from her work in Nigeria, shows how competitive trade and market "preferences" may be reworked through communal rules of apportionment. In the summer of 1997, the country experienced a petrol shortage, and people were lining up to obtain supplies. How did the buying and selling take place? Was there an open market in which prices rose and buyers sorted themselves by ability and desire to pay, or was there communal apportioning based on social values? At one station, the two were uneasily interwoven. The petrol price was roughly in accord with world conditions, but it was localized through communal allocation. Generally, people who had a long-time relationship with the owner and held positions in the local hierarchy, such as the mayor and other officials, were served first, but they did not receive the full amount they requested. A second group, representing commercial and private interests, was served next but at the cost of paying an extra sum to the people, including soldiers, who were keeping order at the station. Next, individuals who had waited in line for a long time received petrol, for an extra payment. Then, the final customers for whom some petrol was saved paid a little bit more money. Along with the soldiers, police and the owner's helpers kept order, and if someone tried to jump the queue he might be jabbed or socially sanctioned.

Thus, within the national conditions of supply and demand, several mutual rules framed the trade, respecting social proximity to the buyer, positions of authority, and the labor of waiting as well as extra payments. The station owner drew on these disparate values and used them to negotiate each case. Buyers generally accepted his tactical uses of the registers, although some tried to subvert the queue. The different social scales did not make up a single system, and their intervals, such as a mayor versus a government official, were not measured. Mutuality and market were combined—with tension, as shown by the need to keep order.[11]

A household also can provide a zone of resistance to trade practices when market earnings are transformed to base. Janet Carsten (1989) tells how this transformation takes place in households on the island of Langkawi off the coast of Malaysia. Men principally fish for a living; they bring their cash earnings home but immediately pass them to women, who keep them for domestic expenses. Women are at the center of the Malay house: they prepare the shared rice meal that is the symbol of domestic and kin unity and is cooked over the hearth that makes up the center of the home. Through this transfer from men to women and into the house for domestic uses, the values of the disjoint individual and the market are transformed to those of the conjoint individual and family unity. The market return becomes part of the base and is used to sustain the home. As Carsten remarks, the women "cook" the money and so transform it from market to home.

Similar dialectics are found in high market economies but often without the careful "washing" that the return in Langkawi undergoes. What does the exchange of work for a wage mean? Is it a private return and the property of the wage earner, or does it have elements of a base trade for a community? For example, who controls a salary earner's return and has rights to the flow? At one extreme the return might be distributed only on the basis of an individual's contributions. Alternatively, does the income earner have special rights to the flow and dole out an intermittent return to his partner, or do spouses share a joint fund that receives all household income? High wages allow for more mutual uses and greater household welfare, but also for the separation of the return among base, individual uses, and new investment. Who makes the judgment and according to what values? High market wages also allow for communal subcontracting. Domestic workers can be hired to supplement the work of maintaining a base, as in the case of caregivers like nannies and domestic workers. But does purchased care create an enlarged set of mutual relationships between householders and caregivers who become family-like, is it a pure trade relation, is it a dialectical combination of both, or is it a market tie mystified as mutuality? (And does this sale of care have a cascading effect on the base of the caregiver who must divert her attention from her own domestic work and sustain it with cash?)

In the United States, the top end of the individual wealth scale has exploded upward, especially in relation to the lower and middle classes, not to speak of less industrialized nations. Some accumulators pass their money to offspring through an inheritance, which is allocation within mutuality, but these registers vary. The money may be apportioned per capita, per stirpes, by need, by gender, by age, or by personal relationships. Similarly, some wealthy capitalists—through social pressure—establish charitable foundations or give to philanthropic organizations and universities, and then explain their gifts by stating that they owe something back to the larger community that supported them. But do these acts cleanse the money of its separatist value? The moral commitments, enabled through market success, vary in amount, timing and direction according to the individual giver's choice. Is this form of giving a calculated selection (with an eye to tax relief), a mutual commitment, or ambiguous? The dialectic of market and mutual values reaches through every domain of economy.

Everyday Mystification: The Appropriation of Features

Trade and mutuality also mystify each other, a process that works from mutuality to trade and from impersonal exchanges to mutuality. Money, for example, may mediate personal relationships or at least be converted to mutuality. Gifts are bought and "given" to intimate family, more distant kin, friends, neighbors, and acquaintances. The money is transformed from an impersonal to an intimate form. Sometimes money is given directly—as at certain weddings—sometimes the gift is presented as a gift card for a store, and sometimes money is loaned interest-free to a friend. But in all cases these interactions involve a degree of ambiguity and tension. For example, Zelizer examines a variety of interactions between intimate or trust relations and economic payments: are they to be interpreted as fees, tips, charity, and bribes, or in other ways? She claims that we use some economic transactions to make and maintain social ties, and people negotiate their meanings. But, Zelizer admits, "[i]t isn't easy. In everyday life, people invest intense effort and constant worry in finding the right match between economic relations and intimate ties" (2005:3). She adds that these mixed ties also occur in the context of longer-term social relations. For Zelizer, "all ongoing social relations (intimate or not) include at least a minimum of shared meanings, operating rules and boundaries" (2005:33). In other words, mutual relationships are necessary and may draw on market returns to sustain and prolong them.

The transformation works in the other direction as well. Market contracts may be veiled as mutuality to enhance individual efforts and commitment. For example, corporations often represent themselves as a family or community, such as the "Wal-Mart family." Corporations may take employees on retreats at resorts (with family members invited), subsidize lunchrooms, and provide nurseries and gyms to promote loyalty. Within a corporation workers with separate contracts may represent themselves as a community. The production team on an automobile assembly line may speak of "its" cars, even in advertising. Construction workers refer to the building they helped create as "theirs," just as a carpenter may sign and hide a piece of wood within a house he helped to construct. Individuals in a corporation also identify with corporate property as if it had been allocated like a base in a community: a worker speaks of his shovel, tractor, chair, office, or desk.[12] Assertions of communal possession and identity arise with respect to intellectual property, too. At a computer institute in Paris, where research groups develop software, sociality emerges among workers and provides "social gratification" (Born 1996:108). As the software product develops and the sense of group possession grows, information needed by others at the institute is increasingly withheld. This assertion of a shared holding may be a protest against the contractual setting in which the work is performed, but it also intensifies commitment, efforts of innovation, and profits for the larger organization. Are these commitments mystifications of contractual relations, are they communal relations, or are they a contradictory combination of the two?

The contingency of these mutual relationships is revealed at the poignant moment of downsizing, when a person is asked to clean out his desk, his computer passwords are frozen, and he is escorted from the building. This moment epitomizes the severing of salary, work, and relationships, or a place in a corporate community. If downsizing has a downside for workers, it has an upside for other corporate members. During the 1990s, an interesting self-critique emerged in the United States when many corporations began to use downsizing to increase productivity. Several years into this movement articles began to appear questioning the tactic because it was said to lead to decreased productivity, loyalty, and morale among the remaining employees; the "best" would seek work elsewhere, leaving a corporation with the least productive and motivated workers. A corporation could fall victim to its attempts at increasing efficiency by destroying the communities on which its success depended. In fact, three economists have analyzed the effects of downsizing. Downsizing did not increase corporate competitiveness or productivity, although that was the stated goal; instead, it decreased unit labor costs. They concluded that downsizing is an effective strategy for holding down wages, raising profits, and transferring income from labor to management, which is "is the dirty little secret of downsizing" (Baumol, Blinder, and Wolff 2003:262). Led by the pull of calculation as well as colonization by the financial realm, downsizing may undermine the mutuality on which corporations depend while increasing the financial well-being of high management.

If corporations mystify themselves as families while contradicting this pose by downsizing, their external presentation is much the same. Companies often reach out to consumers by representing their trade relation as mutuality. Frequent flyer offers, credit card points, and supermarket clubs are part of market trades that offer the persistent buyer a discount. Participants are called "members," and the rhetoric of mutuality is used when inviting participation and communicating with customers—from "Sam's Club" (Wal-Mart) to my local coffee shop that offers me a "loyalty" card. The ideology of community becomes a calculated means for market ends rather than an end itself. Is it an assertion of community or its mystification?

Through the semantic vacancy offered by price fetishism, it may be that we are seized by the "culture industry" and persuaded to purchase by advertising, product labeling, and public display of goods (Horkheimer and Adorno 2002), but corporate promotion and advertising does offer personal identity through belonging to "new" communities, as in the early Apple or Saturn owner groups.[13] Through our choices do we take on the communal "properties" that we purchase in the market? Is the owner of a Ford automobile connected to car that he displays, to other owners, to the human being Henry Ford (and to which one—the ancestor or his descendants in the company)? Branding suggests that we are linked to what we buy and who made the product, and this connection helps formulate our identity through physical or metonymic interaction with that product. Even when an article, such as a shoe or blouse, is made in a light assembly plant by "anonymous laborers" from abroad, its origin may be noted on the label. Some expensive products, such as a hand-knit sweater, may bear a personally signed label (usually by a woman who works at home). These markers are used to convey the mutuality of a home, almost as if the item were a personal gift. This assertion of a connection between corporation and consumer holds even for wrappings, such as labeled shopping bags or paper seals that are placed on new purchases (although in some countries people still bring their own carrying bags to the grocery store).

Slogans also summon mutuality and family relationships as a reason to purchase A large department store used to advertise that "The customer is always right," as if the company had a give-and-take relationship with its shoppers. Other slogans are metaphorical, such as General Electric's motto: "We Bring Good Things to Life." "We" apparently refers to the corporation that creates things just as parents bring children to life, and are connected to what they have produced. But the word "life" also refers to the consumer (as in your life) to whom General Electric brings good things, like a gift. The exchange takes place in the market through the competitive trade of property rights but is represented as a communal tie that connects producer, product, and consumer in a family. Which is the "reality"—the market trade or the happy family?

Consumers may constitute conjoint identities by the connections they make to market products. When we drink a Coca-Cola, do we become "the real thing"? The franchise corporation Burger King says, "Have it your way," meaning that one can choose among having cheese, tomatoes and other additives with a hamburger, and so establish a unique identity in relation to Burger King. But the choices are limited and do not require much time to select, for this product is a "fast food," if only because the narrow range of choice keeps the queues short.[14] Calculative reason is induced in consumption through choice, while corporate cascading mystifies it as mutuality.[15]

The dialectics of mutuality and trade are not confined to formal markets and corporations. Garage sales in the United States combine mutuality and profit making in shifting, sometimes tension-filled practices.[16] Held at a home, a garage sale is a domestic event in that goods come from the house, have been used by a community, and are sold by the homemaker, who is usually female. The owner "gives" the sale, and the charges are low—at "give-away" amounts—but the items are priced and sold as if to deny that the sale is charity. The low charges convert what might otherwise be interpreted as a free gift or an impersonal trade into a moment of give-and-take. People attend garage sales for different reasons, from being thrifty to making money. Purchasers are acquiring some of the tastes and remainders of another, just as sellers are giving something of themselves. But buyer and seller may have conflicting readings of the event: a seller may feel that the object sold is almost a gift, while the buyer may read it as a fair price. A garage sale can be nearly pure trade, an expression of mutuality, or an ambiguous combination.

Other practices resist the mystifying uses of mutuality in the market. The fair trade movement, for example, resists the semantic blandishments of price fetishism and counterbalances, to some degree, the problem of base subsidies. Today fair trade movements advocate certified labeling of products, which increases the transparency of the relation between producer and consumer, and opens the possibility of mutuality between buyer and ultimate producer. Fair trade advocates promote the idea of a partnership between consumer and producer characterized by dialogue and mutual respect. The movement's goals usually are to promote the alleviation of poverty and sustainable development, achieve gender equity in production, enhance working conditions, and ban child labor. Today, there are labeling organizations that certify whether these and other conditions are met so that the consumer has a transparent guarantee. Originally, the fair trade movement focused on handcrafts, but today it is mostly devoted to agricultural products. Consumers in the United States probably know the fair trade movement as it applies to coffee, but many fruits and vegetables are included as well as wine and tea.

Of course, fair trade has its critics. From the left, the fair trade movement may not be sufficiently radical, because it does not challenge the existence of global markets that link "north" and "south," whereas the right may claim that it leads to price distortions and represents a subsidy to producers (although in my experience fair trade coffee is usually competitive with its less transparent counterparts). We might expect this equivocal support, because given the space in which it operates, fair trade is a dialectical movement that embodies economy's tension. It promotes standard economics by supporting markets but increases prices and product information for the consumer to promote mutuality with the original producer.

The Dialectics of Reason

In consumption, the use of calculative reason reaches limits because it is countered by another mode of reason—being thrifty or making savings. Thrift that is nurtured in the communal domain marks the boundaries of calculative reason, even as it is slowly colonized. By thrift, I mean making savings, economizing, and being parsimonious, frugal, or sparing. The thrifty person is careful when expending and stands opposed to the spendthrift. But making savings is not the same as making money. Both practices are means-to-ends directed, however, making money focuses on the relation between means and ends (or the profit obtained), whereas making savings focuses on preserving the means to have a remainder as a precaution for the future. Making savings is a shifting collection of practices. One can make savings by eating less, reusing building materials, repairing a sandal, preserving string, reusing a nail, or finding new uses for discarded materials.

Because making savings often is connected to meeting communal needs, it can be opposed to indulging in wants that are provided through markets. I have found that households in Latin America frequently distinguish between needs they require for maintenance and wants—from alcohol to clothes—that are not required, Similarly, in a recent study of shopping, Miller (1998) finds that most shoppers in North London are neither profligate nor extravagant but concerned with being thrifty. Meanwhile, though they are bound by the budget constraints of their households, thrifty buyers also indulge in "treats," such as stopping for a cup of coffee or eating out. The distinction between needs and wants, however, does not capture the way that making money in the market can draw on making savings for the house. Small-scale agriculture in Colombia, as I described, offers a case of this dialectic. As the people say, "if you can't make savings with the potatoes, you can't make money with the crop for sale." The second practice colonizes the first, just as downsizing can debase a corporation.

Market advertising mystifies this dialectic of communal thrift and calculated gain when it represents purchasing as thrift and a means to build mutuality. Today we are inundated by "sales" that have many forms: sometimes they are held on a particular day, sometimes they consist of remainders or unsold seasonal goods, sometimes they are special offers. But why are they appealing, since anything on sale costs money? Perhaps the buyer can think of himself as a calculating chooser or as a fine trader in the market and so achieve this identity; at the same time, he is a proper community member, because his economies and savings enlarge the household reservoir, like keeping a car one more year or soaking off and using uncanceled postage stamps. In these cases, economizing is recruited by calculative reason to conform to the market project.

Effective advertisements often capture this contradiction between consumer saving and corporate profit, or the need to appeal to mutuality while making money. Consider a failed retailer. In its grandest days, when Sears Roebuck and Co. was the world's largest store, it advertised, "Shop at Sears and Save." In this memorable phrase that combined the embedded and disembedded realms of economy, the merchant linked its purpose of making money ("Shop at Sears") with the consumer's project of economizing money ("and Save"). (I used to wonder if Sears really wanted its customers to walk away with unspent cash or to use their savings in a different part of the store.) Once Sears deviated from this corporate mission and began to sell paintings and upscale goods (or wants), its fortunes lagged: Kmart (with whom it later merged) surpassed it, and the two were overtaken by Wal-Mart, Market projects need to draw on local models, even as they appropriate them for their own purposes.

Cascading and Mystification in Discourse: Disembedding the Embedded

If cascading, mystification, veiling, and debasement are found in everyday practices, they also are encountered in formal models, because economists have added a new bolt to their locker: institutions. New institutionalists focus on market associations, which seemingly brings them closer to including mutuality as part of economy. The institutions explained include clubs, guilds, ethnic groups, and especially property rights, as in the case of Demsetz. Most of these models presume the self-interested person, but they insert another level in the derivational model—that of institutions, which mediate between the individual and exchange. I suggest that this economics is a dialectical combination of mutuality and self-interest. But it starts with the standard assumptions.

The concept of institution refers to formal or written rules, such as property rights and laws, plus informal or unwritten rules, such as shared norms and beliefs as well as enforcement structures. North, who has put forward the most complete new institutionalist perspective, starts with the idea of uncertainty, which humans seek to control and reduce. Beliefs embodied in witchcraft, magic, and religions are non-rational solutions to the existential problem, whereas altering the institutional framework in a rational direction can reduce uncertainty (North

2005:15–16). For North, institutions provide patterns and constraints for organizations within them. They set the rules of the game. In his words, the "continuous interaction between institutions and organizations in the economic setting of scarcity and hence competition is the key to institutional change" (2005:59). North especially emphasizes the significance of property rights with their incentives as defining the rules of the game, and he agrees with Demsetz about the importance of internalizing the effects of externalities.

For most new institutionalists, the idea of "transaction cost" is central, because every exchange has costs of formation, information, monitoring, and completion, and contracts do not cover every contingency or uncertainty. For example, can a trading partner be trusted to deliver the promised quantity and quality of goods on time? How can compliance be enforced, and what can be done about shirking at work or withholding information? Given such problems between contracting parties, they argue, institutions develop to mitigate risk and minimize costs over the longer term, and market competition helps to sort out the more efficient solutions. Institutions are a means within the larger project of achieving market efficiency. They may yield some inefficiencies, due to their historical or "path" dependence, but lasting ones lower transaction costs; and when formal laws arise to structure markets or when other conditions change, older institutions may wither or disappear. Like neoclassical economists, new institutionalists assume the presence of calculative reason but with the difference that they try to show how social forms, beliefs, values, and relationships, in addition to prices, are shaped according to the decisions of the rational actor.

Some institutional economists have turned their attention directly to communities. For example, Aoki and Hayami (2001) argue that communities often stand between the market and the state. They are not rivals of the market but can enhance development in the early stages of market formation. Although such community regulations may offer inferior market equilibriums, they do provide low-cost enforcement of contracts through personal relationships among traders. Greif has offered a number of studies to show that contract enforcement between traders from different communities can be achieved by mechanisms within a community, such as shunning or avoiding outside traders who do not meet their obligations. He calls this the "Community Responsibility System," which embeds an otherwise spot trade. Greif suggests that communities in premodern Europe provided an important complement to the market through such means: "A Community Responsibility System enabled exchange that was impersonal up to one's community affiliation in late medieval Europe. It took advantage of the existing social context, namely, the existence of communities" (Greif 2001:35). With population growth, heightened mobility, and the strengthening of political orders, these systems slowly faded.

Greif, unlike some other new institutionalists who focus only on so-cial relationships, presumes that cultural beliefs influence social organ-ization and that social organization reflects cultural beliefs, as does North. For example, he argues that societies may be divided into col-lectivist and individualist forms "In collectivist societies everyone is expected to respond to whatever has transpired between any specific merchant and agent, whereas the opposite holds for individualist soci-eties" (Greif 1994:919). But shared cultural beliefs also express mutual-ity, which means that his collectivist and individualist forms of trade are dependent on local models.

Greif tends to use game theory in support of his explanations, but other authors provide different derivations. Aoki (2001), for example, assumes that traders have preference rankings for both economic out-comes and for social standing, such as reputation, esteem, or higher status. These two preference scales are exchangeable or commensurate, so that what one loses in one can be compensated by a gain in the other, or the reverse, For example, an actor who breaches market obligations may be excluded from festivals and ceremonies (Aoki 2001:108). These are linked games, and the key idea is that sociality is not only subjected to a measuring rod but that this measuring rod is part of a larger util-ity function that includes economic events and outcomes. In both ex-amples, according to the theorists, the calculating actor is everywhere and there is no tension or contradiction between mutuality and market: if the cost of maintaining a community is higher than the benefits, it disappears.[17]

Goodbye to Pensée Sauvage

Inevitably, given the tendency to cascade a universal model into the realm of mutuality, at least one new institutionalist, Janet Tai Landa, has applied the approach to ethnography in order to demonstrate its power, expand the reach of economics, and claim that a new institution-alist approach can lead to the "unification of the social sciences"(Landa 1994:38). Goodbye to one hundred years of anthropology, and to Mali-nowski and Mauss.

Landa starts her tale with an encounter between the rational chooser and another maximizer: "Imagine a world," she says, "in which there are no clubs and in which the state affords no protection of contracts" (1994:117). Traders are opportunistic, so breach of contract is always a possibility. This moment of uncertainty marks Landa's entry point. Drawing on the concepts of rational choice, property rights, and trans-action costs, she tries to explain the emergence or origin of trade in-stitutions, such as ethnic trader organizations and gift exchange as responses to contract uncertainty. In the language of economists, she argues that rules of trade are generated *endogenously* rather than *exoge-*

nously, or that rational choosers generate the social institutions within which they can carry out rational choice.

For Landa, institutions are rules that specify roles and expectations. Like other new institutionalists, she inserts a new level in the derivational model. Operating between individuals as rational choosers and pricing outcomes, institutions are a means to the end of acquisition, because they function to assure regularities of trade and economize on its costs (Landa 1994:23). Landa attacks traditional functionalist theory in sociology because it does not explain how norms emerge; however, she continuously evokes the notion of function in her story (Landa 1994:5, 13, 29, 116, 134, 155). But this reliance on a functionalist account is hardly surprising, because in her model institutions or valued social relationships are not satisfying ends. They are instruments in the toolkit of the maximizing actor. Landa explains:

> From a comparative institutional perspective, contract law, ethnic trading networks, and gift-exchange can be viewed as alternative governance structures or economic organization in different historical contexts that function to constrain traders from acting opportunistically by breach of contract. The existence of exchange externalities arising from breach and the transaction costs involved in internalizing the externalities are crucial for the emergence of constraints—formal legal norms or informal social norms—against opportunism. (1994:28)

Landa continues that institutions and trading groups are "clubs" that function as alternatives to legal contracts backed by law. She assumes that the costs of belonging to such a club are lower than the benefits (Landa 1994:126), although she presents no calculations to support the argument.

Landa brings this argument to the heart of anthropology when she applies her derivational model to the realm of kinship. Drawing on the language of Meyer Fortes, she claims that "[k]inship relations are the irreducible jural and moral relations, and kinsmen are thus the most reliable people with whom to trade" (1994:109), which is not what Fortes intended. Next, she invokes Fortes's phrase—the "calculus of relations"—which originally referred to the realm of kinship (Fortes 1969:50, 107) to argue that locating these social positions, with their rights and obligations, is an ingenious strategy or efficient screening device that enables traders to pick up nonprice signals for predicting the behavior of a potential partner (Landa 1994:109). By employing this pick-anything-out-of-context strategy, she avoids mentioning Fortes' central argument that kinship and descent relations embody what he called the "axiom of amity," which might also be glossed as the principle of mutuality. Fortes even surmised that amity might be imbibed with "mother's milk."[18] He was arguing that a calculus of kin relations helped individuals determine their degree of social amity rather than trade relationships.

Here Landa's misreading of Fortes is especially disingenuous, because he always vigorously distinguished between moral ties and voluntary contracts, and claimed that kin must share "without putting a price on what they give" (1969:238). Fortes urged that economic processes "have never been incontrovertibly shown to be the ultimate *raison d'être* of such [kinship] institutions, norms, and relationships regarded as an internal system" (Fortes 1969:229). Landa misconstrues and inverts his argument to legitimate her own, that kinship functions to provide a screening device for trade.[19] Then, generalizing on this misrepresentation, Landa claims that all clubs, including kin organizations and ethnic groups, have signaling devices so that members can identify themselves and know whom they can trust. Such signals include flags, totems, clothing (such as Scottish tartans), and the dietary laws of Jews. (Landa adds that the *chai*, worn about the neck, has replaced the Star of David as the emblem of religious identity and information device for Jews.) Such signals reduce a trader's search and information (or transaction) costs. Anything and everything is grist for her derivational model—including the kula.

The Trobriand Islands' kula provides Landa's principal illustration of institutional growth "where the legal framework ... is not well developed" (Landa 1994:28). As every anthropology student knows, the kula consists of two opposite circuits of exchange: armshells are passed in one direction against a flow of necklaces from the other. The original work dates to Malinowski (1922) who showed that these open-ended, delayed exchanges involve chains of debts and credits, are surrounded by ceremonies, spells, and rituals, and are connected to gender relations, productive activities, canoe building, kinship obligations, and the achievement of rank and prestige. Through his analysis of the kula, Malinowski firmly established the importance of context or meaning in use, and of social give-and-take or reciprocity. Since Malinowski, the kula has been extensively discussed in the anthropological literature, and it was used by Mauss (as well as Polanyi) to exemplify the role of the gift or reciprocity, which he sharply distinguished from market trade (as did Fortes).[20]

But Landa follows a different trail: for her, "the Kula Ring is an institutional arrangement that emerged *primarily* in order to economize on transaction costs of intertribal commercial exchange in stateless societies" (1994:143, italics added). She claims that the kula functions to cover the costs of transport, setup, search, contract negotiation, and enforcement for the Trobriand Islanders who engage in ordinary trade (*gimwali*). According to Landa, the entire kula network, which links the Trobriands and other islands, emerged through the action of self-interested traders (even though the relationships are built on reciprocity). Landa adds that the ring pattern of the kula is an efficient two-market system because it economizes on traders' costs of acquiring goods in other markets; the opposed exchange cycles make up an efficient way to barter valuables across group boundaries, because each kula participant, as a middleman, participates in only two adjacent markets, which is more efficient than attending several markets on different islands or a central marketplace. The ring pattern also allows sanctions to work chainlike throughout the entire region: word about unreliable participants will efficiently circulate. Finally, the associated magical rites and mortuary rituals of the kula are efficient signaling devices for identifying people who are or can be members of this exclusive trading club (Landa 1994:xii). The entire system of social relationships, magical rites, myths, and expectations emerged, of course, "by an 'invisible hand' process" (Landa 1994:160).

In contrast to Landa, I do not think the kula is reducible to a derivational model based on calculative reason. A few years ago, a number of experts on the kula gathered to review and compare their findings on this widespread exchange. They found such diversity in the ways it is practiced that Edmund Leach, who was a student of Malinowski and an expert on the kula, concluded that there is "no such thing as THE KULA" but rather a number of overlapping ways that certain valuables are passed around. He suggested that "[t]he nearest approach to a 'common' scheme of values in the whole set is that originally perceived by Mauss: social relationships entail 'prestations'—obligatory gift giving" (Leach 1983:536). Other contributors concur that social communication is a fundamental part of the kula. Scoditti, who studied an island near the Trobriands that was part of the kula, found that on their expeditions the people carried only small amounts of material resources to a kula district in the Trobriands, and that these goods were offered as solicitory gifts to kula partners; they were not used in barter (*gimwali*) (Scoditti 1983:257). Embracing Malinowski's original interpretation, he stated that "[the] kula continues whether resource transfer is high or low, that it is possible to acquire shells and partners without other material resources at all, and that nothing they receive from subsidiary kula transactions is essential to their everyday lives…. Kitavans do not see trade (gimwali) as intrinsically linked to and a function of the kula" (Scoditti 1983:265).

Finally, among other authorities, I cite Thune, who studied the island of Normanby, which has a relatively marginal position in the kula. He explained that "[the] simultaneous gimane (barter) of kula valuables is a more reasonable strategy for Duau [a district of Normanby] kula traders to pursue than is formal delayed exchange which requires greater control over and consequent trust of one's muli (trade partner). Indeed some younger less important traders explicitly say they gimane in the kula out of recognition of their weakness and in hope of eventually building a major kula position" (Thune 1983:359–360). The people of Normanby turn Landa's entire argument on its head because they barter to enter the high-status kula, and not the reverse. Whom should we believe—the derivational modeler or the local voices?

I cite Landa, then, to show how a new institutionalist or derivational model that is built on the foundation of rational choice has been deployed to "explain" the emergence and "function" of reciprocity, mutuality, verbal spells uttered over trees and canoes, mortuary food distributions, and other aspects of culture that North considers to be nonrational. Landa, however, mystifies these local practices that are done for their own sake as being done for the sake of sustaining trade. By cascading her market model, Landa dialectically converts mutuality into its opposite and turns local beliefs into fabrications: the kula becomes an illusion of the Trobrianders, reciprocity becomes a fantasy of escape from homo economicus, and both are contingencies. Unlike Demsetz in the case of property rights, Landa recognizes that mutual ties exist, but they are rationally derived. Unlike Becker, she does not place mutual ties within the subjective preferences of rational actors but derives them as a consequence of self-interest. Whereas Becker elides and Demsetz silences local practices, Landa colonizes them. These rhetorical strategies veil local models by cascading a universal one and denying economy's dialectical structure.

And so we return to Polanyi's division. Although worried about the economic transformation Europe had experienced, Polanyi held that market models do work for market economies, because the economy there is disembedded. In contrast, I argue that the division is a continuing dialectic in all economies, where it assumes different historical forms and degrees of tension. Disembedded economies cannot exist without mutuality; however, market practices and models erase their contingency and dialectically undermine their existence by continuously expanding the arena of trade, by cascading, by appropriating materials, labor, and discourse, and by mystifying and veiling the mutuality on which they are built. This process reaches its apogee in financial markets, to which we now turn.

Notes

1. In a recent work Callon (1998a:19–20) focuses on market framing, "which allows for calculation and consequently makes possible the emergence of calculative agencies." In the case of a strawberry market that was established in France, he speaks of the "existence of a perfectly qualified product, existence of a clearly constituted supply and demand, [and] organization of transactions allowing for the establishment of an equilibrium price" (1998a:20). To account for framing, he draws on Bourdieu's recounting of the Maussian notion of the gift along with the concepts of externalities and Coasian transaction costs. But Callon (1998b) also says that framing is imperfect and speaks of market overflows that can either be measured as externalities or made objective through social

science knowledge and brought to the bar of negotiation. My notion of the market arena is similar, but I do not think Callon sees the "inside" and the "outside" or the internalization of externalities in a sufficiently dialectical manner. He constitutes the outside as remainders from the inside and not as local models. In effect, Callon sees economy only through the lens of the market.

2. This material is drawn from Berndt (1951), which I have discussed at greater length elsewhere (2001).

3. See, for example, Fukuyama (1995), Gambetta (2000), and Hollis (1998).

4. For a comparative example from East Germany of the way trust within enterprises was lost, see Thelen (2005).

5. The fieldwork was carried out with Dr. Alberto Rivera.

6. See, for example, Gibson-Graham (2006), Kasmir (1996), the Community Economies Collective (2001), Whyte (1999), and Whyte and Whyte (1988).

7. For one comparative study of regions, see Bagnasco and Sabel (1995). On France, see Lorenz (2000).

8. According to *Business Week*, the goal of "hundreds of respected U.S. companies ... is to skirt the rules of consolidation, the bedrock of the American financial reporting system and the source of much of its credibility" (28 Jan. 2002). For discussion of the Enron case, see also Henwood (2003) and Toobin (2003).

9. On the place of social networks in markets, the role of labor markets, and a broader discussion critical of many neoclassical and new institutional models, see Granovetter (1985). Missing from his critique of the concept of the atomic individual, and his use of the idea of networks, is the realization that networks involve overlapping interests or values.

10. Ben-Yami (2004) provides a general discussion of this same process in relation to neoliberal models.

11. Communal allocations exemplify socially embedded preferences. For example, the Haka Chins sacrificed water buffalo to gain merit and prestige, and the holder of the ritual would apportion meat within his community: different joints of the beast were allocated to specific social positions but the portions could vary in size and could be a combination of joints. The recipients included the village headman and blacksmith, but prior feast-givers and their widows, as well as certain kin of the sacrificer, were included as well. Community provided the frame or preference registers for the apportionment but individuals mixed and weighted these registers. Calculation and mutuality were combined (Stevenson 1937).

12. Humphrey (2002b) offers a similar observation about property in markets but also provides an example from socialist Mongolia (in the 1970s) where an individual claimed a horse that was brigade property as a kind of personal possession. When against his will the horse was presented to someone outside the brigade, the man refused to drive horse carts until it was returned, She interprets his claim to the horse as the realization of "person-thing" relations that emerge through use, but the man's assertion might also be seen as his way of connecting to objectified property as if it were an apportionment of base and of asserting a place in the local brigade; alienating the horse severed his community position.

13. The connecting process occurs in many ways. For example, through the division of labor, one corporation purchases its resources from another: in the

classic arm's length case, the butcher purchases animals from the cattleman; the baker procures flour from the miller, who bought his resource from the farmer. But today, products may be presented as threads linking one producer to another, and offered to the consumer as a conglomerate community. These "communities" of corporations are advertised: an Apple computer contains an Intel chip; synthetic products from 3M, Dupont, or Gore-Tex are advertised as components in clothes and shoes that are branded as products of another manufacturer, NutraSweet is advertised as a constituent of diet drinks that are competitors. Automobiles embody branded radios, speakers, or tires that are advertised with the vehicle. Conversely, sometimes the connections between corporations are silenced. Dashboards of different brand cars may be produced by the same supplier but not labeled; different brands in the General Motors "family" of cars may use the same engines (an occurrence that caused a minor scandal some years ago). What does cross-branding mean? Do the products present the consumer with a cooperative community, or do they represent impersonal market trades embedded one within another?

14. Product differentiation also may be linked to the constitution of ethnic identity and cultural diversity (Zelizer 1999).

15. In contrast, see Campbell (1987), who claims that modern consumerism, unlike production, is induced through a romantic, as opposed to the Protestant, ethic. But both are examples of calculative reason.

16. I draw some of this material from Herrmann (1997).

17. For an institutionalist analysis by an anthropologist see Ensminger (1992), especially 176–181.

18. "It is conceivable—and I for one would accept—that the axiom of amity reflects biological and psychological parameters of human social existence. Maybe there is sucked in with the mother's milk, as Montaigne opined, the orientation on which it ultimately rests" (Fortes 1969:231).

19. Her new institutionalist argument oddly repeats the more Marxist argument of Worsley (1956), which was countered by Fortes (1969); see also Sahlins (1976).

20. The literature on the kula is enormous. See Weiner (1976) for a revision of Malinowski's ethnography and interpretation, and the collected essays on the exchange in *The Kula* (Leach and Leach 1983).

6

Making Money

Money is a tool of exchange. Its uses range from maintaining mutuality to facilitating competitive trade; it can even be traded for itself. Money can measure the size of an obligation or be used to indebt others. In some economies several monies are used, and a single money can serve multiple purposes. The importance of money varies by economy, but almost everywhere narratives explain why it is legitimate just as it has local meanings.

In contrast to most views, I see money as a composite instrument that is constructed through different modes of reason: analogy, metaphor, substitution, calculation. Money also is used in different value spheres that include commensuration, community, commerce, and finance. The figurative processes by which money is built vary according to the value realm in which it is used. As a unit of account or measuring rod, money expresses reason by analogy. In the realm of mutuality or community, money is usually constructed through metaphor. In the commercial realm it is built through metaphor and substitution, and in the financial realm calculative reason is central. These four ways of employing money sometimes conflict, overlap, and colonize one another. When money is traded for money in the financial sphere, it cascades into and generally governs the other realms.

My figurative approach to money and its realms does not fit standard ones. Economists bring their toolkit to the study of money and connect it to people through their preferences for obtaining, holding, and exchanging it. Economists speak with authority about the supply and demand for money, inflation and deflation, fiat versus commodity money, Gresham's law, and the velocity of circulation. They address inverted yield curves, discounting, liquidity preference, the overnight rate, and deficit spending as well. For most economists, money operates only in the commercial and financial spheres, which are markets. They usually distinguish three functions of money. First, it is a medium of exchange without which people would need to barter. Sometimes economists offer stories about how money emerged from barter to ease the problem that wants are rarely coincident: the seller of one good cannot always find a seller of the good she wants who wants to buy what she has to offer. Money lubricates trade, and makes it more efficient. Second, money is a store of value, which means it can serve as a medium of exchange. Sometimes economists distinguish commodity money from fiat money as different stores of value and types of legitimacy. Commodity money might be gold, silver, salt, or another general good that has tangible uses and "holds" value; fiat money is issued and backed by a state (or government) that assures its value. Third, for economists, money is a unit of account that assesses the relative value of objects.[1] It is a measuring rod for comparing commodities in exchange.

Anthropologists bring ethnography and interpretation to the understanding of money. Through innumerable studies, we have shown how there may or may not be monies or part-monies in other cultures: When people use pearlshells or salt to obtain goods, are they using money? Anthropologists also have shown that people may have several monies that are used in distinct circuits. One traditional issue concerns these spheres of exchange. Do some economies contain separate exchange circuits?If so, why are they not converted into one sphere through arbitrage and the use of a single currency?[2]

Anthropologists attend to the local meanings of money as well, for it may evoke conflicting sentiments and contradictory meanings. For example, money can be respected as an instrument of freedom, reviled as the work of the devil, blamed as the instrument of change, viewed as socially corrosive, or honored as the embodiment of national identity. A few anthropologists have turned their attention to our theories and practices. Hart argues that money is a memory bank or a way of remembering our connections to others (2001). Money, he says, is a symbol of our relationship to community and helps to anchor "identity in a collective memory" that might be the state, a sense of nationhood, a local community, or even global markets created through the internet (2002). Gregory distinguishes between "savage money," which is found in our current state of "free market anarchism" or "disorganized capitalism" (1997:1, 3), and the "domesticated money" that is associated with the domain of the house.

My project is different, because none of these explications attends to the figurative processes by which money is constructed. I shall not be asking how money is physically made, how government and bank action can make money by adding to its circulation, or how one makes money through trade; by "make" I mean the way money is symbolically built and how its construction is related to its differing uses.

I distinguish four uses of money, each of which draws on a figurative process. First, money as a *unit of account* is built through analogical reason. The unit of account function is necessary for the other uses but it does not separate money from other measuring rods or modes of commensuration. Second, money is a *means* to form or liquidate obligations; this use is constructed through metaphoric reason. "Means money" is used within the *communal sphere* of economy, where it substitutes for specific things, services, or social positions connected to a shared base. These first two processes are found in most if not all economies. Third, money can be a general *medium* of exchange, constructed through metaphor and substitution. This money stands for value positions rather than specific goods, services, and social roles. "Medium money" is used in markets and pertains to the *commercial* sphere. Abstracted from particular things and services, it enables price formation, regardless of social context. The second and third processes, or money as a means and money as a medium, are different because money as a means of exchange points to mutually defined objects or services for which it substitutes, whereas medium money points to value positions whose places it may take. These two forms of money are dialectically related, as are the communal and commercial spheres, and one is sometimes used as if it were the other. Both these monies serve as stores of value. Finally, when money is exchanged for itself over time, it is both the means and the end of trade, because it is traded at a price, which is the rate of interest. Such means-ends or derivational money pertains to financial markets and is constructed through calculative reason.

When viewed across economies, the four processes of money traverse the spectrum from local to derivational models. In high market economies, money provides a measure, a means, and a medium for exchange, as well as serving as the means and ends of trade. This money's shifting price for itself reverberates in the financial realm and cascades into the commercial sphere, so that market money principally comes to "mean" means-to-ends behavior; instrumental reason is produced and reproduced through its use. By contrast, in mutual contexts, this final use usually does not appear: money can be a measuring rod, a substitute means, and sometimes a medium, but not a way to gather interest. In these contexts, money often embodies or stands for a community's base or sacra. Thus, a people's claim that market money is evil, that it disrupts social relationships, or that it has magical powers frequently refers not to money itself, to loss of control, or to the goods it secures but to the debasement its use brings through the calculative practices it invokes, the relationships it disrupts, and the subjectivity it requires. Here then lies a way to answer the often evaded but century-old question: What is the difference between "primitive" monies and "Western" money? Are cowries, pearlshells, Kula valuables, pigs, or cows money? How are they similar to and different from "modern" money?[3] Money's uses display the tension in economy just as its variant constructions draw on different forms of reason and legitimating narratives. To explicate these variations, I begin with money's figurative constructions and then turn to the dialectics of money in the communal, commercial, and financial realms of economy.

Analogy and Proportion

Money is a ruler or gauge of comparative value: it has a well-known role as numeraire. To provide a unit of account is money's first task, because without it the others cannot be performed. This measurement role of money is built on analogical reason; money provides an index for what is made commensurate. Relations between items, such as apples and oranges, are compared to relations between the counters, just as the use of a thermometer creates an analogy between its relations of degrees and relations of heat, or between the height of mercury in a glass tube and warmth. Twenty-five degrees centigrade means that the heat of one object stands to that of another as 25 degrees stands to 23 (or other) degrees.[4] If two apples exchange for three oranges, a package of each with these quantities will be marked with the same money sum that allows them to be compared to each other, and to other tagged goods. Proportion or ratio relations of things and services are expressed through money. This relation between units of money on the one hand and things and services on the other is one-directional. Like a meter stick, money units are projected on entities by counting, tagging, and recording the relation of one to another.

The measurement role of money can be purely notional, as in the case of barter transactions in which a currency is not used but the trades are made against an agreed money standard. The euro was a notional counter and denominator of different monies before it became more than a measuring rod. (Once it was issued in place of separate national currencies and its uses expanded, the euro's value against other moneys seemed to rise.) Price tags in stores exemplify the measurement function: they display how a seller assesses a good in relation to other goods. In theory, goods with price tags might be purchased through barter, if there is a coincidence of wants.

Not all measures such as baskets, hands, and paces are money, even if they share this measurement feature. In the Peruvian Andes, Enrique Mayer (2002:153) notes, barter takes place by comparing weight, volume, or number of units. Different systems are used to compare weight; volume might be measured by sacks made of wool, jute, or plastic, or by containers ranging from small gourds, to large pots, to baskets, to tin receptacles. Thus, one can barter x pots of fava beans for y pots of barley, or m sacks of potatoes for y sacks of corn: the pots and the sacks are measuring rods but not objects of exchange.

The Andeans also use money to measure barter, but this money is only a unit of account and is not even possessed. For example, Andean highlanders barter their sheep for maize offered by valley farmers. The exchange rate varies and is negotiated against an old Peruvian currency that no longer circulates. Using this accounting system, known as *unay precio,* in 1969 farmers offered 20 ears of dried maize at 10 centavos, while highlanders offered one pelt of wool at 30 centavos so that 60 pairs of maize ears were exchanged for a woolen pelt. Use of the obsolete money allows people to exchange local products at rates independent of their nationwide market equivalents without having to possess the national currency. In the 1969 example, a sheep owner would have received more maize for his wool by selling his pelt for the national money and purchasing maize with his receipts. Yet use of the old measuring rod allowed the shepherds and farmers to resist the impact of the larger market, to maintain long-term relationships that favor one or the other over time, and to assure that both have a steady supply of needed things (Mayer 2002:153–155). Mutuality and commerce are mixed. As we shall see, in high market economies, such communal currencies, based on different measuring rods, also have emerged to separate local, mutual exchanges from impersonal market ones.

Finally, currencies themselves may be assessed in relation to another measuring rod. In some postcolonial and transglobal contexts, for example, a national currency may be measured by another money that has the role of unit of account. At one time, the British pound served this role in some colonies. Today, the dollar seems to occupy this position now that gold no longer provides a standard, but the euro is emerging as a contender and competitor with the dollar for the role of principal measuring rod and memory device.

Community Currency: Money as a Means

In barter, one item substitutes for another. But money also may substitute for what it measures. In the first analogical process, the value of things is tagged by their places on a numerical scale. In this second one, an accounting unit measures goods, services, and positions, and it substitutes for them.

This communal money replaces a specific range of objects and services only; it is not a marker of value in general. Consider a plantation that issues scrip.[5] The scrip is issued according to the amount of work a laborer performs; there is no other way to earn it. The scrip both measures a part of the whole of work on the plantation and pays for the work undertaken. In turn, the scrip can be redeemed at the plantation's store, where the laborer apportions it among the available goods. It represents rights to a proportion of the stock of goods for which it can be substituted and has no use outside this specified realm. Sometimes the scrip cannot be given to or exchanged with other holders, and the goods on offer might be a single item for which the scrip is redeemed. Work, thus, is substituted by scrip, which is substituted by goods. The scrip goes from owner to worker to store to owner. The transactions are set by the rate at which the scrip is exchanged for labor, and by the market price (and markup) of the goods in relation to that transaction. This double exchange is not barter, because scrip is an intermediary in the exchange of work for goods, nor is it reciprocity, because the amounts are earned by contract and precisely measured, and the exchange is closed on redemption. The scrip is a tangible *means* for settling debts, although it could be marks in a ledger or on a computer. It is used in a one-directional transaction; scrip transforms work to goods but is not gained for goods (that a worker offers to the store) or employed to buy the work of other tenants. Used in the context of differential power, its recipients must trust that a store will be stocked and that the scrip will be honored.

The use of scrip involves both analogical reason and metaphoric substitution: the work of the tenant and the goods of the store are first seen in terms of their places on a measuring rod; then, the counters become a substitute for the work performed and the goods offered. Substitute items are widely encountered in ethnography, from cucumbers that stand in place of cows and are eventually redeemed, to notches on a stick that substitute for different trade debts from goats to gold.[6] Similarly, frequent flyer coupons that reduce the cost of the next airplane fare, government welfare stamps that can be redeemed only for certain "basic" foods, coupons sent in the mail or placed in newspapers that reduce the cost of designated items in a store, and promotional discounts offered to specific recipients (sometimes without issuance of the actual coupons) are forms of scrip.[7] These are one-way transactions: a customer does not bring food to a store to be redeemed by a coupon or government stamps.

Even credit cards are a form of scrip, in one of their functions. For a fee or other qualifying right, the cardholder has claims to market money held by the issuer and to having the issuer pay the seller in his stead. (Hence, stores run credit checks on the cardholder to see if his right to the stock of money is valid.) Like scrip, the sum of money available to the card or scrip holder is specified, is accessible only by him, and often can be used only at a limited range of stores. Some credit cards issued by a chain of gas stations can only be used at their pumps; department stores issue charge cards that provide access only to goods in their stores. The cards offer a form of scrip within the community made up of the store and its customers. Sears had a charge card for use in its stores, but some years ago it issued the "Discover" card, which could be used at any store that would accept it; this card was both a narrow and broad form of scrip (before it was sold by Sears).

Most banks issue ATM debit cards that provide claims to the issuance of cash at the bank through personal assets held there. But through an ever-shifting maze of rules these cards may be used at some ATM's of other banks—sometimes at a cost levied by the issuing bank, sometimes at a charge levied by the bank with the ATM, sometimes by both, and sometimes at no cost. The transaction charges also shift when one is outside an ATM region or state, and they are yet different when the ATM card is "honored" at an overseas location. For the rational actor these regulations are tiresome because she must absorb a large amount of information at personal cost in order to maximize her use of the card. In this case, an ATM card is a form of scrip that allows banks to extract money, under the label of transaction cost, when it is used outside a region or even when the available scrip on the card is converted to a general currency. As a form of scrip, the bank card is one-directional: the bank does not deposit its money with the cardholder in order to have a credit of scrip from him. In all cases, scrip users constitute a community that recognizes a specified range of one-way substitutions.

Nonmarket forms of means money also are found. A long-standing question in ethnographic studies concerns whether local currencies are money. Considering money as a measure and substitute that refers to a specified range of things and services helps to explicate local currencies. Like scrip, ethnographic monies point to specific objects or services for which they substitute. Recent research suggests that many local currencies are "base monies" that provide a measure and substitute, linked to continuing social relationships or a community of users. Consider some examples.

Over the years Andrew Strathern has provided rich studies of the Mount Hagen people of Papua New Guinea. Recently he has considered the people's use of pigs and pearlshells in exchange, as well as their handling of state money. The Mount Hageners identify with their land, as do others throughout New Guinea (Strathern and Stewart 1999). According to the Mount Hageners' narrative, the land is connected to the ancestors and provides for clan continuity and the living. Through its products, such as pigs and garden foods, land is "the ultimate locus of the embodiment of the person" (Strathern and Stewart 1999:175). Pigs are raised on clan land (although they are sometimes initially brought to a home through exchange). By the space they occupy and the crops they consume, pigs embody the ancestors, fertility, and the females who raise them. They are the "basic form of wealth" (Strathern and Stewart 1999:170). Pigs, which point to the "locus" of society, are used in a variety of transactions, such as payments at marriage and compensation for deaths, injuries, and insults. To sustain the land's fertility, pigs also are sacrificed to the ancestral spirits. At the major fertility cult ceremonies, when pigs are sacrificed, their meat is distributed to many people so that communal fertility and the base are manifested and shared.

Pearlshells, which are the second form of currency the Mount Hageners use, are appreciated for their aesthetic and religious meanings. Pearlshells are likened to people's skin, while their growth rings stand for sustained reproduction or fertility, because one ring follows another as the shell grows. Pearlshells also are likened to Sky Beings and to female spirits who bring fertility and well-being. With these several meanings, the shells express the identity and agency of all their prior owners (including both their physical being and social position). Like pigs, the shells are used competitively, but they are acquired through external trade. Unlike pigs, the pearlshells are not distributed at cult ceremonies; instead, they are worn as indicators of fertility, wealth, and the presence of the Spirit. Wearing them creates social relationships and induces further exchanges (Stewart and Strathern 2002). Attracted in exchange by magic, large ones are kept at home, where they help "pull" others to their owner. The use of pearlshells is relatively new; only in the mid twentieth century did they begin to be intensively used in rituals and transactions. However, today they have "been added to the basic form of pig and pork gifts" that are used in ceremonies and exchanges (Strathern and Stewart 1999:172).

Pearlshells and pigs are local currencies or means money because they are measuring rods or units of account and substitutes for that which they measure. Pigs encapsulate the ancestors and fertility that make up the base of society, and the community of people who sustain the land's richness. Pearlshells designate the fertility of the pigs that provides the agency for gathering them in exchange. Both local monies, embellished by metaphors, extend the base by circulating its vitality among people. With reason, pigs are the main payment in bridewealth and other forms of compensation, because they restore and create mutuality through the shared holding. Like scrip, both pigs and pearlshells are "redeemed" at ceremonies. Trust in their efficacy comes with commitment to the Mount Hagen mode of conducting material life.

This way of considering local money in relation to mutuality explicates many other ethnographic cases. In some instances, narratives about the heritage, base, and identity are especially revealing. For example, a Kwanga man of Papua New Guinea traditionally gathered and displayed his ritual heat and potency by producing pigs and yams on his land, and by avoiding certain foods and restraining his sexual relationships. Ritual heat provided him with the force to organize others and to collect wealth for exchanges between patrilineages that rearranged social positions during initiations and adoption ceremonies. Men accumulated pigs, but their collections were put together in a group's offerings to other groups so that personal display was done in "the service of exhibiting communal potency" (Brison 1999:154). Because equivalent exchanges between groups in the larger community were valued, men who had accumulated a substantial number of pigs were adopted by less endowed groups so that community balance in material life and ritual heat was preserved. In the twentieth century, state money began to be acquired by the Kwanga through external trade; at first, this money was accumulated and transferred within the community along with the pigs. Like them it referred to ritual potency and communal harmony. Eventually, people were attracted by the increase in choice and profit-making activities that state money yielded. Families and lineages used the external money for profitable investments, which began to undermine the community cohesion that had previously been achieved through the transfers of pigs or base money. Local money, constructed through analogy and substitution, began to be replaced by commercial money that drew on other figurative processes, and debasement occurred.

The Urapmin, who also live in Papua New Guinea, use valuable shells called *bonang*. These shells are their preeminent wealth item, and "Urapmin reckon the prices of pigs and other expensive items as often in terms of bonang as of money" (Robbins 1999:91). Bonang embody sexuality, death, and the ancestral figures of the community. Among Urapmin, the shells are a currency of communal relationships; they are symmetrically exchanged at death ceremonies and dispute resolutions, although as bridewealth they are transferred in a one-sided, measured exchange, because the groom's side is "buying the woman's bones" (Robbins 1999:91). In fact, through adroit marriage arrangements individuals can accumulate bonang, but this mode of accumulation is criticized because people say a man should depend on his kin to accumulate the bonang needed for a marriage, just as the receipt of bonang as bridewealth must be dispersed among the bride's people. Only with non-Urapmin are the shells used in impersonal trade to obtain goods. Indeed, because bonang are a currency of communal relationships, accumulations of them should be achieved only through external trade. Bonang, then, seemingly have a bifurcated use. Within the community, they are the measure of value and a substitute used for social ends, but outside they are an ordinary trade item.

How do the Urapmin explain their way of accumulating bonang through external trade? Does this practice undermine its position as a local or means currency? Are bonang actually a commercial, medium of exchange whose local quantity is controlled by the volume of external trade? Several narratives that have to do with bonang's "base" or "origin" explain why they are amassed through external trade (Robbins 1999:87). According to these stories, the shells first come from Urapmin, then move outside, and finally must be drawn back through trade. In one story, a Urapmin man dies, is burned and putrefied, and then passes through a spirit who vomits him in the form of bonang shells. The spirits wrap his shell remains in leaves and send them to another village, where the people turn the shells into finished bonang. Eventually, say the spirits, the shells must "find their way to the children of the deceased, for they are part of his body" (Robbins 1999:

88). Thus, the shells are in fact "made" of the community; and the Urapmin trade some of their low-value material goods to obtain from non-Urapmin the high-value shells that embody their ancestors and community. The notion of a base, with its symbolism of keeping, self-sufficiency, and autarchy, helps illuminate this need to re-collect the dispersed bonang. Both a measure and a substitute, bonang embody village sacra that are the spiritually transformed ancestors. Dispersed to other groups as ancestral remains, they are regained through trade to be used in internal exchanges and rites that sustain the group. They are a base money.

The Tolai on the island of New Britain off the coast of New Guinea use *tambu*, also a shell money. Over the course of a century, anthropologists and others recorded the uses of tambu in times of local stability and change. Much discussion has surrounded tambu concerning whether or not it is like market money; over time its uses have varied as well.[8] Today tambu is used in conjunction with the national currency, and it is spent in both external and internal exchanges but in very different ways. Tambu consists of the shells of a mollusc found on the north coast of the island. The shells are accumulated and saved in large rolls, which are called fathoms. But as Scarlett Epstein tellingly observed, "I never met a Tolai who knew how many single shells made up one fathom. My Tolai assistant, to whom I first put the question, was completely perplexed and could not grasp why I wanted this piece of information" (1968:148). Tambu is a measure and a means, and it is accumulated for social uses, but it is not tallied.

Tambu is a communal currency and a store of value that can be used to secure ornamental wares or a spouse, repair damages to others, and celebrate social changes. Among Tolai, tambu is loaned but interest is not collected; rather, the borrower offers an advance payment unrelated to the size of the loan or its duration (Scarlett Epstein 1964:61). Thrift in the use of tambu and hoarding are common, because it is distributed in large quantities at funerals for the "ancestors' gratification" (Salisbury 1970:279).[9] Large amounts of tambu also are used to change or reorient relationships as well as a person's status at birth and marriage. At ceremonies such as funerals, the host distributes tambu from the large rolls; others throw it down at the feet of fellow attendees to ingratiate, repay, make peace, and be convivial with them. One ethnographer observed that national money pertains to food, whereas tambu is part of the sacred and is bound up with the afterlife (A. L. Epstein 1979:159); some said it connects the living to the dead, and is their god. The distribution of a dead person's tambu helps ease his soul, and if tambu is not distributed his spirits haunt his descendants (Scarlett Epstein 1968:57). Like a thread from the ancestors, tambu connects people in the community when it is publicly apportioned (or "redeemed") in sizable sums (Salisbury 1970:193).

Tambu also is used commercially to obtain food; however, in markets tambu is exchanged only with other Tolai. It is paid in small sums for Tolai-produced goods, such as taro, and it enters (in the early 1960s) less than 10 percent of the transactions. The purpose of such trade is to secure a needed item or a small amount of tambu for social use. Just as tambu loans do not yield interest, trade with tambu exchanges is not profit-oriented. In markets, Tolai also use the national currency but to purchase goods, such as chickens and imported items. Given the different exchange rates, Tolai traders in theory could buy local goods in tambu at home and sell them for the national currency in a market; the money received could then be used to purchase market goods for resale to Tolai in tambu. Such traders would secure a greater quantity of tambu than they started with: adroit arbitrageurs could accumulate tambu outside the traditional ways. But Tolai rarely purchase external goods with tambu, while outside traders rarely have tambu with which to purchase Tolai goods or have much interest in their products, such as taro (Scarlett Epstein 1964:58). The two currencies are kept separate. Tambu is a base or communal (means) money, separated from most commercial uses, for which the Tolai use the national currency. This currency separation was changing when most of the fieldwork was undertaken, but the difference between the monies neatly displays the breach and the tension between mutuality and trade.[10]

Communal money is not "private" property to be alienated completely outside a community, because ethnographically it may represent ancestors, fertility, sacred powers, or spirits that constitute the base of a community and seal social relationships. Kept within a community, where it helps to constitute identity, this money is a substitute for other communal things and relationships, though like scrip (such as an ATM card) it sometimes is used commercially as well.

Commercial Money: A Medium of Exchange

Medium money substitutes for value positions or relationships. Like local or means money, it provides a measuring rod, a means for canceling debts, and a way of storing wealth or value. But this money is also used in two-way exchanges, is not limited to particular things and services, and permits a wide range of choice in use. Holding this money for display or as a personal precaution—that is, keeping it from circulation—has a pronounced effect on the level of market activity, as Keynes argued. This form of money usually is issued and controlled by a state or transnational authority (as in the case of the euro). Its management is a prime concern of national and cooperating governments. Overseeing the increase and contraction of its supply usually is the task of a central bank.

Deployed in the commercial sphere, medium money is separated from its holder in trade. Today, such money seems to have no anchor or base, although the dollar (like other currencies) once was linked to gold. When the United States severed its fixed price in relation to gold, it became, in Gregory's phrase, "savage money." Many currencies, however, bear impressions of royalty, presidents, or other leaders, and the dollar carries the inscription "In God We Trust": these are narratives to bolster users' faith that they are members of a community that has a base—in the sacred realm.

Just as this form of money may give hints of having a base, through impressions on the currency and fixed exchange rates with rare metals, the uses of commercial (medium) and community (means) money often are dialectically connected.[11] For example, means money can be used like medium money. The Tolai do exchange *small* amounts of their tambu in markets for goods, though only with other Tolai. The Baruya of New Guinea produce blocks of salt and apportion some of it among themselves along lines of kinship and friendship for local consumption. But they also use it as a currency in competitive trade outside the community, although when a salt block returns as currency it may be kept as a memory of relationships forged outside the community (Godelier 1977). Sometimes base money and medium money become "dueling currencies" when the local one, used to maintain relationships and generate activities, is confronted with an expanding state money. Each stands for different social features and values (Gewertz and Errington 1995).

Conversely, commercial money can be turned to scrip-like uses. It can become a means for securing a specific property in a communal context, as in the case of the Kwanga, who initially used state money in their social exchanges. Commercial money also may be treated like community money in household budgeting.[12] As Zelizer (1999) observes, a family may earmark a general medium of exchange for specific uses by sorting the physical currency into separate jars or labeled envelopes: so much goes for entertainment, so much for food, and so much for transportation and other budgeted items. When a labeled container or envelope is empty, a separate container cannot be used to underwrite it until the next apportionment of the general currency, which may be done weekly, monthly, or at another interval. We also convert commercial money to communal money or scrip when we buy coupons, such as theater or airline tickets, that have limited uses. Poker chips, purchased by commercial money, signal membership at a table where risk and opportunity are limited by the number of chips available, but this scrip can be converted back to the medium money.

The lure of transforming commercial money to base money as representing community or nationhood is shown by the occasional calls to return to the gold standard. In post-Soviet Russia some people argue

that the value of the ruble should be determined by the natural resources of the nation that have moral substance, which lend social
identity and authenticity, rather than by the nation's produced products that are traded (Lemon 1998). According to this narrative, the ruble
should express a community of people with their base. Hart recounts
that some older theories or stories about market money claimed that
it expressed the "folk"; he suggests that the euro, by transcending national borders and being delinked from any state, may eventually lead
to new assertions of national communities with alternative subcurren-
cies (2002). In everyday practices, we also convert commercial money
to a sense of community by writing on it in hopes of hearing from a
stranger, saving the first dollar earned, copying it, and occasionally
smoking it. We even call this form of money "bread" as if it were the
staff of life, our base.

Financial Money: The Means and End of Trade

Most market money (aside from the Islamic world) can be exchanged
for itself at a cost: it can be rented for a period of time to earn interest
as the price of using it. This money becomes the substance of trade and
self-referring, because it is secured as an end in exchange for itself as a
means. Financial or derivational money induces calculative reason, as
it refers to the quantifiable relation between means and ends. As a
measure, money signals ratio relations between goods; as a community
means and a commercial medium, it provides for the enactment of
means-to-ends relations; but as an item exchanged for itself, money
comes full circle, because it is the instrumentality of itself. Given the
end or sum to be repaid after a specified period of time, the interest rate
can be derived, or given the interest rate the end can be figured.

But how is trust in financial money established? The occasional calls
to use commodity money or to back paper money with precious metals may be motivated by the desire to have an anchor for this commitment. But faith in money today is often based on a belief in its issuing
economy or controlling authority, such as a central bank, whose putative intentions are the good of the economy. The Federal Reserve Bank
in the United States has significant powers. It issues money for government spending through the purchase of bonds (or subtracts it by buying bonds), which can have an inflationary or deflationary effect; it
raises and lowers the reserve amounts that its banks must hold and
thus can or cannot loan; above all, it changes the government (or risk-
less) interest rate through open market operations and the overnight
rate it charges its component banks. The bank's powers over the interest rate of derivational money affects money's other uses, although the
bank does not fully control the expansion of credit throughout the pri-

vate banking sector. The powers of the Federal Reserve are also connected to the rhetorical power of its chair, and to the belief that people have in his or her understanding of the commercial sphere of the economy. Financial managers often await his emergence and oracular statements in a public setting, much like a divine king. The chair of the Federal Reserve becomes a symbol of faith in the transactions of the economy, although the Board of the Federal Reserve is principally made up of bankers and not merchants.[13] Who governs the governors at the apex?

Does the probity of the Federal Reserve ensure trust in money? I suggest that derivational money requires a commitment by its users to a market as opposed to a self-sufficient economy. Market participants must trust that others will be traders with goods to offer and desires to purchase, and they must have faith in the laws and norms surrounding the commercial and financial arenas of trade. Above all, each trusts that others are using money to calculate means-to-ends connections: derivational money is assured by the belief that others are disciplined by the subjectivity of calculative reason, which produces what it induces. Through the unending trade of financial money, formal or calculative reason becomes a commitment or substantive mode of rationality, in Weber's terms. In this use the tool is not simply a means or a medium of exchange, because as both means and end it has no instrumentality other than to show, by its accumulation, that it has served as a tool in successful exchanges for itself. Money, the instrument used for the sake of something else, is dialectically turned into a tool for its own sake.

The derivational use of money provides it with considerable power in the economy, because its rates of exchange reverberate across exchanges and cascade into other realms. For example, consider again a credit card. It is a means or communal money, because it conveys rights to use money at a specific bank (linked to an issuer, a receiver, and an acceptor), and it is a medium or commercial money, because it can be used to purchase almost any goods and services. But when the debit on the card is not paid to the bank on time, this money is subjected to an interest charge figured in relation to a prevailing interest rate that is partly determined by the national and global cost of money. A credit card translates prices in the financial sphere to the commercial one and local realms, and the financial use controls the others according to its discipline of seeking the highest ratio of benefits to cost.

Financial money not only colonizes other spheres but also debases them in the sense of drawing a return from them. It affects the distribution of income. Consider a simplified picture of distribution by spheres (see Table 3).

Each year production yields an increase (or decrease) above (or below) initial costs. This increment is distributed among the communal, commercial, and financial realms. One portion of the surplus may be

Table 3 | *Market Distribution*

Communal	Commercial	Financial
Government Support (Taxes, Duties, Other attachments)	Wages Salaries	Interest Dividends - Profit Rents
Religious Groups (Tithes, Donations)		
Foundations (Donations)		

used for communal services supplied by a government and supported through taxes, duties, and other collective assessments. This division is part of the community/market dialectic. A second portion of the surplus may augment workers' wages and administrators' salaries. This division is part of the wage and class struggle. A third portion flows to the lenders of capital in the form of dividends, rents, and interest. For example, a corporate balance sheet displays its liabilities or obligations to others, which include current debts, long-term debentures to finance the corporation, and retained earnings, which are the shareholders' (or capital owners') property. Whether the returns on these obligations are labeled "rents," "interest," or "dividends"—depending on the type of property held—all are payments for the use of financial capital.

The use of financial money creates a flow from its consumers or debtors to its providers or creditors. The commercial realm returns not only the original capital (when it is withdrawn) but also an increment that flows to the financial realm. For simplicity the different financial returns might all be called interest. We have many narratives and theories explaining why one, another, or all of these financial receipts are just or unjust. For example, interest on a loan may be justified as the reward for abstention, for waiting to consume, for undertaking a risk, or for providing liquidity. Rent may be seen as the reward for providing a scarce resource, such as fertile land. On the other hand, by a labor theory of value, both rent and interest may be viewed as appropriations from the worker. From an anthropological standpoint, these and other explanations are moral narratives. The categories rent, dividends or profit, and interest are neither natural nor given, but locally constituted, even if their sizes can be mathematically derived.

I see the flow of interest from debtors to creditors as a product of the cascading effects of money that is competitively traded for itself. As this realm of trade expands, financial money increasingly flows to the sites where it receives the highest rate of return and debases the communal and strictly commercial uses of currency by drawing on and converting them to its mode of reason. The colonization occurs in the use of theory as well. An early and famous controversy in anthropology concerned the use of Rossel Island (Yela) money. In the early 1920s, W. E. Armstrong, a trained economist, visited the island and studied the role of its shell valuables (Armstrong 1924, 1928). He claimed that the separate, named classes of shell valuables in each of two currencies were related by time: a lower valuable borrowed for one social use had to be repaid with a higher valuable after a period of time. Armstrong adduced the formula for compound interest to explain the practices—because the Rossel Islanders were collecting calculated interest, he argued, they had developed money. Afterward a number of anthropologists contested his interpretation; John Liep (1983) went to Yela, restudied the system, and showed that Armstrong's analysis was incorrect because interest was neither calculated nor collected on borrowed valuables. The controversy between the economist and anthropologists revolves about the use and projection of a derivational model on a communal or means money. It illustrates how "natural" and deeply engraved the universal form was (and remains) in economics.

Financial Resistance

Resistance to colonization by financial money has taken many forms, including religious prohibitions and questions about the morality of gathering interest. For example, several forms of communal and commercial currencies are currently being tried. Two of the more prominent ones are LETS schemes and Ithaca HOURS. The key feature is that neither involves payments of interest on loans. But there is more, for each is used in both commercial and communal ways: they are media of exchange in the commercial realm and a means for building social relationships in the communal sphere. (Rotating credit associations, observed by anthropologists, often do not collect interest; many of these loans have been used for household or ritual consumption. But Vélez-Ibañez (1983) also reports that in Mexico people speak about "saving to save," meaning that participation converts a means-to-ends practice into an end alone; thrift can be a mode of substantive rationality.

The acronym LETS (which beckons togetherness) usually stands for Local Exchange Trading System.[14] In a LETS scheme a commercial money is created and used within a trading community. The range of goods for which this money may be exchanged varies by the size of the group and its participants. Among the members, debits and credits may be accumulated but carry no interest charge. A LETS program defines a market arena, proscribes the collection of interest, allows a specific range of goods to be offered, and sometimes emphasizes community values or themes. For example, a LETS scheme could be organized around the trade of organic foods or environmentally soft goods. Sometimes a currency or tangible medium is not used; the money is a notional unit of account, and debts and credits in the trading community are simply recorded (Hart 2001). Such plans emphasize commerce and contain the financial realm. They may also represent an attempt to limit the impact of global merchants, such as chain stores, that do not accept the local money.

A LETS program (and an HOURS scheme, which is slightly different) is more than a commercial venture, because it involves mutuality. Raddon (2003:130) notes that many outside observers and theorists promote community currencies as a way to increase local employment and economic activity, but participants usually are attracted by the possibility of creating community, meeting needs, or spending ethically. Her study, based on interviews and local voices, displays the different forms of tension that members experience: all agree that the currency is not a financial end but some treat it as an instrument of mutuality, whereas others emphasize its commercial aspect, and many shift between the two and are conflicted. For example, some people associate LETS exchanges with reciprocity and with barter, because in barter two parties must meet and converse: both may feel that they are establishing a mutual relationship by obtaining something the other has directly produced. Some people enter the scheme to expand their circle of friends. Others claim that a LETS currency leads to greater economic equality, especially when time is used as the measuring rod. Still others do not think time alone is the way to commensurate, because it leaves out varying skills. (HOURS schemes tend to emphasize labor time as the measuring rod.) There are also some counterintuitive gender differences: men tend to value the exchange as a form of reciprocity, because it provides a release from their normal economic relations, whereas women want a fair trade because they desire self-respect and want their vended domestic services to be fully valued. Others experience tension between the two values: should an exchange be part of an ongoing relationship of reciprocity or a trade, measured in the currency unit, by time or by skill? Raddon concludes that for many participants these schemes are not about replacing state money or increasing employment but about expanding the local experience of trade; for them, trade should not be colonized by calculative reason and competition.

After Interest: Derivatives

Financial money, whether held, loaned, or invested, is always subject to the risk of loss. Debts may not be repaid, investments may go sour, and inflation may depreciate money's buying power. For many years people have found ways to mitigate market risk through financial instruments and institutions, such as the joint stock company and limited partnerships. But after Markowitz's work in the early 1950s on portfolio selection (with its trade-offs between risk and reward), a revolution in financial thinking and products emerged. Risk was commoditized and became a private property that could be bought and sold in the financial sphere. Through the purchase and sale of risk, parties can hedge and speculate with their investments. Risk is commoditized by (1) breaking it into types or components; (2) projecting its historical performance or variations as probabilities from the past to the future; (3) comparing it to other forms of risk; and (4) buying and selling it. This way of managing risk involves both metaphoric reason, by which the future is "seen as" the past, and the mystification of uncertainty or contingency as if it were measurable as probability. (Risk and uncertainty are encountered in the communal realm, too, but they are usually managed through norms of sharing and reciprocity.[15])

The significance of market risk, I argue, transcends its emergence as a form of property. Commensurating and commoditizing risk is the clearest and perhaps ultimate use of a universal or derivational model in the market. Risk transactions reverberate in the financial sphere and cascade into the other value domains, as if they were abstracted from all other modes of exchange. For most people, the purchase and sale of risk seems far removed from everyday experience. But this is wrong, for risk transactions rely on information about a local context. Risk trades belie the idea that calculative reason alone describes the market economy and display a derivational model's incompleteness.

Most risk transactions take place through the formation and sale of derivatives, which were conceptualized and developed after Markowitz. Their growth, following the breakthrough of the Black-Scholes pricing formula in the 1970s, has been startling: for example, according to a Federal Reserve Bank survey (nd:3), in the United States daily foreign exchange turnover (which includes swaps, spot trading, and forward transactions) increased 82 percent between 2001 and (April) 2004, when it amounted to $461 billion. Daily turnover for other derivatives markets (including forward rate agreements, interest rate swaps, cross currency swaps, and foreign exchange and interest rate options) rose 164 percent to $355 billion at the same date (Federal Reserve Bank nd:7). In 2004 as well, the daily turnover of global derivatives was estimated to be one half the size of the United States' economy (*Financial Times*, 19 July 2006:25). In the year 2006, the total annual value of derivative contracts exceeded $450 trillion (*Wall Street Journal*, 20 March 2007:C1). The growth rate in the use of derivatives has been so large that they now swamp traditional futures contracts. Similarly, over 50 percent of the daily transactions on the New York and London stock exchanges are made by hedge funds. Derivative transactions have global spread today.

Derivatives include puts and calls on stocks, credit swaps, futures contracts, warrants, options, interest rate swaps, and other instruments. Like other financial entities, they are a form of private property but have no material existence other than the paper on which they are written or the computer where the contract is stored. They may be traded in specific market arenas, but many are exchanged over the counter outside normal oversight.

The term derivative is used for these commodities because their value depends on another underlying asset, whose price usually changes over the duration of the contract. I use the word in a triple sense. A derivative does refer to an underlying asset from which its value is derived. But this value is putatively derived mathematically or deductively, as in a universal model. In the calculus, it can also be related to a first (velocity) and a second derivative (the change in velocity). One might also suggest that the derivative is a postmodern financial product, because it deconstructs traditional modes of holding or forms of organization, such as the corporation, by distributing their parts to new owners.

Let us turn to the construction and use of a derivative. Consider, first, traditional forward contracts, such as grain futures that are transacted on commodity exchanges, as derivatives that *hedge against risk*. In these markets, a farmer can pledge to deliver his harvest at a specified price in the future. The price takes into account the delivery date and the projected commodity price (due to natural conditions and national or global production) at the time of completion. The contract is a hedge: the farmer receives the surety of vending his harvest, and the buyer has the certainty of receiving the contracted quantity of grain. The farmer may not receive the highest price at the time of completion, but he insures against a price fall; the buyer may not pay the lowest price, but he hedges against a price rise.

A stock option as a derivative is similar but involves *leveraging* capital as well. For example, a buyer may purchase the right to buy a number of corporate shares at a specified price at a future date.[16] At the expiration date, the option is exercised or allowed to lapse, depending on the stock's movement. If the price of the stock at expiration is higher than the option price, the buyer of the option may exercise his "call." He then owns the stock at its contracted price plus the cost of the option, and makes a profit (or loss) on the remainder. If he does not exercise his call because the price is not sufficiently high, the seller retains the stock but gains the price of the option. Because the buyer puts up only the cost of the option rather than the full cost of the stock, he leverages his money: for example, if the cost of the option is $10.00 (regardless of the stock's price) and the buyer makes $15.00 on the stock (its market price less the contracted price), his rate of return is 50 percent, due to the leveraging.

Derivatives above all commoditize *risk*. As an example of risk, consider a homeowner who wishes to assure the market price of his house. Desiring to hedge the downside risk, he buys insurance against specific events, such as fire, wind, or hail damage. For a price, the insurance company accepts this downside risk. Such insurance does not cover fluctuations in the market price of the house, and it may exclude other events such as flooding or earthquakes. But if one of the insured events occurs, the homeowner makes a call on the risk option that he bought. In this transaction, the house's price risk (for specific events) is commoditized. (The insurance company packages together a number of such contracts and may sell parts of a package to yet other insurers in order to hedge its risks.)

A derivative, then, is a financial commodity that prices an asset's price risk for a specified time. The derivative's price is derived from the volatility of the asset's price, or we might say that it is the price of a change in the price of an asset. With derivatives, a new financial process emerges: instead of money being traded for money for a price over time (as in interest rates), money can be traded for a *change* in the price of money (or any asset) over time. As the price of a price, a derivative commoditizes the probability of price movements. Because of this feature, derivatives (like stock options) allow for considerable leverage in the use of capital, which does not happen with labor or natural resources.

How is the risk or the probability of a change in an asset's price constructed? As one example of the statistical derivation, consider the risk of a stock. Its historically shifting values can be entered on a Cartesian graph that plots its past prices over time. A least squares line can then be calculated, and with this information, the stock's volatility around its mean (or its standard deviation and variance, which is the square of the standard deviation) can be figured. This historical plot of volatility defines the stock's risk, which can be small or large. What the Black-Scholes formula showed was that a stock's option price is determined not by its closing price but by its volatility around its mean. Some have a larger variation than others, or higher risk than others. With this mathematical discovery, risk was separated from stock price, commensurated, commoditized, and became a property that could be traded in the financial realm. Today, measurements of risk have not only become highly sophisticated but are applied to innumerable entities and events.

But what is this statistical calculation of risk measuring? Consider here a mutual fund. Its portfolio of stocks exhibits price volatility over time. Presumably, the fund's risk—in relation to a benchmark—is due to the manager's "style" of stock selection, which can be opaque to most investors. The reasons for interest rate variations (or risk) across currencies are even less clear. Feeding into the value changes of a currency are events, such as hurricanes, earthquakes, revolutions, political shifts, wars, the actions of a central bank, the IMF, and economic downturns and upswings. If the risk of a fund manager might be derived from his historical performance, exchange rate changes are even more susceptible to a break between known history and the uncertain future.

As mentioned, derivatives deconstruct a property into separate features that can be bought and sold. For example, 3M could be seen as a technology stock, a resource stock, an international stock, or another vehicle. Instead of purchasing the stock, which represents rights to its total assets, an investor might buy a derivative that links its price to an underlying measure, such as a technology, resource, or international index around which it shows variability. Conversely, 3M might decide to focus on its core activities or ones in which it has a comparative advantage: for example, it might see itself as an innovative, technological, industrial corporation with skills in marketing. But it also bears the risks of exchange rate fluctuations and real estate exposure. By engaging in the derivatives market, it can outsource these risks to others who specialize in managing them, such as international bankers and property insurance companies. (Similarly, the homeowner specializes in holding and living in his home and not in speculating in the real estate market; he outsources as well.) Because derivatives decouple or outsource qualities of a property, one might term them a "postmodern" way of investing. (If derivatives deconstruct a corporate body, perhaps the risk of a human part might be traded as a derivative. We take out health insurance, but why not commoditize the risk of heart or kidney failure?)

Derivatives are used not only to hedge foreign currency positions or the movements of stocks and bonds, but also to connect conditions in different markets and nonmarket events. For example, a derivative might link the weather in the western plains of the United States with the value of the Argentine peso on the assumption that weather conditions in the United States affect its beef production, which influences the size of Argentine beef exports and leads to a change in the peso/ dollar exchange rate. Such connections that determine a derivative's value could create an incentive to interfere in local conditions in order to change a payoff, such as seeding clouds, inciting a run on a nation's currency, or employing mercenaries to topple a political order and a nation's money. Because derivatives leverage an investment, the cost of changing local outcomes might be less than the projected gain on the derivative. Even as derivatives reduce financial risk by hedging, they can increase volatility on the ground through feedback and cascading calculative reason into local practices.

Feedback is not the only way derivatives may affect other spheres in markets. Derivatives, it is sometimes said, take the pressure of managing risk off end parties and place it in the market, where it can be bought and sold; the risk is off-loaded or transferred. For example, hedge funds can allocate risk in the market, which is made up of individual buyers who bear part of the risk by holding it, laying part of it off on others, or combining it with contrary risks. The risk is distributed. This process, however, may distinguish different sorts of participants. Some market actors may desire to hedge risk through a derivative; others may be speculating and leveraging their money. But these bettors may not have the assets to cover their leveraged position if the future is not as they speculated. Spectacular meltdowns may occur, as in the case of Barings Bank or LTCM. And these meltdowns can have a reverberating effect on the financial and other spheres.

The central problem is that past statistical performance is often used to project future price variability, a method that leaves out contingent events and uncertainty. Information and knowledge are central. Derivatives are mostly constructed in the information and financial centers of the world, such as Chicago, New York, and London, but local knowledge of events and people may be needed. For example, in 2006 the hedge fund Amaranth had a meltdown of assets due to a trader's reckless bets on natural gas futures that did not behave as expected. In a few weeks the market disruption was managed; but with the occurrence of a large unexpected event, such as a nuclear explosion, a tidal wave, or the overthrow of a major government, the global distribution of risks could lead to a collapse of financial obligations that would dwarf previous banking sector crises. More formally stated, when long-tailed or small-probability risks occur, such as a Hurricane Katrina or a Russian default on bonds, the financial sphere has no backing, except to distribute the adverse effects among many investors. And even if they lose money, capital holders and capital-endowed economies usually are better able to survive in times of crises, in contrast to small national economies and individual debtors, as well as other members of an economy, who may become destitute when a government tightens spending, raises interest rates, lowers subsidies, and shrinks welfare plans in response to a run on its currency, as in the case of the Thai Baht.

Thus, we return to economy's dialectic. Embodying calculative reason, derivatives illustrate the power of a derivational model to accumulate wealth and its limits, because their construction requires local knowledge and they affect lives that are not part of this world. Instruments in the financial sphere that are forged in the name of capital efficiency, derivatives display the incompleteness of calculative reason, which they so splendidly represent. This sphere of financial exchange is always open to contingency, which cannot be derived—a problem that has become especially salient through the globalization of capital. But for most of us uncertainty is represented and mystified as calculable risk through the construction of derivatives.[17]

Notes

1. See, for example, Stiglitz (1993) and Shubik (2000).

2. See, for example, Barth (1967), Bohannan (1955, 1959), Douglas and Isherwood (1979), Parry and Bloch (1989), and Sillitoe (2006).

3. This literature is extensive, and the debate about "What is money?" and whether "they" have it quickly expands into larger questions about what is economy: Are markets found elsewhere, is homo economicus universal? For some of this literature, see Armstrong (1924, 1928), Einzig (1966), and Melitz (1974).

4. I assume for the moment that a money scale is constant: there is no change in the supply and velocity of money, or in the volume of things for which it is exchanged, just as the thermometer in theory measures equally in all environments.

5. I abstract from Peloso's (1999) description of plantations in Peru.

6. Evans-Pritchard describes that a cucumber may take the place of an ox in sacrifice among the Nuer, but the relation is one-directional or scrip-like: "a cucumber may be called an ox but an ox cannot be called a cucumber ... these are not statements of identity" (Evans-Pritchard 1956:141). Properties from one are attributed to the other in certain contexts but not in reverse. In some Kachin areas, a traveling trader recorded different debts, from goats to gold, as notches on a bamboo stick; the notched stick was a measuring rod and a convenient scrip (Leach 1954:146).

7. Douglas (1967) draws a parallel between "primitive" monies and coupons to much effect; she also emphasizes rationing and control as part of this nexus.

8. I have drawn on Danks (1888), A. L. Epstein (1963, 1969, 1979), Scarlett Epstein (1964, 1968), and Salisbury (1962, 1970).

9. I return later to the idea that thrift is often linked to preserving a holding and is closely related to the obligations of mutuality.

10. Other relevant ethnography on base money is presented by Breton (2000), Foster (1998), Keane (2001), and Thurnwald (1934).

11. Keane (2001), with others, emphasizes the mobility of money between "ceremonial" and market uses.

12. In Lawonda (Indonesia) when the people began to use national money, they first allocated or budgeted it according to their traditional hierarchy of exchanges; thus, a buffalo might be sold to pay university fees, or garden goods could be sold to pay a school fee, but a horse would not be sold to pay for a secondary school fee or for ordinary food (Vel 1994:70–71).

13. The chair of the Federal Reserve Bank in the United States should not be able to make money through actions of the bank. But the Federal Reserve earns money through its operations, and its component banks are made up of interested bankers.

14. I draw principally on the study by Raddon (2003), who observes that LETS can also stand for Local Employment and Trading System, Local Energy Transfer System, or Let's Eat Together Soon!

15. An older argument between James Scott and Samuel Popkin revolved about peasant and communal management of risk; Scott (1976) explored the relationships in which peasants were enmeshed to see how far they helped

assure subsistence, especially in times of need; Popkin (1979:18) argued for a "deductive understanding" and saw peasants in terms of rational decision-making.

16. A corporation may also grant options or warrants to its officers, in which case the holder has no risk, especially if the option is backdated as has recently occurred.

17. This entire section was being copyedited when the subprime mortgage crisis emerged in the United States. It illustrates the several points about the miscalculation of risk, long-tailed probabilities, the separation of local knowledge from calculative reason, the hunger for gain, and the sometimes crushing and cascading effects of the financial realm on everyday life.

⊗ 7

SEEKING A BALANCE

With the demise of communism and various forms of socialism, with the withering of the welfare state and the increasingly contested place of welfare plans in most nations, and with continuing pressures to privatize common tasks and spaces, market economics ever more guides material and social practices throughout the globe. The transcendence of market society seems to be the condition and promise of modernity. Remnants and achievements of central planning and socialism can be found, as in Cuba, and remains of the welfare state endure, as in the Nordic nations, but with heightened transnational flows, the "promissory notes" of modernity have been adopted in many parts of the world. The expression "promissory notes" refers to the cultural aspirations, hopes, and projects that modernity beckons; but for Björn Wittrock (2000), to whom we owe this phrase, and for many others, the historical emergence of modernity is visualized primarily as a political and social process that ushered in the heightened role of agency and reason in the making of society, and the possible achievement of moral values such as liberty, freedom, and equal rights for all.[1]

If today modernity also means the emergence of diverse forms of state organization, new mixes of religion and politics, and a growing reflexivity about these processes—as in the development of the social sciences—then we may agree with the revised notion that there are "multiple modernities" (Dædalus 2000, vol.129:1). But these and other accounts of modernity seem to omit the presence of a singular economic form—global, market trade—whose emergence marked a break with traditional economy and whose presence provides the cement for the multiplicities of modernity. Are diverse ideologies, and political and social arrangements, independent of economy? The new understanding of modernity seems to presume that it is a political, social, and ideological movement disconnected from material practices that affect people and change their world.

In contrast to the revised concept of modernity, by the mid twentieth century the word modernization had come to mean economic reorganization after the pattern of the "advanced" industrial economies, such as the United States.[2] This narrative revolved about the emergence of "economy" from communal restraints, and as centrally planned economies faded, this story should have become even more compelling. But if modernization theories of the economy, such as Rostow's (1960), as influenced by the legacy of Durkheim and Parsons, are now viewed as unilinear and imbued with the idea of progress copied after the United States and other industrialized nations, and if the idea and practice of "development" is now critiqued as a postcolonial project (Escobar 1995), how can we understand economic conditions today without deploying the lens of the rational actor as expressed in microeconomics, the new institutionalism, or versions of evolutionary economics? We lack accounts of globalization with economies that have diverse configurations, technologies, and cultures.

Today, we are told in news media and theoretical discourse that the new global economy will bring greater material welfare to everyone. But the new high market economy is not simply about hyperconsumption and the throwaway culture, just-in-time inventories, shortened and specialized production lines, the use of outsourcing, or space-time compression. It is not just multitasking or attending to several consumption activities at once—as epitomized by use of the cell phone— or paying for more domestic activities, such as eating out or consuming ready-made foods using the microwave. It is not only buying over the internet, nor is it paying for the gender of one's child or agonizing over the cost of prolonging a loved one's life. It revolves about the increasing dominance of markets and calculative reason in social life.

Engendered by competitive trade and disciplined by the exchange of money for itself, calculated selection is the engine of high markets. It fuels the drive for profit, because monetary profit is the index of its fruitful practice, while incessant consumption is the zone of its public display. Reaching a pinnacle in the financial sphere, where it is practiced for its own sake, as signaled by the ratio Δ Capital/Capital, calculative reason has become the shared culture of the market. This practice denies mutuality, because with the exchange and alienation of private property, objects separate rather than join people.

I return to the Weberian image of the "iron cage" (Weber 2002). The iron cage does not, as against some interpretations, mean being caught within rational, depersonalized bureaucracies (with specialization and the rapidity of communications and transport, large modern projects are continuously broken up by "creative destruction" anyway). I refer instead to the way we make our identity through rational choice and the continual act of selecting.[3] Choices proliferate as the market widens, but their completion is no longer the finality, because choosing has become the dominant realization and subjectivity of what we are: efficient beings. In explanatory discourse and life, utility maximization itself has become a subjective "preference," exemplifying what economists call "learning-by-doing," although they may have a less reflexive sense of the expression in mind. As this "utility-maximizing, forward-looking behavior" (Becker 1993:386) spreads across subjectivities, "getting the incentives right"—an oft-repeated phrase—becomes a principled way to change behavior.[4] But deploying this model on others, for good or ill, objectifies them, even if done in the name of the actor's own altruistic preferences, for the other is emptied of alternative modes of reason and emotion, except the passion to calculate and maximize. These consequences, I believe, were the core of Weber's fearful vision. The iron cage contains rats racing for a reward of pellets in a maze we have built. Are we turning these animals into a vision of ourselves, or have we put ourselves in the cage?

My position is neither Weber's—that we can gain some understanding of the growth of markets in terms of religious or ideological forces—nor Polanyi's, that the market was disembedded in a one-time event. There may have been a moment when modern markets were increasingly loosened from communal forms, but impersonal arenas of trade long existed, if controlled by states and smaller entities. Even if these two historical interpretations are not entirely helpful in understanding economy's dynamics, I would not revert to economism as a heuristic method, for economy includes more than markets. I have been trying to show what we can learn from an anthropological approach and ethnography in thinking about economy, and I have been offering a different language for material life. Everyone is both a socially embedded or conjoint actor who is constituted by social relationships and ideas, and a disjoint chooser with aspirations, hopes, desires, and wants. We traverse this disjunctive terrain everyday with ease, with distress, and often without notice. I want to bring this perspective to conscious reflection and discussion because it has dramatic effects on everyone.

Economy contains two value realms: mutuality and markets. Mutual transactions include allotting, apportioning, and reciprocity (which are often intermingled). Markets include commerce or the trade of goods and services (which include ideas), and finance or the trade of money and financial instruments. Competitive trade leads to the reification of calculative reason. Independent of contexts, its purest expression is in the financial sphere, through which it increasingly governs economic action yet requires a local setting in the commercial and mutual spheres for its realization. Of course, there are many varieties of capitalism, such as shareholder capitalism, stakeholder capitalism, and welfare capitalism. Markets can be slanted toward pure laissez-faire, laissez-faire with regulation, state planning, state ownership, state ownership of natural resources, or the commercial realm. But these are variations of the dialectic, because through price reverberations, competitive trade cascades into the realm of mutuality, debases its foundation, and turns into the market fundamentalism of the rational actor, about which we build stories, such as the Protestant Ethic. The cultural construction of calculative reason is created and re-created by practices of trade, but it is incomplete and contingent because it depends on a transcendent context that it also denies. Moreover, it has been contested in a variety of ways, from controlling interest rates and limiting what may become a commodity, to raising trade barriers, to forming local action groups, to the surfacing of terrorism. Our contemporary crisis is not just the ever-present potential for commercial or financial downswings and recessions; rather, the cascading impact of the calculated financial sphere increasingly defines identities, subjects the commercial and mutual realms to its bottom-line discipline, and affects development, the distribution of wealth, environmental behavior, and our understanding of freedom.

Equity or Efficiency?

Today we use the shorthand description "efficiency versus equity" to capture the value "trade-off" that many perceive between smart markets and fairness. But the shorthand usually is not explored. Efficiency refers to a perfect market in which competitive trades take place until no one could achieve a better position without someone else moving to a worse one. In economists' terms this is Pareto optimality, which is the first theorem of economics. This narrative does leave out the impact of monopolies and imperfect information. But more important, competitive equilibrium is achieved given an initial distribution of resources, or what the participants bring to trade, also known as their endowments. Economics is relatively silent about this initial distribution except to address Pareto improvement and potential Pareto improvement through redistribution. The trump card is that more efficient outcomes lead to greater growth. For some economists, growth or a rising standard of living overall even helps to shape the "moral character of a people," because it fosters "greater opportunity, tolerance of diversity, social mobility, commitment to fairness, and dedication to democracy" (Friedman 2005:4), which is heady stuff. Who can argue with that? Yet this world vision is contested by people who do not find it to be an unalloyed good.

The concept of equity is very different from efficiency or growth, and it seems to pale in relation to the practical and intellectual force behind them. In fact, as the reader notices I have not used the term "equity," because it places too much emphasis on the material sphere. Instead I speak of "sharing," which occurs in multiple ways according to local values of mutuality, and concerns the linkages between people. But so what? The crucial concern, I argue, is that growth depends on mutuality and community. Let us consider that idea.

The Dialectics of Growth: From Rags to Riches

Economic growth, I suggest, ultimately depends on the dialectics of trade and mutuality. As Schumpeter long ago argued (1934), development comes from innovations. The pace of innovations may be heightened through market participation, because markets can offer opportunities for "new combinations," but innovation is not a function of calculative reason: it depends on communication, connections, and creative contributions that draw on many forms of reason. To understand why I think market innovations emerge in a dialectical process let us recall the idea of remainders as they are found in the mutual realm.

Remainders are something like market spillovers, but they are not externalities. An externality, to repeat, is the effect of a market practice on others; it can be positive or negative as in the examples of excess irrigation water or pollution. An externality falls outside market trade and is not private property—hence its name. But both positive and negative externalities can be measured against market goods, and as private property they can be legally assigned to the issuer or to the affected, with the result that they are brought into markets through raising or lowering the costs of market producers or consumers. The concept of externalities is framed within the market model.

Remainders start with the idea of thrift. Making savings means having a leftover. After a material practice, there may be an extra, such as a harvest, an implement, or a piece of material. In the economies I know, remainders are kept as a reserve for the future. Sometimes remainders are recycled or imaginatively reused in the quest to be thrifty, as in the case of a Guatemalan householder who inverted a ceramic bowl to use as a chimney cap in order to keep rain from dripping down onto his wife's cooking hearth (Gudeman 2001).

Remainders come either from the self or from others. For example, a field owner may give others permission to glean his field, or leftover seed may be given to others, sometimes in the hope of receiving a different strain in the future. Sifting through garbage, securing out-of-date food from a grocery store, or picking up rags, which have become common practices in many parts of the world, are thrifty actions that make use of market remainders. In the language of the market, remainders are spillovers, which are not precisely defined but seem to refer to unmeasured externalities or the indirect effects of public expenditures. My examples of remainders or spillovers have a material form, and I surmise—without a statistical study—that it is the less wealthy classes of an economy who most frequently make use of them.[5]

Remainders and spillovers also provide ideas; they are information, not in the Austrian sense of price signals but in the form of interpretable objects, as in the case of the ceramic bowl turned into a chimney cap. In rural areas with domestic economies, people freely copy the successful seeding patterns of others. In anthropology, this type of spillover was known as "diffusion," which certainly must be a factor in the material growth that has occurred outside markets. Similarly, I have recorded the case of a rural Guatemalan man who built an earthquake-proof and larger furnace for baking commercial bricks for sale. Due to his proximity and conversations with paid construction workers, he learned how steel rods were used to reinforce the concrete walls of urban buildings and applied this technique to the floor of his new furnace. For him, walls became floor. He was a creator and innovator who applied a market technique in a new way (Gudeman 2001).

How do these local, unrecognized, and often obscure practices help us understand market growth? There have been many theories of economic growth; some are formal, some are local, and some pertain to one or another of economy's realms. Material growth may be attributed to the acts of gods, to ancestors, to the finding of gold or silver, to the finding of new resources, to an increased population and enlarged labor force, to building machines, or to saving and investing. Within economics many of these ideas have been winnowed into what is known as Old Growth Theory and New Growth Theory (Warsh 2006).

Old Growth Theory is associated with the work of Solow (1956, 1997). It starts with the idea that adding labor and machines leads to growth. Solow showed that over time, capital accounts for about one third of total production, while labor accounts for about two thirds. The implication, given diminishing returns to capital, was that "[i]ncreasing machines was *not* a feasible way to sustain growth" (Easterly 2002: 51). Increasing the savings rate for investment also would not create long-run growth due to diminishing returns. To explain the rise in labor productivity, Solow turned to the external advance of scientific knowledge that supports technological change. For example, space exploration has led to the development of new materials that in turn have been incorporated in a multitude of market products: basic and applied science stimulate market growth. In the language of economists, Solow saw technological change as an exogenous variable: it was not created by market transactions but emanated from factors, such as scientific change and the action of entrepreneurs. Solow's ideas had both theoretical and policy implications (such as encouraging government support of science), but they also display the limits of the standard model. Growth occurs and is important, whether it is measured as a rising gross domestic product for a nation or as per capita output, but how can economics explain it, if the source is an exogenous variable?

New Growth Theory, which emerged in the 1980s and 1990s (and has many contributors, such as Lucas [2002] and Romer [1990]) ends up—or tries to end up—making technological change an endogenous variable, one within the market realm.[6] A central idea is that spillovers occur when the division of labor increases along with economies of scale. New ideas and complementary or supplementary products are the unintended effects of growth itself: a bread knife and cutting board supplement the baker's new bread; a candleholder is developed after candles are produced. Software develops as the use of computers and the internet expand. Larger automobiles lead to new forms of tires. Spillovers are endogenous effects of a growing market economy. Increasing returns that accrue to monopolies lead to spillovers, which lead to increasing returns. Success breeds success.

But spillovers, like remainders, must be imaginatively reinterpreted to serve in a new context, which is a very different sort of rationality from calculative reason, involving innovation in Schumpeter's sense (1934). Elsewhere (1992, 2001) I have described Schumpeter's notion of "creative destruction" as involving figurative reason, because it draws on metaphor, metonymy, and other modes of thought. It deconstructs (destruction) as it recreates (creative). The innovator is both a disjoint or singular agent and a conjoint person; she is a disembedded and embedded actor who depends on others in order to act for the self, which returns us to spillovers and the necessity of mutuality. Spillovers appear to be a "free gift" because they fall outside contractual relations and do not obligate the taker to provide a return. But a spillover becomes a leakage only if someone is around to respond to it. Spillovers require a communicatory space; they become seepages only in the context of a degree of mutuality. People listen, interpret, ask questions, offer suggestions, and are stimulated to have new ideas in communication with others. Of course, spillovers can be singularities, when one person appropriates an idea from another, but even so spillovers play on and make a short-lived base between people across the boundaries of private property. Some well-known examples of this process are the industrial districts of northern Italy (Bagnasco and Sabel 1995) and Silicon Valley, in which engineers communicated across the boundaries of corporations to solve problems or find new angles (Saxenian 1994). Innovation is an additive process that builds on a legacy of knowledge.[7] Today, the open access and speed of the internet seem to heighten the spillover process; Castells argues that innovation is "the primordial function" of the internet, which is a "collective intellect" (2001:100, 101).[8]

To be an engine of growth, spillovers require mutuality and yet something more. Reverting to an old, mostly rejected idea, I suggest that innovation as a collective process is closely akin to what Durkheim (1995 [1912]) termed "collective effervescence." Put forward a century ago, collective effervescence for Durkheim was the origin of religious conceptions and by extension the collective ideas of society. His example was the Australian corroboree, in which people from groups gathered once a year and through their interaction created, recreated, and revitalized their sense of commonality. Earlier Durkheim had hinted at this same conception in *The Division of Labor in Society* (1933 [1893]) when he noted how specialization, interaction, and mutual dependence increase through greater population and moral density, especially with the growth of cities.[9] Durkheim's insight is reflected in the latest versions of New Growth Theory. For example, in his account of economic growth, Lucas (2002:58–59) turns to the importance of interaction, stimulation, and the rise of cities, which is to say that growth rests on establishing communality outside contractual relations.

If innovation rests on a "free gift" from the realm of mutuality to market entrepreneurs, we must consider the dialectic of reciprocity. The embedded, conjoint, innovative agent is indebted to a social heritage, a base on which he relies. Should some fruits of an innovation, which are normally realized as private property and profit, be reciprocated through apportionment and allotment? Competitive markets give rise to the use of calculative reason but do not cause economic growth, except through the division of labor and economies of scale. Spillovers increase with this growth, but the key to development is connecting people through a base of communication, things, and shared practices. This needed, mutual part of economy falls outside market calculations, which if carried to their conclusion destroy the base on which they rest. Mutuality, I am suggesting, provides the needed piece in practices (and theories) of economic growth, which was Adam Smith's original concern.

Development

We should not conflate development with growth. To whom should we apply the concept of "lesser development"—economies with a more mutual or a more market orientation? What does development mean—a rising GNP per capita or enhanced welfare? Even this dichotomy is ambiguous, because indices of living standards may include nonmonetary measures, such as infant mortality and life expectancy, while improvement in these ratios is often attributed to economic growth.[10] The meaning of welfare is unclear as well. Does it refer to the availability of schooling, to literacy, to psychological health, or to a combination of factors? And who should define welfare—an international agency, a nation, or a local group?

Today, inequalities within and between nations are astounding and growing. For example, in 1992 the Gini coefficient (which measures income inequality) for Sweden was 25 and the top 10 percent of the population received 20.1 percent of yearly income, whereas in the United States, for 1997, the Gini coefficient was 40.8 and the top 10 percent secured 30.5 percent of the nation's income. Few developed nations exceeded the income disparities in the United States, although many less developed ones did.[11] The Human Development Report for 2005 provides an even grimmer picture. It shows that the combined income of the world's 500 richest individuals is larger than that of the poorest 416 million, and the 2.5 billion people who comprise 40 percent of the world's population and live on less than $2.00 per day receive only

5 percent of the world's income (United Nations Human Development Report 2005:4). Even as globalization in trade and ideas proceeds, the national disparities registered by the human development index grow larger.

The expansion of calculative reason, the growth of choice, has not brought the welfare that is promised through trickle-down theories of economic growth, for income distribution does not change dramatically with growth: markets do not equalize wealth. To the contrary, two economists concluded, "in recent decades growth and increases in inequality have been positively correlated" (Piketty and Saez 2006:7). Even if growth is not always correlated with greater income disparities, it does not bring about greater equality either within national economies or between them (Blim 2005). I cannot speculate on the complicated connection between wealth and welfare conceived as happiness; but if happiness is linked to the relationships we establish, then increased or constant wealth disparities, signaling a lack of mutuality or community, can hardly be counted as an increase in welfare, even in the face of economic growth.[12]

Foreign aid from the United States has done little to alter this situation. Years ago I spoke with the man who would become President Carter's Secretary of State; when I urged that greater attention be given to the rural areas of less developed countries, he explained that over 90 percent of US aid was provided as loans and tied to spending in the US, while only about 2% was allocated for humanitarian purposes. According to recent critiques and reports, he provided a largely accurate picture that remains true today (Henry 2003; Perkins 2004). The United States often cycles its aid money (and oil money expenditures) back through large corporations, such as Bechtel, offering a kind of governmental pump-priming that becomes the debt of other countries.

Let us also consider the distribution and development issues on the international scale through the three different perspectives of the International Monetary Fund (IMF), the World Bank (WB), and the World Trade Organization (WTO). Other organizations operate in the development sphere, from nongovernmental organizations (NGOs) to national governments. But these three are the principal global actors, with their different spheres of influence, different projects, and different impacts on human relationships. The International Monetary Fund loans money to nations to enhance economic and financial management. With the aim of implementing growth through national macroeconomic and structural changes, it offers borrowing nations technical assistance and monitoring (termed "surveillance") of their performance by ratios, such as the borrower's exchange rate and balance of payments positions, in order to promote currency exchange stability and avoid competitive exchange rate reductions.[13] One stated purpose of the IMF is to eliminate foreign exchange restrictions that hamper the growth of world trade.[14] But the case has yet to be made that capital flows, between nations and in the hands of interested parties, have much to do with the welfare of most humans. The IMF operates in the financial sphere of economy. In Veblen's words, the "captains of finance" populate it. Joseph Stiglitz (2002) observes that it represents the interests of finance ministers and international bankers (who often circulate between it and the private banking sector). Arguing that the IMF adheres to a strict view of "market fundamentalism" (2002:221), he suggests that the Washington Consensus policies of the IMF (austerity, privatization, market liberalization) have become ends rather than means, and proposes that the IMF's push for "capital account liberalization was *the single most important factor leading to the* [recent Asian financial] *crisis*" (2002:99). Stiglitz suggests that an economic "structure" must be in place for such policies to be useful, but he does not provide a picture of such a structure, except to suggest a go-slow policy with safety nets for the unemployed.

The purpose of the World Trade Organization (WTO), which is the successor to the General Agreement on Tariffs and Trade (GATT), is to facilitate the flow of trade throughout the world.[15] It deals with the agreements signed between nations concerning international commerce. Providing a forum for negotiations, it also is concerned with settling transnational disputes. The WTO primarily promotes the elimination of trade barriers or obstacles to commercial trade in order to achieve more competitive world markets in goods and services. Some barriers (such as tariffs) are allowed, as in the case of regional trading blocs of nations or when unfair trading practices that hamper a nation are encountered. But the WTO's overriding purpose is to promote open competition in the market arena. In recent years, meetings of the WTO have been marked by demonstrations concerning the environment, the plight of less competitive nations, and the problems of small farmers and others throughout the world who are affected by the shifting rules of world trade that often come under the influence of Western Europe, the United States, and the WTO. If the IMF conforms to Veblen's image of the captains of finance, the WTO is populated by the "captains of industry." It focuses on the realm of commerce. Neither the IMF nor the WTO is organized to promote the mutual realm of economy.

The World Bank, which supports local projects throughout the globe that have sustainable economic, social, and environmental benefits, is the third principal actor on the world's economic development stage.[16] It has a broad mandate and supports projects that affect health, education, the environment, public sector governance, and sustainability, among others. In recent years, the World Bank has increasingly turned to using local-level information, recognizing local communities, and designing projects that meet basic needs or alleviate poverty (it has declared a war on poverty). But it specifies that any supportable project must have a quantifiable, overall positive rate of return, which is often derived through the attribution of shadow prices. Operating partly in the communal realm, it nonetheless draws on the commercial and financial sectors, and employs the language of calculative reason or of the market, to judge where its financial and technical support will be directed.

The three major actors (as well as transnational corporations and banks) have effectively seized some control and governance of the global economic community, whose purpose they define as one of increasing market participation and productivity (which they sometimes modify by striving to eradicate poverty or create gender equity). The IMF, WB, and WTO replicate the divisions and language of the market realm. But does capital market liberalization that favors monetary interests build development? Does enhancing commerce through lowering trade barriers lead to development for less competitive areas? Does development through selected projects, using the language of the market realm, promote welfare? Surely we do not need to be caught in the rhetoric that market efficiency achieved through trade is the singular economic good.

I view development differently. Development cannot start from the reified financial sphere, nor should we expect it to be brought about by lowering trade barriers and promoting international commerce. It means more than constructing a transparent system of property rights (as the new institutionalists insist is key), loaning money, or supporting projects. Instead, it must mean recasting development in light of local dialogues about mutuality and trade. The purpose of development must be opened to reasoned discussion and not rely on the logic of means-to-ends calculation. I have sometimes harbored the view that Cuba, with its achievements in education, health, education, and sense of national identity, has built a base around which a defined market arena could be sustained. Because base building is a slow—not a "quick fix"—process, in order to foster development we need to consider more than investing in financial, human, social, and cultural "capital."

Considering development in this way will require new projects, new forms of assistance, greater respect for the capacities of others, and a new way of thinking based on a concept of economy as locally constructed around mutuality and market. We might start with the serious task of considering governance of the global market, which will be difficult to change. Good governance as the IMF defines it (floating exchange rates, no cronyism, no corruption) is market oriented and pertains to national economies. But what community governs the governors, including the transnationals? History is not on my side in this endeavor, but we could begin with the many local efforts that think globally, such as the International Labor Organization, fair trade movements, and others. I advocate seeing them in light of economy's dialectic: they are communities that help set the boundaries of the global market arenas. We need as well to loosen up the meaning of community to thinking about multiple, emergent, overlapping communities that act on the outside of markets and within them.

This way of viewing development could lead us to rethink the meaning of "foreign aid." Again, we can draw a perspective from the domain of mutuality and sharing. Instead of formulating aid as a contractual loan, we can see it as long-term reciprocity that connects economies or nations; foreign aid could be, like economy itself, a combination of mutuality and market, or reciprocity and contract. For example, a central impetus for contemporary aid programs was the Marshall Plan; initiated by the United States after World War II, it helped parts of Western Europe rebuild over the subsequent years. It had, of course, elements of self-interest, such as combating the influence of communism. But as early as 1954, the United Kingdom set up the Marshall Fellowships scheme for graduating college students in the United States (later Germany responded with a Marshall fund as well). This act of reciprocity allowed United States citizens to share in the national community of the United Kingdom and strengthened understanding between the two nations. Should foreign aid be conceived in terms of reciprocity, or a two-way, if incommensurate, transaction? At a national level we need to leaven self-interest with sharing and live with the uncertainty of return that reciprocity brings.

More broadly, economies, as unstable combinations of trade and mutuality, can have shifting purposes and values. We must rid ourselves of the sterile opposition between communism and capitalism to think in terms of diverse economies with multiple aims. A "developing" economy might emphasize growth in productivity, seen as output per labor hour, output per land area, or output per capital investment. An economy might aim for growth in its GNP, high financial profit making, or market efficiency. Alternatively, it could aspire to have full employment by governmental (community) investments. But these projects focus on the market realm, and an economy could also be aimed at promoting its mutual domain through education and health programs, the eradication of poverty, and greater welfare services. None of these goals is the same, though some seem to be conflated under the single market category of a growing GNP.

There are many ways to diminish the wealth inequalities within nations that undermine the lives of citizens. For example, Kerala (India), which is one of the poorest states in the world, achieved high literacy and life expectancy rates, combined with low infant mortality and birth rates, through a strong program of mutuality or redistribution, without a high growth rate in GNP (Franke and Chasin 1989). Similarly, an understanding of the centrality of the mutual domain can lead to offering no-cost long-term loans and grants, and combinations of mutual and private investments. Understanding the place of markets may lead to shortening the workweek to spread employment, as France has tried.

More broadly yet, we can set new market arenas. What do we want outside the market to save our bodies, share welfare, and provide space for the enhancement of subjectivities other than calculative reason? What should be traded in competitive markets, and what might be stipulated as already commensurate? For example, social security payments, pegged to a cost of living index, are a stipulated trade (or price) for a payment made (through taxes) earlier in life and by current wage earners. The exchange rate is set by the state. But how do we conceptually justify this welfare rate or erect boundaries on markets? What persuasions can be devised for other stipulations? One problem is our habit of accepting calculative reason to justify choice. Thus, a benefits/cost ratio is usually invoked to decide what can and should be in the market. In using this conceptual device, however, we allow market reason to decide who and what may enter its field of play. Conversely, we sometimes do not use calculations when market actors impinge on shared holdings. According to some reports Wal-Mart is able to keep employee wages low because many of their living costs, such as health care for children, tax credits for low-income families, and housing assistance are subsidized by the US taxpayer. These accounts suggest that the annual welfare bill for Wal-Mart's 1.2 million underpaid US employees is $2.5 billion (*The New York Review of Books,* 16 December 2004: 88). Taxes are diverted from national welfare to subsidize and enlarge Wal-Mart profits. (Let us recall the reverse: marginal farmers in Latin America and elsewhere subsidize low-cost food by diverting some of their "low-cost" communal production to markets.)

The problem is not *how* to create equity and development, which is not so hard conceptually, but summoning the language, the knowledge, and the communal commitment to do so, which requires a new understanding of how economy operates. When we allow the interest-bearing function of money to roam freely according to the model of free choice and efficiency, we let the financial realm determine the shape of economies through its cascading power that draws a return. Traditionally, labor unions, Luddites, communists, and others have opposed capital power with responses ranging from destroying equipment, to go-slow tactics, to strikes, to apathy, to alienation. Today we are encountering new responses around the globe, some of which are grouped under the category "terrorism." We ascribe diverse motivations to these actors, from religious fanaticism to irrationality. But given my view of economy, I wonder why we do not translate the name of the most widely known network of dissenters: Al-Qaeda means "the foundation" or "the base." This "community" provides an ideological and material foundation for violent dissent; we would do well to gain a deeper understanding of the dialectics by which it is produced.

Environment

Environmental issues might be approached in a similar way. The problem has many aspects, such as protecting fish, terrestrial animals, mineral resources, and water supplies; avoiding pollution of the air, earth and water; preserving natural spaces and farmland; slowing the use of dams and river controls; and stopping global warming.[17] Some observers claim that cost/benefit analysis, with the attribution of shadow prices to the degradations, should be used so that the quantitative trade-off between the economic return and environmental debasement may be assessed. Depending on the ratio of the two (which is a price), appropriate legal or political action can be taken. Others suggest that the negative "externalities" should be handled directly through the market mechanism. By assigning the negative externalities (as private property) to their producer or to a consumer, the cost of repair or damage can be legally attributed to one or the other party; either the pollution will continue with lower profits or higher costs to some, or it will be stopped. The effect will be accounted for through the market, which provides the most efficient and desirable uses of capital. Alternatively, pollution rights or quotas may be issued and then traded among those who are damaging the environment; as a corporation through technological improvements lowers the release of its damaging byproducts, it may trade its rights to higher polluters for a monetary return.

But these solutions assume that the people polluting and affected are market actors, and they veil the larger issue: Should we make people price pollution in order to elicit trade-offs (or prices) and "leave it to the market?" Market management of spillovers does not invariably debase community and the material world; however, this governance process not only expands the space for trade but also presumes that trade (versus abstention) provides the only reasoned way to solve the problem. The modern practice of carbon trading may be the worst of these activities, because it does not stop or diminish the release of carbon dioxide into the atmosphere (Lohmann 2006).

If economy is a dialectical mix of mutuality and market within an environment, can we not place boundaries around markets by stipulating a "zone of the incommensurable" through social institutions, laws, and informal practices?[18] In addition to detrimental fertilizers, pesticides, and effluents, what do we want outside the market to save our bodies and provide space for the development of other subjectivities? What should be traded in competitive markets, and how do we justify erecting borders around markets? I am suggesting that we expand our concept of the base, because we always face uncertainty and lack of knowledge. Should we not act with prudence or thrift, which are hallmarks of reasoned action in the realm of mutuality and in uncertain situations? The problem is our habit of accepting calculative reason to justify all choices. Thus, a cost/benefit ratio is usually invoked to decide what can and should be in the market. In using this narrative device, however, we allow market reason to decide who and what may enter its field of play. Should the players set the rules? Should we not preserve the environment as part of our legacy for making creative bases in the future?

Return to Reason

My anthropological position on economy also turns our consideration to the projects of enhancing human agency and freedom. Surely, freedom means not only the liberty to select among goods and services produced by free women and men or to vote and choose a political order; it must also mean the liberty to question what we mean by freedom. Some years ago, Isaiah Berlin distinguished between "negative" and "positive" freedom (Berlin 1969). More recently, Amartya Sen (2002) has addressed what he terms "procedural" and "opportunities" freedom. Even if their formulations are not congruent, both resemble my distinction between the value realms of mutuality and trade.

By *negative freedom* Berlin means the space or arena in which a person or group is left to do or to be without interference from others. This field of action could be likened to a vacuum in which nothing obstructs the self. In contrast, *positive freedom* means the individual is free to be his own master or to have mastery over any space where he can exercise choice and realize his inner self. This freedom is identified with rational control (1969:138) and liberation achieved by reason (1969:144). But Berlin suggests that the positive form of freedom can lead to totalitarianism. Because positive freedom lies at the heart of demands for self-direction, or the right to do what one wishes, one can come to believe there is only one (correct) way to live (1969:169). The real self also may be conceived as something wider than the individual, such as the church, the state, or the nation. Both conceptions can justify imposing one's will on others and coercing them to conform to a single ideal of freedom, and if freedom means self-mastery, how should one comport with others who oppose one's projects, except by force (1969:132–133, 140)? Because positive freedom can lead to oppressing others who have a different sense of self, Berlin opposed defining the real self or the true nature of humans in the quest to define freedom. For him, liberty must start with holding off someone who trespasses on a space, or with negative freedom (1969:158). Berlin argues for pluralism, because values are not commensurable and cannot be compared by a "slide-rule operation" (or a Benthamite calculation, as Mill well knew) (1969:170–171). For Berlin, every conception of liberty must include an area of negative freedom. Berlin does not apply his concepts to the market; however, in my terms mutuality provides an arena of negative freedom in which market actors exercise positive freedom.

Sen's approach is similar but slanted toward market freedom. He differentiates between *opportunity* and *procedural* freedom but adds that both forms must be subjected to "reasoned scrutiny." Sen observes that economists have tended to focus mostly on the opportunity aspect of freedom, which are the choices that individuals can and do make. Under opportunity freedom, Sen includes not only whether a person has the freedom to choose according to her preferences but also the freedom to choose or develop these preferences. Rational choice theory focuses on this domain. In contrast, procedural freedom pertains to questions such as whether others intrude or obstruct choice, and whether one is free to select. Sen comments that procedural liberty cannot be determined through instrumental calculations or by homo economicus (2002:25, 28, 50), and he adds that rules for the overall arrangement cannot be put to a vote because that would require a prior constitution or vote. But Sen does not state how this ethical arena is formed. He explains that there is "an irreducible role of a class of generally acceptable values (perhaps 'agreed' in some loose and inexact sense), without that class itself being put to some kind of *formalized* [italics added] determination. In this difficult exercise there is need for an ethical structure not unlike what Adam Smith attributed to the role of the 'impartial spectator'" (2002:626). Sen relates his two notions of freedom to Berlin's but places far more importance on positive freedom or the opportunity aspect of choice (2002:586), which could lead his view into the "totalitarian" difficulties with which Berlin was concerned. But Sen adds the check that both freedoms must be subjected to a higher order, reasoned scrutiny or critical assessment.

Both opportunity and positive freedom in the political sphere broadly correspond with the image of a "free market." In neoliberal discourse today, the two are aligned through the argument that the free market brings political liberty. In contrast, what I have termed mutuality or community is more closely aligned with procedural or negative freedom, because it sets the space within which individual choices can be made. My notion of community is not fully coincident with Berlin's, because community may set the space for choice but can turn totalitarian when a group subjects members to its exclusive will; to follow Sen this form of freedom must be subjected to critical scrutiny or heightened social reflexivity.

This dialectic of positive and negative freedom, and of opportunity and procedural freedom, has direct relevance for the often-confused moral stances of anthropology. After the founding of the UN, the American Anthropological Association uniquely refused to sign the subsequent charter of Human Rights out of concern for cultural relativism and cultural as opposed to individual rights. But this emphasis on cultural autonomy was an embarrassment in light of Nazism and genocide, which could not easily be condemned by that form of relativism. Anthropology has since been reconsidering its relativist position. But we might do better to see our contribution as an important voice in a dialogue between the two sorts of freedom, which in turn would allow us to develop a stronger role in the development problems of today, because its purposes, too, would be seen in light of this human dialectic.

Today, the exercise of opportunity freedom, seen as the liberty to select and relate means and ends, has become an end itself; through competitive trade it cascades into the space for procedural freedom by subjecting it to calculation. Precisely here I reiterate Berlin's plea for value incommensurability. If a promissory note of modernity was enlarged freedom, an important source of this ideal was the economic sphere where increased reliance on trade was taking place. If market freedom, in the historical unfolding of modernity, provided a powerful metaphor for other spheres, it has now become its own necessity, because it draws on a single form of reason that has no end. Today this image of freedom is becoming the single model of liberty. But if we feel compelled to exercise this freedom, and do not encounter rational choice itself as a selection, it is but an illusion of liberty. Freedom lies not in opportunity freedom alone but in deploying both forms, whose application and balance is discussed and negotiated in an open conversation. To what degree do we want practical reason with its embodiment in free markets to define its own range of application? Does freedom mean accepting the image that we produce of ourselves in the market, and widening its application across political, familial, and other life spheres, or does it mean imagining and deploying different models of ourselves?

A major project of modern anthropology is to enhance and expand our horizons through interpreting and reinterpreting practices. This human conversation is not located in the market; nor, given the established institutional spaces, does it have a single forum. I am suggesting a cultural shift in how we think about economy. The transcendent economic freedom brought by modernity is not to burst all constraints on trade and expand markets but to define their arenas, to critically assess the balance between economy's two sides, and to build new local models. If social reflexivity is a condition and achievement of modernity, then it must mean the freedom to reflect on the conditions of both economy and freedom itself.

Notes

1. Therborn argues that modernity should be thought of as a time period, rather than a set of institutions or forms, and that today many different modes of modernity are "entangled" (Therborn 2003).

2. For a recent and critical review of modernization theories in the social sciences, see Ruttan (2003).

3. See Scaff's (1989) discussion.

4. Stigler and Becker (1977:76, 77): "widespread and/or persistent human behavior can be explained by a generalized calculus of utility-maximizing behavior," while "families maximize a utility function of objects of choice."

5. For a fascinating collection of innovative uses of remainders, see Arkhipov (2006).

6. See Easterly (2001), Helpman (2004), and Warsh (2006).

7. I have elsewhere provided examples of innovation as a communal process (1992, 2001). For discussion of some of the issues, see von Hippel (1988) and Christensen (1997).

8. Some companies have been using the internet to solve scientific problems by describing them on a website, advertising for solutions, and rewarding the best ideas, so relying on a form of distributed intelligence (*Boston Globe,* 21 August, 2006, E1).

9. See also Durkheim (1953[1924]) and Simmel (1997:174–185).

10. For a discussion of the presumed link between per capita gross domestic product and other dimensions of the standard of living see Easterlin (2000).

11. *World Development Report 2000/2001*:182–183. For 1993, the Central African Republic registered a Gini coefficient of 61.3, and the consumption share of the top 10 percent of the population was 47.7 percent.

12. For recent studies of happiness, see Frey and Stutzer (2002) and Haidt (2006).

13. For an earlier on-the-ground account of the way the IMF operates, with experts flying in and out of a country and without any local knowledge cooking unreliable figures so that a country can receive funds, see Klitgaard (1990).

14. This information is drawn from the IMF's articles of agreement, under "Purposes" as stated in Article I. The material is widely available and can be found on the IMF website (www.imf.org).

15. For general information about the WTO, see its website (www.wto.org).

16. Information about the World Bank can be found at its website (www.worldbank.org).

17. See, for example, Gore (2006), Speth (2004).

18. The problem, of course, is global and not national. The *Wall Street Journal* (17 June 2005) recently reported that the sacred glacier of the Quechua, a people located in the highlands of Peru who used it in ceremonies, is disappearing. World pollution and warming—led by consumption in the United States—is debasing the mutuality of others. A Quechua base literally is disappearing, to the detriment of their well-being.

References

Abolafia, Mitchel Y. 1996. *Making Markets: Opportunism and Restraint on Wall Street*. Cambridge: Harvard University Press.

———. 1998. "Markets as Cultures: An Ethnographic Approach." In *The Laws of the Markets,* ed. Michael Callon, pp. 69–85. Oxford: Blackwell Publishers.

Adorno, Theodor W. 1973. *Negative Dialectics.* New York: Continuum Publishing.

Akerlof, G. A. 1970. "The Market for 'Lemons': Quality Uncertainty and the Market Mechanism." *Quarterly Journal of Economics* 84, no. 3: 488–500.

Alchian, Armen A., and Harold Demsetz. 1973."The Property Rights Paradigm." *Journal of Economic History* 33, no. 1: 16–27.

Anderson, Benedict. 1991. *Imagined Communities.* Rev. ed. London: Verso.

Anderson, David G. 1998. "Property as a Way of Knowing on Evenki Lands in Arctic Siberia." In *Property Relations,* ed. C. M. Hann, pp. 64–84. Cambridge: Cambridge University Press.

Aoki, Masahiko. 2001. "Community Norms and Embeddedness: A Game-Theoretic Approach." In *Communities and Markets in Economic Development,* ed. Masahiko Aoki and Yujiro Hayami, pp. 96–125. Oxford: Oxford University Press.

Aoki, Masahiko, and Yujiro Hayami. 2001. "Introduction: Communities and Markets in Economic Development." In *Communities and Markets in Economic Development,* ed. Masahiko Aoki and Yujiro Hayami, pp. xv–xxiv. Oxford: Oxford University Press.

Appadurai, Arjun. 1986. "Introduction: Commodities and the Politics of Value. In *The Social Life of Things,* ed. Arjun Appadurai, pp. 3–63. Cambridge: Cambridge University Press.

Aristotle. 1984. *The Complete Works of Aristotle.* Ed. Jonathan Barnes. Princeton: Princeton University Press.

Arkhipov, Vladimir. 2006. *Home-Made.* London: FUEL.

Armstrong, W. E. 1924. "Rossel Island Money: A Unique Monetary System," *The Economic Journal* 34, no. 135: 423–429.

———. 1928. *Rossel Island.* Cambridge: Cambridge University Press.

Arrow, Kenneth J. 1990. "Kenneth J. Arrow." In *Economics and Sociology,* Richard Swedberg, pp. 133–151. Princeton: Princeton University Press.

Bagnasco, Arnaldo, and Charles F. Sabel, eds. 1995. *Small and Medium-Size Enterprises.* London: Pinter.

Bailey, A.G. 1937. *The Conflict of European and Eastern Algonkian Cultures, 1504–1700.* Publications of the New Brunswick Museum, Monographic Series, No. 2.

Baldwin, John W. 1959. "The Medieval Theories of the Just Price, Romanists, Canonists, and Theologians in the Twelfth and Thirteenth Centuries." *Transactions of the American Philosophical Society* 49, part 4: 3–92.

Barth, Fredrik. 1967. "Economic Spheres in Darfur." In *Themes in Economic Anthropology,* ed. Raymond Firth, pp. 149–174. London: Tavistock.

————. 2002. "An Anthropology of Knowledge." *Current Anthropology* 43, no. 1: 1–18.

Baumol, William J., Alan S. Blinder, and Edward N. Wolff. 2003. *Downsizing in America.* New York: Russell Sage Foundation.

Baumol, William J., Robert E. Litan, and Carl J. Schramm. 2007. *Good Capitalism, Bad Capitalism, and The Economics of Growth and Prosperity.* New Haven: Yale University Press.

Becker, Gary S. 1976. *The Economic Approach to Human Behavior.* Chicago: University of Chicago Press.

————. 1981. *A Treatise on the Family.* Cambridge: Harvard University Press.

————. 1993. "Nobel Lecture: The Economic Way of Looking at Behavior." *The Journal of Political Economy* 101, no. 3: 385–409.

————. 1996. *Accounting for Tastes.* Cambridge: Harvard University Press.

Becker, Karin, and Barbro Klein. 2003. "Med Svenska ögan - Ett Mångkulturellt Odlingsområde 1990 och 2000." In *Stadens Odlare,* ed. Christina Westergren, pp. 151–181. Stockholm: Nordiska museets och Skansens årsbok.

Benería, Lourdes. 2003. *Gender, Development, and Globalization.* New York: Routledge.

Ben-Yami, M. 2004. "Fisheries Management: Hijacked by Neoliberal Economics." *Post-Autistic Economics Review* 27, no. 27: 15–20. Online at http://www.btinternet.com/~pae_news/review/issue27.htm.

Berlin, Isaiah. 1969. *Four Essays on Liberty.* Oxford: Oxford University Press.

Berndt, Ronald. 1951. "Ceremonial Exchange in Western Arnhem Land." *Southwestern Journal of Anthropology* 7, no. 2: 156–76.

Bestor, Theodore C. 2004. *Tsukiji: The Fish Market at the Center of the World.* Berkeley: University of California Press.

Blim, Michael. 2005. *Equality and Economy.* Walnut Creek: AltaMira Press.

Boettke, Peter J. 1989. "Evolution and Economics: Austrians as Institutionalists." *Research in the History of Economic Thought and Methodology* 6: 73–89.

Bohannan, Paul. 1955. "Some Principles of Exchange and Investment Among the Tiv." *American Anthropologist* 57, no. 1: 60–70.

————. 1957. *Justice and Judgment Among the Tiv.* London: Oxford University Press.

————. 1959. "The Impact of Money on an African Subsistence Economy." *The Journal of Economic History* 29, no. 4: 491–503.

Bohannan, Paul, and Laura Bohannan. 1968. *Tiv Economy.* London: Longmans, Green and Co.

Boisard, Pierre. 2003. *Camembert: A National Myth.* Trans. Richard Miller. Berkeley: University of California Press.

Bollier, David. 2002a. *Silent Theft: The Private Plunder of Our Common Wealth.* New York: Routledge.

————. 2002b. "Ruled by the Market: Reclaiming the Commons." *Boston Review* 27, no. 3-4. Online at http:// bostonreview.mit.edu/BR27.3/contents .html.

Born, Georgina. 1996. "(Im)materiality and Sociality: The Dynamics of Intellectual Property in a Computer Software Research Culture." *Social Anthropology* 4, no. 2: 101–116.

Bourdieu, Pierre. 1990. *The Logic of Practice.* Trans. Richard Nice. Stanford: Stanford University Press.

———. 1984. *Distinction: A Social Critique of the Judgment of Taste.* Trans. Richard Nice. Cambridge: Harvard University Press.

Boyer, Robert. 1997. "The Variety and Unequal Performance of Really Existing Markets: farewell to Doctor Pangloss?" In *Contemporary Capitalism,* ed. J. Rogers Hollingsworth and Robert Boyer, pp. 55–93. Cambridge: Cambridge University Press.

Braudel, Fernand. 1982. *The Wheels of Commerce.* Trans. Siân Reynolds. New York: Harper and Row.

Breton, Stéphane. 2000. "Social Body and Icon of the Person: A Symbolic Analysis of Shell Money Among the Wodani, Western Highlands of Irian Jaya." *American Ethnologist* 26, no. 3: 558–582.

Brison, Karen. 1999. "Money and the Morality of Exchange Among the Kwanga, East Sepik Province, Papua New Guinea." In *Money and Modernity: State and Local Currencies in Melanesia,* ed. David Akin and Joel Robbins, pp. 151–161. Pittsburgh: University of Pittsburgh Press.

Burkett, Larry. 1993. *The Family Budget Workbook.* Northfield Publishing.

Callon, Michel. 1998a. "Introduction." In *The Laws of the Markets.* ed. M. Callon, pp. 1–57. Oxford: Blackwell.

———. 1998b. "An Essay on Framing and Overflowing: Economic Externalities Revisited by Sociology." In *The Laws of the Markets,* ed. M. Callon, pp. 244–269. Oxford: Blackwell.

Campbell, Colin. 1987. *The Romantic Ethic and the Spirit of Modern Consumerism.* Oxford: Basil Blackwell.

Carpenter, Jeffrey P. 2005. "Endogenous Social Preferences." *Review of Radical Political Economics* 37, no. 1: 63–84.

Carrier, James G. 1995. *Occidentalism: Images of the West.* Oxford: Clarendon Press.

———. 1998a. "Introduction." In *Virtualism: A New Political Economy,* ed. James G. Carrier and Daniel Miller, pp. 1–24. Oxford: Berg.

———. 1998b. "Abstraction in Western Economic Practice." *Virtualism: A New Political Economy,* ed. James G. Carrier and Daniel Miller, pp. 25–47. Oxford: Berg.

———. 2001. "Social Aspects of Abstraction." *Social Anthropology* 9, no. 3: 239–252.

———. In press. "Simplicity in Economic Anthropology: Persuasion, Forms and Substance." In *Economic Persuasions,* ed. Stephen Gudeman. New York: Berghahn.

Carrier, James G., and Daniel Miller. 1998. *Virtualism: A New Political Economy.* Oxford: Berg.

Carsten, Janet. 1989. "Cooking Money: Gender and the Symbolic Transformation of Means of Exchange in a Malay Fishing Community." In *Money and the Morality of Exchange,* ed. J. Parry and M. Bloch, pp. 117–141. Cambridge: Cambridge University Press.

———. 2004. *After Kinship.* Cambridge: Cambridge University Press.

Castells, Manuel. 2001. *The Internet Galaxy.* Oxford: Oxford University Press.

Christensen, Clayton M. 1997. *The Innovator's Dilemma: When New Technologies Cause Great Firms to Fail.* Boston: Harvard Business School Press.

Coase, R. H. 1988. *The Firm, the Market and the Law.* Chicago: Chicago University Press.

Coleman, James. 1994. *Foundations of Social Theory*. Cambridge: Harvard University Press.

Collingwood, R. G. 1989. *Essays in Political Philosophy*. Oxford: Clarendon Press.

Conway, Janet. 2004. "Citizenship in a Time of Empire: The World Social Forum as a New Public Space." *Citizenship Studies* 8, no. 4: 367–381.

Coyle, Diane. 2007. *The Soulful Science*. Princeton: Princeton University Press.

Community Economies Collective. 2001. "Imaging and Enacting Noncapitalist Futures." *Socialist Review* 28, nos. 3–4: 93–135.

Daedalus. 2000. 129, no. 1. *Multiple Modernities*.

Dahl, Gudrun. 1998. "Wildflowers, Nationalism and the Swedish Law of Commons." *Worldviews: Environment, Culture, Religion* 2: 281–302.

Daly, Herman E., and Joshua Farley. 2004. *Ecological Economics*. Washington, D.C.: Island Press.

Danks, Benjamin. 1888. "On the Shell-Money of New Britain." *Journal of the Anthropological Institute of Great Britain and Ireland* 17: 305–317.

de Soto, Hernando. 1989. *The Other Path*. New York: Harper and Row.

Demsetz, Harold. 1967. "Toward a Theory of Property Rights." *American Economic Review* 57, no. 2: 347–359.

Diderot, D. 1751. "Art." In *Encyclopédie, ou Dictionnaire Raisonné des Sciences, des Artes et des Métiers*, ed. D. Diderot and D'Alembert, vol. I, pp. 713–717. Paris: Briasson, David, Le Breton, Durand.

Dominquez, Joe, and Vicki Robin. 1992. *Your Money or Your Life*. New York: Penguin.

Douglas, Mary. 1967. "Primitive Rationing." In *Themes in Economic Anthropology*, ed. Raymond Firth, pp. 119–147. London: Tavistock.

Douglas, Mary, and Baron Isherwood. 1979. *The World of Goods*. New York: Basic Books.

Dumont, Louis. 1970. *Homo Hierarchicus*. Trans. Mark Sainsbury. Chicago: University of Chicago Press.

Durkheim, Emile. 1933 [1893]. *The Division of Labor in Society*. Trans. George Simpson. Glencoe: The Free Press.

———. 1953 [1924]. *Sociology and Philosophy*. Trans. D. F. Pocock. London: Cohen and West.

———. 1995 [1912]. *The Elementary Forms of Religious Life*. Trans. Karen E. Fields. New York: The Free Press.

———. 1960. *Montesquieu and Rousseau*. Ann Arbor: University of Michigan Press.

Easterlin, Richard A. 2000. "The Worldwide Standard of Living Since 1800." *Journal of Economic Perspectives* 14, no. 1: 7–26.

Easterly, William. 2001. *The Elusive Quest for Growth*. Cambridge: The MIT Press.

Einzig, Paul. 1966. *Primitive Money*, Rev. ed. Oxford: Pergamon Press.

Elster, Jan. 1989. *The Cement of Society*. Cambridge: Cambridge University Press.

———, ed. 1986. *Rational Choice*. New York: New York University Press.

Ensminger, Jean. 1992. *Making a Market*. Cambridge: Cambridge University Press.

Epstein, A. L. 1963. "The Economy of Modern Matupit." *Oceania* 33, no. 2: 182–215.

———. 1969. *Matupit*. Canberra: Australian National University Press.

————. 1979. "*Tambu*: The Shell-money of the Tolai." In *Fantasy and Symbol: Studies in Anthropological Interpretation*, ed. R. H. Hook, pp. 149–205. London: Academic Press.

Epstein, Scarlett. 1964. "Personal Capital Formation among the Tolai of New Britain." In *Capital, Saving and Credit in Peasant Societies*, ed. Raymond Firth and B. S. Yamey, pp. 53–68. Chicago: Aldine.

————. 1968. *Capitalism, Primitive and Modern*. Lansing: Michigan State University Press.

Escobar, Arturo. 1995. *Encountering Development*. Princeton: Princeton University Press.

Espel, Wendy Nelson, and Mitchell L. Stevens. 1998. "Commensuration as a Social Process." *Annual Reviews of Sociology* 24: 313–343.

Evans-Pritchard, E. E. 1956. *Nuer Religion*. Oxford: Clarendon Press.

Federal Reserve Bank of New York. Nd. *The Foreign Exchange and Interest Rate Derivatives Markets: Turnover in the United States, April 2004*. New York: Federal Reserve Bank.

Feeny, David, Susan Hanna, and Arthur F. McEvoy. 1996. "Questioning the Assumptions of the 'Tragedy of The Commons' Model of Fisheries," *Land Economics*, 72, no. 2: 187–205.

Ferry, Elizabeth Emma. 2005. *Not Ours Alone*. New York: Columbia University Press.

Fine, Ben. 1998. "The Triumph of Economics; Or, 'Rationality' Can Be Dangerous to Your Reasoning." In *Virtualism: A New Political Economy*, ed. James G. Carrier and Daniel Miller, pp. 49–73. Oxford: Berg.

Firth, Raymond. 1936. *We, The Tikopia*. London: George Allen & Unwin.

————. 1951. *Elements of Social Organization*. Boston: Beacon Press.

————. 1964. *Essays on Social Organization and Values*. London: The Athlone Press.

————. 1965 [1939]. *Primitive Polynesian Economy*. London: Routledge and Kegan Paul.

————. 1966. *Malay Fishermen: Their Peasant Economy*. New York: W. W. Norton & Co.

Folbre, Nancy. 2001. *The Invisible Heart, Economics and Family Values*. New York: The New Press.

Fortes, Meyer. 1969. *Kinship and the Social Order*. Chicago: Aldine.

Fortune, R. F. 1963 [1932]. *Sorcerers of Dobu*. Rev. ed. New York: E. P. Dutton.

Foster, Robert J. 1998. "Your Money, Our Money, the Government's Money: Finance and Fetishism in Melanesia." In *Border Fetishisms: Material Objects in Unstable Places*, ed. Patricia Speyer, pp. 61–90. New York: Routledge.

Foucault, Michel. 1979. *Discipline and Punish*. Trans. Alan Sheridan. New York: Random House.

Frank, R. H., T. Gilovitch, and D. T. Regan. 1993. "Does Studying Economics Inhibit Cooperation?" *Journal of Economic Perspectives* 7, no. 2: 159–171.

Franke, Richard W., and Barbara H. Chasin. 1989. *Kerala: Radical Reform as Development in an Indian State*. San Francisco: Institute for Food and Development Policy.

Freeman, J. D. 1958. "The Family System of the Iban of Borneo." In *The Developmental Cycle in Domestic Groups*, ed. J. Goody, pp. 15–52. Cambridge: Cambridge University Press.

————. 1970 [1955]. *Report on the Iban.* London: Athlone Press.

Frey, Bruno S., and Alois Stutzer. 2002. *Happiness and Economics.* Princeton: Princeton University Press.

Friedman, Benjamin M. 2005. *The Moral Consequences of Economic Growth.* New York: Alfred A. Knopf.

Friedman, Milton. 1953. *Essays in Positive Economics.* Chicago: University of Chicago Press.

Fukuyama, Francis. 1995. *Trust.* New York: The Free Press.

Gambetta, Diego, ed. 2000. *Trust: Making and Breaking Cooperative Relations,* Electronic edition, Department of Sociology, University of Oxford, http://www.sociology.ox.ac.uk/papers/trustbook.html.

Gardner, Howard. 2004. *Frames of Mind.* New York: Basic Books.

Gell, Alfred. 1982. "The Market Wheel: Symbolic Aspects of an Indian Tribal Market." *Man* 17, no. 3: 470–491.

Georgescu-Roegan, Nicholas. 1971. *The Entropy Law and the Economic Process.* Cambridge: Harvard University Press.

Gewertz, Deborah B., and Frederick K. Errington. 1995, "Dueling Currencies in East New Britain: The Construction of Shell Money as National Cultural Property." In *Occidentalism,* ed. James G. Carrier, pp. 161–191. Oxford: Clarendon Press.

Gibson-Graham, J.K. 1996. *The End of Capitalism (As We Knew It): A Feminist Critique of Political Economy.* Oxford: Blackwell.

————. 2006. *A Postcapitalist Politics.* Minneapolis: University of Minnesota Press.

Gladwin, Thomas. 1970. *East is a Big Bird: Navigation and Logic on a Puluwat Atoll.* Cambridge: Harvard University Press.

Godelier, Maurice. 1977. *Perspectives in Marxist Anthropology.* Trans. Robert Brain. Cambridge: Cambridge University Press.

————. 1986. *The Mental and the Material: Thought in Economy and Society.* Trans. M. Thom. London: Verso.

Godoy, Ricardo. 1990. *Mining and Agriculture in Highland Bolivia.* Tucson: University of Arizona Press.

Goetzmann, William N., and K. Geert Rouwenhorst. 2005. "Introduction: Financial Innovations in History," *The Origins of Value,* ed. William N. Goetzmann and K. Geert Rouwenhorst, pp. 3–16. Oxford: Oxford University Press.

Gore, Al. 2006. *An Inconvenient Truth.* Emmaus, PA: Rodale.

Graeber, David. 2001. *Toward An Anthropological Theory of Value.* New York: Palgrave.

Granovetter, Mark S. 1973. "The Strength of Weak Ties." *American Journal of Sociology* 78, no. 6: 1360–1380.

————. 1985. "Economic Action and Social Structure: The Problem of Embeddedness." *American Journal of Sociology* 91, no. 3: 481–510.

Green, Duncan. 2003. *Silent Revolution: The Rise and Crisis of Market Economics in Latin America.* New York: Monthly Review Press.

Gregory, C. A. 1997. *Savage Money.* Amsterdam: Harwood.

————. 2002. "The Anthropology of the Economy." *The Australian Journal of Anthropology* 13, no. 3: 361–362.

Greif, Avner. 1993. "Contract Enforceability and Economic Institutions in Early

Trade: The Maghribi Trader's Coalition." *The American Economic Review* 83, no. 3: 525–548.

——. 1994. "Cultural Beliefs and the Organization of Society: A Historical and Theoretical Reflection on Collectivist and Individualist Societies." *The Journal of Political Economy* 102, no. 5: 912–950.

——. 2001. "Impersonal Exchange and the Origin of Markets: From the Community Responsibility System to Individual Legal Responsibility in Premodern Europe," In *Communities and Markets in Economic Development*, ed. Masahiko Aoki and Yujiro Hayami, pp. 3–41. Oxford: Oxford University Press.

Gudeman, Stephen. 1976. *Relationships, Residence and the Individual.* London: Routledge & Kegan Paul.

——. 1978. *The Demise of a Rural Economy.* London: Routledge.

——. 1986. *Economics as Culture.* London: Routledge.

——. 1992. "Remodeling the House of Economics: Culture and Innovation." *American Ethnologist* 19, no. 1: 141–154.

——. 1998. "Banishing the Other from the Market: The Development Economics of W. A. Lewis." *Paideuma* 44: 125–37.

——. 2001. *The Anthropology of Economy.* Malden: Blackwell.

Gudeman, Stephen, and Mischa Penn. 1982. "Models, Meanings and Reflexivity." In *Semantic Anthropology,* ed. David Parkin, pp. 89–106. London: Academic Press.

Gudeman, Stephen, and Alberto Rivera. 1990. *Conversations in Colombia.* Cambridge: Cambridge University Press.

Guyer, Jane I. 2004. *Marginal Gains.* Chicago: University of Chicago Press.

Habermas, Jürgen. 1984. *The Theory of Communicative Action,* vol. 1. London: Heinemann.

——. 1987. *The Theory of Communicative Action,* vol. 2. Cambridge: Polity Press.

Haidt, Jonathan. 2006. *The Happiness Hypothesis.* New York: Basic Books.

Hann, Chris, ed. 1995. *Property Relations.* Cambridge: Cambridge University Press.

Hardin, G. 1968. "The Tragedy of the Commons," *Science* 162, no. 3859: 1243–1248.

Hart, Keith. 2000. "Kinship, Contract, and Trust: The Economic Organization of Migrants in an African City Slum." In *Trust: Making and Breaking Cooperative Relations,* ed. Diego Gambetta, pp. 176–193. Electronic edition. Department of Sociology, University of Oxford, http://www.sociology.ox.ac.uk/papers/trustbook.html.

——. 2001 [2000]. *Money in an Unequal World.* New York: Texere.

——. 2002. "The Euro: New Wine in an Old Jar?" Online at http://www.thememorybank.co.uk/publications/euro_new_wine,

Hausman, Daniel M. 1992. *The Inexact and Separate Science of Economics.* Cambridge: Cambridge University Press.

Hayek, Friedrich A. 1948. *Individualism and Economic Order.* Chicago: University of Chicago Press.

——. 1960. *The Constitution of Liberty.* London: Routledge & Kegan Paul.

——. 1967. *Studies in Philosophy, Politics and Economics.* Chicago: University of Chicago Press.

————. 1976. *Law, Legislation and Liberty,* vol. 2. London: Routledge & Kegan Paul.

————. 1978. *New Studies in Philosophy, Politics, Economics and the History of Ideas.* Chicago: University of Chicago Press.

Helgason, Agnar, and Gísli Pálsson. 1998. "Cash for Quotas: Disputes Over the Legitimacy of an Economic Model of Fishing in Iceland," In *Virtualism: A New Political Economy,* ed. James G. Carrier and Daniel Miller, pp. 117–134. Oxford: Berg.

Helgesson, Gert. 2002. *Values, Norms and Ideology in Mainstream Economics.* Uppsala: University Printers.

————. 2005. "Rationality in Economy: An Interdisciplinary Debate." In *Peopled Economies: Conversations with Stephen Gudeman,* ed. Staffan Löfving, pp. 29–62. Uppsala: Interface.

Helpman, Elhanan. 2004. *The Mystery of Economic Growth.* Harvard: Harvard University Press.

Henry, James S. 2003. *The Blood Bankers.* New York: Four Walls Eight Windows.

Henwood, Doug. 2003. *After the New Economy.* New York: The New Press.

Herrmann, Gretchen M. 1997. "Gift or Commodity: What Changes Hands in the U.S. Garage Sale?" *American Anthropologist* 24, no. 4: 910–930.

Herskovits, Melville J. 1953 [1940]. *Economic Anthropology.* New York: W.W. Norton.

Hewitson, Gillian. 2001. "The Disavowal of the Sexed Body in Neoclassical Economics." In *Postmodernism, Economics and Knowledge,* ed. Stephen Cullenberg, Jack Amariglio, and David F. Ruccio, pp. 221–245. London: Routledge.

Von Hippel, Eric. 1988. *The Sources of Innovation.* New York: Oxford University Press.

Hirschman, Albert O. 1977. *The Passions and the Interests: Political Arguments for Capitalism Before Its Triumph.* Princeton: Princeton University Press.

Hollis, Martin. 1998. *Trust Within Reason.* Cambridge: Cambridge University Press.

Holmes, Douglas R. 1989. *Cultural Disenchantments: Worker Peasantries in Northeast Italy.* Princeton: Princeton University Press.

Horkheimer, Max. 1994. *Critique of Instrumental Reason.* New York: Continuum Publishing.

Horkheimer, Max, and Theodor W. Adorno. 2002. *Dialectic of Enlightenment.* New York: Continuum Publishing.

Humphrey, Caroline. 2002a. *The Unmaking of Soviet Life: Everyday Economics After Socialism.* Ithaca: Cornell University Press.

Humphrey, Caroline. 2002b. "Rituals of Death as a Context for Understanding Personal Property in Socialist Mongolia." *Journal of the Royal Anthropological Institute* 8, no. 1: 65–87.

Humphrey, Caroline, and Katherine Verdery. 2004. "Introduction: Raising Questions About Property." In *Property in Question,* ed. Katherine Verdery and Caroline Humphrey, pp. 1–25. Oxford: Berg.

Husserl, Edmund. 1970 [1954]. *The Crisis of European Sciences and Transcendental Phenomenology.* Trans. David Carr. Evanston: Northwestern University Press.

Hutchins, Edwin. 1995. *Cognition in the Wild.* Cambridge: MIT Press.

Hutchinson, Sharon E. 1996. *Nuer Dilemmas.* Berkeley: University of California Press.

Iannucci, Lisa. 2000. *The Unofficial Guide to Minding Your Money.* Foster City, CA: IDG Books Worldwide.

Jacobsen, Joyce. 2004. "Economic Man." In *The Social Science Encyclopedia,* 3rd ed. Ed. Adam Kuper and Jessica Kuper, pp. 274–276. London: Routledge.

Jaggar, Alison M. 1983. *Feminist Politics and Human Nature.* Totowa: Rowman & Allanheld.

Jameson, Fredric. 1991. *Postmodernism, or, The Cultural Logic of Late Capitalism.* Durham: Duke University Press.

Kasmir, Sharryn. 1996. *The Myth of Mondragan.* Albany: State University of New York Press.

Keane, Webb. 2001. "Money Is No Object." In *The Empire of Things: Regimes of Value and Material Culture,* ed. Fred R. Myers, pp. 65–89. Santa Fe: School of American Research Press.

Keynes, John Maynard. 1964 [1936]. *The General Theory of Employment, Interest, and Money.* New York: Harcourt, Brace and World.

Klamer, Arjo. 2004. "Cultural Goods are Good for More than Their Economic Value." In *Culture and Public Action,* ed. Vijayendra Rao and Michael Walton, pp. 138–162. Stanford: Stanford University Press.

Klein, Barbro. 1993. "Fences, Fertilizers, and Foreigners: Moral Dilemmas in the Swedish Cultural Landscape." *Journal of Folklore Research* 30, no. 1: 45–59.

Klein, Naomi. 2002. *No Logo.* New York: Picador.

Klitgaard, Robert. 1990. *Tropical Gangsters.* New York: Basic Books.

Knight, Frank H. 1921. *Risk, Uncertainty and Profit.* Chicago: University of Chicago Press.

Kolakowski, Leszek. 1978. *Main Currents of Marxism,* vol. 1. Oxford: Oxford University Press.

Kopcke, Richard W., Jane Seddon Little, and Geoffrey M. B. Tootell. 2004. "How Humans Behave: Implications for Economics and Economic Policy." Online at http.www.bos.frb.org/economic/neer/neer2004/neer04a.pdf.

Landa, Janet Tai. 1994. *Trust, Ethnicity, and Identity.* Ann Arbor: University of Michigan Press.

Lane, Robert E. 1991. *The Market Experience.* Cambridge: Cambridge University Press.

Leach, Edmund R. 1954. *Political Systems of Highland Burma.* London: G. Bell and Sons.

———. 1983. "The Kula: An Alternative View." In *The Kula,* ed. Jerry W. Leach and Edmund Leach, pp. 529–538. Cambridge: Cambridge University Press.

Leach, Jerry W., and Edmund Leach. 1983. *The Kula: New Perspectives on Massim Exchange.* Cambridge: Cambridge University Press.

Leacock, Eleanor. 1954. "The Montagnais 'Hunting Territory' and The Fur Trade." *American Anthropological Association,* memoir no. 78, vol. 56: 5.

Lemon, Alaina. 1998. "'Your Eyes are Green Like Dollars': Counterfeit Cash, National Substance, and Currency Apartheid in 1990s Russia." *Cultural Anthropology* 13, no. 1: 22–55.

Lessig, Lawrence. 2001. *The Future of Ideas: The Fate of the Commons in a Connected World.* New York: Random House.

Lévi-Strauss, Claude. 1969 [1949]. *The Elementary Structures of Kinship.* London: Eyre & Spottiswoode.

Liep, John. 1983. "Ranked Exchange in Yela (Rossel Island)." In *The Kula*, ed. Jerry W. Leach and Edmund Leach, pp. 503-525. Cambridge: Cambridge University Press.

Linder, Steffan. 1970. *The Harried Leisure Class*. New York: Columbia University Press.

Locke, John. 1960 [1690]. *Two Treatises of Government*. Ed. Peter Laslett. Cambridge: Cambridge University Press.

———. 1975 [1690]. *An Essay Concerning Human Understanding*. Ed. P. H. Nidditch. Oxford: Clarendon Press.

Löfving, Staffan, ed. 2005. *Peopled Economies: Conversations with Stephen Gudeman*. Uppsala: Interface.

Lohmann, Larry. 2006. "Carbon Trading." *Development Dialogue*, vol. 48. Uppsala: The Dag Hammarskjöld Centre.

Lorenz, Edward H. 2000. "Neither Friends nor Strangers: Informal Networks of Subcontracting in French Industry." In *Trust: Making and Breaking Cooperative Relations*, ed. Diego Gambetta, pp. 194–210. Electronic edition, http://www.sociology.ox.ac.uk/papers/lorenz 194-210.pdf.

Lucas,Robert E., Jr. 2002. *Lectures on Economic Growth*. Cambridge: Harvard University Press.

Lukács, Georg. 1971 [1922]. *History and Class Consciousness*. London: Merlin Press.

Macpherson, C. B. 1962. *The Political Theory of Possessive Individualism*. Oxford: Clarendon Press.

———. 1979. "Property as Means or End." In *Theories of Property: Aristotle to the Present*, ed. Anthony Parel and Thomas Flanagan, pp. 3–9. Waterloo, Canada: Wilfrid Laurier University Press.

McCay, Bonnie J., and James M. Acheson, eds. 1987. *The Question of the Commons*. Tucson: University of Arizona Press.

McLean, John. 1932. "Notes of a Twenty-five Years' Service in the Hudson's Bay Territory." Ed. William S. Wallace. *Publications of the Champlain Society*, vol. 29, Toronto.

McMurtry, John. 2001. "The Life-Ground, the Civil Commons and the Corporate Male Gang." *Canadian Journal of Development Studies* 22, Special Issue: 819–854.

Malinowski, Bronislaw. 1961 [1922]. *Argonauts of the Western Pacific*. New York: Dutton.

———. 1978 [1935]. *Coral Gardens and Their Magic*. New York: Dover Publications.

Marglin, Stephen A. 1990. "Losing Touch: The Cultural Conditions of Worker Accommodation and Resistance." In *Dominating Knowledge*, ed. Frédérique Apffel Marglin and Stephen A. Marglin, pp. 216–282. Oxford: Clarendon Press.

———. 1996. "Farmers, Seedsmen, and Scientists: Systems of Agriculture and Systems of Knowledge." In *Decolonizing Knowledge*, ed. Frédérique Apffel Marglin and Stephen A. Marglin, pp. 185–248. Oxford: Clarendon Press.

———. 2007. *The Dismal Science*. Cambridge: Harvard University Press.

Marks, S. A. 1976. *Large Mammals and a Brave People*. Seattle: University of Washington Press.

Markus, Hazel, and Shinobu Kitayama. 1998. "The Cultural Psychology of Personality." *Journal of Cross-cultural Psychology* 29, no. 1: 63–87.

———. 2003. "Models of Agency: Sociocultural Diversity in the Construction of Action." In *Cross-Cultural Differences in Perspectives on the Self,* ed. Virginia Murphy-Berman and John Berman. Nebraska Symposium on Motivation 49: 18–74.

Markus, Hazel, Patricia Mullally, and Shinobu Kitayama. 1997. "Selfways: Diversity in Modes of Cultural Participation." In *The Conceptual Self in Context,* ed. Ulric Neisser and David Jopling, pp. 13–61. New York: Cambridge.

Marx, Karl. 1995 [1865]. *The Poverty of Philosophy.* New York: Prometheus Books.

———. 1988. *Economic and Philosophic Manuscripts of 1844.* New York: Prometheus Books.

———. 1973 [1857–8]. *Grundrisse.* New York: Vintage Books.

———. 1967 (1867). *Capital* vol. 1. New York: International Publishers.

Maurer, Bill. 2002. "Anthropological and Accounting Knowledge in Islamic Banking and Finance: Rethinking Critical Accounts." *J. Roy. Anthrop. Inst.* (N.S.) 8: 645–667.

———. 2005. *Mutual Life, Limited.* Princeton: Princeton University Press.

Mauss, Marcel. 1979. *Sociology and Psychology: Essays.* Trans. Ben Brewster. London: Routledge & Kegan Paul.

Mayer, Enrique. 2002. *The Articulated Peasant: Household Economies in the Andes.* Boulder: Westview Press.

———. 2005. "Households and their markets in the Andes." In *A Handbook of Economic Anthropology,* ed. James G. Carrier, pp. 405–422. Cheltenham: Edward Elgar.

Meek, Ronald L. 1973. *Studies in the Labour Theory of Value,* 2nd ed. London: Lawrence and Wishart.

Melitz, Jacques. 1974. *Primitive and Modern Money.* Reading, MA: Addison-Wesley.

Middleton, John. 2003. "Merchants: An Essay in Historical Ethnography." *Journal of the Royal Anthropological Institute* (N.S.) 9, no. 3: 509–526.

Miller, Daniel. 1998. *A Theory of Shopping.* New York: Cornell University Press.

Mintz, Sidney W. 1961. "*Pratik*: Haitian Personal Economic Relationships." In *Symposium: Patterns of Land Utilization and Other Papers,* ed. Viola E. Garfield. pp. 54–63. Seattle: American Ethnological Society.

———. 1985. *Sweetness and Power.* New York: Viking Penguin.

Mirabeau, Marquis de, and Quesnay, Francois. 1973 [1763]. *Precursors of Adam Smith.* Ed. R. L. Meek, pp. 104–13. London: Dent.

Muldrew, Craig. 1993. "Interpreting the Market: The Ethics of Credit and Community Relations in Early Modern England." *Social History* 18, no. 2: 163–183.

———. 1998. *The Economy of Obligation: The Culture of Credit and Social Relations in Early Modern England.* New York: St. Martin's Press.

Nas, Peter J. M. 2002. "Masterpieces of Oral and Intangible Culture." *Current Anthropology* 43, no. 1: 139–148.

Neusner, Jacob. 1990. *The Economics of the Mishnah.* Chicago: University of Chicago Press.

Niezen, Ronald. 1998. *Defending the Land.* Needham Heights: Allyn and Bacon.

North, Douglass C. 2005. *Understanding the Process of Economic Change.* Princeton: Princeton University Press.

Oliven, Ruben George. 1998. "Looking at Money in America." *Critique of Anthropology* 18, no. 1: 35–59.

Oschinsky, Dorothea. 1971. *Walter of Henley.* Clarendon Press: Oxford.

Ostrom, Elinor. 1990. *Governing the Commons: The Evolution of Institutions for Collective Action.* Cambridge: Cambridge University Press.

Parry, J., and M. Bloch, eds. 1989. *Money and the Morality of Exchange.* Cambridge: Cambridge University Press.

Parsons, Talcott. 1966. *Societies: Evolutionary and Comparative Perspectives.* Englewood Cliffs: Prentice-Hall.

Parsons, Talcott, and Neil J. Smelser. 1956. *Economy and Society.* New York: The Free Press.

Peloso, Vincent C. 1999. *Peasants on Plantations.* Durham: Duke University Press.

Perkins, John. 2004. *Confessions of an Economic Hit Man.* New York: Penguin.

Pietz, William. 1985. "The Problem of the Fetish, I." *Res* 9: 5–17.

Piketty, Thomas, and Emmanuel Saez. 2006. "The Evolution of Top Incomes: A Historical and International Perspective." Working Paper 11955, National Bureau of Research. Online at http://www.nber.org/papers/w11955.

Polanyi, Karl. 1944. *The Great Transformation.* New York: Farrar and Reinhart.

———. 1968. *Primitive, Archaic, and Modern Economies.* Ed. George Dalton. Garden City: Anchor Books.

Popkin, Samuel L. 1979. *The Rational Peasant.* Berkeley: University of California Press.

Porter, Theodore. 1995. *Trust in Numbers: the Pursuit of Objectivity in Science and Public Life.* Princeton: Princeton University Press.

Povinelli, E. A. 2001. "Radical Worlds: The Anthropology of Incommensurability and Inconceivability. *Annual Reviews of Anthropology* 30: 319–334.

Putnam, Robert D. 2000. *Bowling Alone: The Collapse and Revival of American Community.* New York: Simon and Schuster.

Quesnay, François. 1972 [1758–59]. *Tableau Économique.* Trans. and ed. Marguerite Kucynski and Ronald L. Meek. London: Macmillan.

Raddon, Mary-Beth. 2003. *Community and Money: Men and Women Making Change.* Montreal: Black Rose Press.

Radin, Margaret Jane. 1996. *Contested Commodities.* Cambridge: Harvard University Press.

Raz, Joseph. 1986. *The Morality of Freedom.* Oxford: Clarendon Press.

Ricardo, David. 1951 [1815]. *The Works and Correspondence of David Ricardo,* vol. 4. Ed. Piero Sraffa. Cambridge: Cambridge University Press.

———. 1951 [1817]. *On the Principles of Political Economy and Taxation,* ed. Piero Sraffa. Cambridge: Cambridge University Press.

Richards, Audrey. 1939. *Land, Labour and Diet in Northern Rhodesia.* London: Oxford University Press.

Robbins, Joel. 1999. "This Is Our Money: Modernism, Regionalism, and Dual Currencies in Urapmin." In *Money and Modernity: State and Local Currencies in Melanesia,* ed. David Akin and Joel Robbins, pp. 82–102. Pittsburgh: University of Pittsburgh Press.

Robbins, Lionel. 1969 [1935]. *An Essay on the Nature and Significance of Economic Science*. 2nd ed. London: Macmillan.

Romer, Paul M. 1990. "Endogenous Technological Change." *The Journal of Political Economy* 98, no. 5: S71–S102.

Rose, Carol M. 1994. *Property and Persuasion: Essays on the History, Theory, and Rhetoric of Ownership*. Boulder: Westview Press.

Roseberry, William. 1996. "The Rise of Yuppie Coffees and the Reimagination of Class in the United States." *American Anthropologist* 98, no. 4: 762–775.

Rostow, Walt Whitman. 1960. *The Stages of Economic Growth*. Cambridge: Cambridge University Press.

Rousseau, Jean Jacques. 1913 [1762]. *The Social Contract*. Trans G. D. H. Cole. London: J. M. Dent and Sons Ltd.

Ruttan, Vernon W. 2003. *Social Science Knowledge and Economic Development*. Ann Arbor: University of Michigan Press.

Sahlins, Marshall. 1972. *Stone Age Economics*. Chicago: Aldine.

———. 1976. *Culture and Practical Reason*. Chicago: University of Chicago Press.

Salisbury, Richard F. 1962. "Early Stages of Economic Development in New Guinea." *Journal of the Polynesian Society* 71, no. 3: 328–339.

———. 1966. "Politics and Shell-Money Finance in New Britain." In *Political Anthropology*, ed. Marc J. Swartz, Victor W. Turner, and Arthur Tuden, pp. 113–128. Chicago: Aldine.

———. 1970. *Vunamami: Economic Transformation in a Traditional Society*. Berkeley: University of California Press.

Saxenian, Annalee. 1994. *Regional Advantage: Culture and Competition in Silicon Valley and Route 128*. Cambridge: Harvard University Press.

Scaff, Lawrence A. 1989. *Fleeing the Iron Cage: Culture, Politics, and Modernity in the Thought of Max Weber*. Berkeley: University of California Press.

Schumpeter, Joseph A. 1934 [1926]. *The Theory of Economic Development*. Cambridge: Harvard University Press.

Schwartz, Barry. 2004. *The Paradox of Choice: Why More is Less*. New York: HarperCollins Publishers.

Scoditti, Giancarlo M., and Jerry W. Leach. 1984. "Kula on Kitava." In *The Kula*, ed. Jerry W. Leach and Edmund Leach, pp. 249–273. Cambridge: Cambridge University Press.

Scott, James C. 1976. *The Moral Economy of the Peasant*. New Haven: Yale University Press.

Sen, Amartya K. 1977. "Rational Fools: A Critique of the Behavioral Foundations of Economic Theory. *Philosophy and Public Affairs* 6, no. 4: 317–344.

———. 2002. *Rationality and Freedom*. Cambridge: Harvard University Press.

Shipton, Parker. 1989. *Bitter Money: Cultural Economy and Some African Meanings of Forbidden Commodities*. American Ethnological Society Monograph Series No. 1. Washington, D.C.: American Anthropological Association.

Shubik, Martin. 2000. "The Theory of Money." Santa Fe Working Paper. Online at http://www.santafe.edu/sfi/publications/Working-Papers/00-03-21. pp. 1–32.

Sillitoe, Paul. 2006. "Why Spheres of Exchange?" *Ethnology* 45, no. 1: 1–23.

Simmel, Georg. 1971. *On Individuality and Social Forms*. Chicago: University of Chicago.

———. 1990. *The Philosophy of Money.* 2nd Ed. David Frisby. Trans. Tom Bottomore and David Frisby. London: Routledge.

———. 1997. *Simmel on Culture.* Ed. David Frisby and Mike Featherstone. London: SAGE Publications.

Smith, Adam. 1976 [1759]. *The Theory of Moral Sentiments.* Indianapolis: Liberty Classics.

———. 1976 [1776]. *The Wealth of Nations.* Chicago: University of Chicago Press.

Sneath, David. 2004. "Property Regimes and Sociotechnical Systems: Rights over Land in Mongolia's 'Age of the Market.'" In *Property in Question,* ed. Katherine Verdery and Caroline Humphrey, pp. 161–182. Oxford: Berg.

Solow, Robert M. 1956. "A Contribution to the Theory of Economic Growth." *The Quarterly Journal of Economics* 70, no. 1: 65–94.

———. 1997. *Learning From "Learning By Doing."* Stanford: Stanford University Press.

Sombart, Werner. 1967 [1915]. *The Quintessence of Capitalism.* Trans. and ed. M. Epstein. New York: Howard Fertig.

Speck, Frank G. 1926. "Land Ownership Among Hunting People in Primitive America and the World's Marginal Areas." *Twenty-second International Congress of Americanists (Rome)* 2: 323–332.

Speth, James Gustave. 2004. *Red Sky at Morning.* New Haven: Yale University Press.

Stewart, Pamela J., and Strathern, Andrew. 2002. "Transformations of Monetary Symbols in the Highlands of Papua New Guinea." *L'Homme* 162 *Questions of Money:* 137–156.

Strathern, Andrew, and Pamela J. Stewart. 1999. "Objects, Relationships, and Meanings." In *Money and Modernity: State and Local Currencies in Melanesia,* ed. David Akin and Joel Robbins, pp. 164–191. Pittsburgh: University of Pittsburgh Press.

Strathern, Marilyn. 1988. *The Gender of the Gift: Problems with Women and Problems with Society in Melanesia.* Berkeley: University of California Press.

———. 1993. "Entangled Objects: Detached Metaphors." *Social Analysis* 34, no. 4: 88–98.

———. 1999. *Property, Substance and Effect: Anthropological Essays on Persons and Things.* London: The Athlone Press.

Stevenson, H. N. C. 1937. "Feasting and Meat Division Among the Zahau Chins of Burma." *Journal of the Royal Anthropological Institute* 65:15–32.

Stigler, George J., and Gary S. Becker. 1977. "De Gustibus Non Est Disputandum." *The American Economic Review* 67, no. 2: 76–90.

Stiglitz, Joseph E. 1993. *Economics.* New York: W.W. Norton & Co.

———. 1997. *Principles of Micro-Economics.* 2nd ed. New York: W.W. Norton & Co.

———. 2002. *Globalization and Its Discontents.* New York: W.W. Norton & Co.

Swedberg, Richard. In press. "The Concept of Interest as Rhetoric – or as a Useful Social Science Concept?" In *Economic Persuasions,* ed. Stephen Gudeman. New York: Berghahn.

Taleb, Nassim Nicholas. 2005. *Fooled By Randomness.* 2nd ed. New York: Random House.

Tambiah, Stanley J. 1990. *Magic, Science, Religion, and the Scope of Rationality.* Cambridge: Cambridge University Press.

Taussig, Michael. 1980. *The Devil and Commodity Fetishism in South America.* Chapel Hill: University of North Carolina Press.

Thelen, Tatjana. 2005. *The Loss of Trust: Changing Social Relations in the Workplace in Eastern Germany.* Halle/Saale: Max Planck Institute for Social Anthropology. Online at http://www.eth.mpg.de.

Therborn, Göran. 2003. "Entangled Modernities," *European Journal of Social Theory* 6, no. 3: 293–305.

Thune, Carl Eugene. 1984. "Kula Traders and Lineage Members: The Structure of Village and Kula Exchange on Normanby Island." In *The Kula,* ed. Jerry W. Leach and Edmund Leach, pp. 345–368. Cambridge: Cambridge University Press.

Thurnwald, Richard C. 1934. "Pigs and Currency in Buin: Observations About Primitive Standards of Value and Economics." *Oceania* 5, no. 2: 119–141.

Tilly, Charles. 2001. "Relational Origins of Inequality." *Anthropological Theory* 1, no. 3: 355–372.

Toobin, Jeffrey. 2003. "End Run at Enron: Why The Country's Most Notorious Executives May Never Face Criminal Charges." *The New Yorker* October 27th: 48–55.

Toulmin, Stephen. 1992 [1990]. *Cosmopolis.* Chicago: University of Chicago Press.

———. 2001. *Return to Reason.* Cambridge: Harvard University Press.

Trawick, Paul. 2001. "The Moral Economy of Water: Equity and Antiquity in the Andean Commons." *American Anthropologist* 103, no. 2: 361–379.

Turgot, A. R. J. 1898 [1770]. *Reflections on the Formation and the Distribution of Riches.* New York: Macmillan and Co.

United Nations Human Development Report 2005. Online at http://hdr.undp.org/reports/global/2005/

Veblen, Thorstein. 1914. *The Instinct of Workmanship: and the State of the Industrial arts.* New York: Macmillan.

———. 1983 [1921]. *The Engineers and the Price System.* New Brunswick: Transaction Books.

Vel, Jacqueline. 1994. *The Uma-Economy.* Wageningen, The Netherlands: Thesis, Wageningen University.

Vélez-Ibañez, Carlos G. 1983. *Bonds of Mutual Trust.* New Brunswick: Rutgers University Press.

Verdery, Katherine. 2003. *The Vanishing Hectare.* Ithaca: Cornell University Press.

Vico, Giambattista. 1970 [1744]. *The New Science of Giambattista Vico.* Trans. Thomas Goddard Bergin and Max Harold Fisch. Ithaca: Cornell University Press.

Vitebsky, Piers. 2001. "Withdrawing from the Land: Social and Spiritual Crisis in the Indigenous Russian Arctic." In *Postsocialism: Ideals, Ideologies and Practices in Eurasia,* ed. C. M. Hann, pp. 180–195. London: Routledge.

———. 2005. *Reindeer People.* London: Harper.

Vohs, Kathleen D. et al. 2006. "The Psychological Consequences of Money." *Science* 314, no. 5802: 1154–1156.

Von Mises, Ludwig. 1976 [1933]. *Epistemological Problems of Economics.* Trans George Reisman. New York: New York University Press.

Warsh, David. 2006. *Knowledge and the Wealth of Nations.* New York: W.W. Norton & Co.

Weber, Max. 1958 [1904–05]. *The Protestant Ethic and the Spirit of Capitalism.* Trans. Talcott Parsons. New York: Charles Scribner's Sons.

———. 1976 [1909]. *The Agrarian Sociology of Ancient Civilizations.* Trans. R. I. Frank. London: NLB.

———. 1978 [1956]. *Economy and Society.* Ed. Guenther Roth and Claus Wittich. Trans. Ephraim Fischoff et al. Berkeley: University of California Press.

———. 1961 [1923]. *General Economic History.* Trans. Frank H. Knight. New York: Collier Books.

Weiner, Annette. 1976. *Women of Value, Men of Renown.* Austin: University of Texas Press.

White, Harrison C. 2002. *Markets from Networks: Socioeconomic Models of Production.* Princeton: Princeton University Press.

Whitehead, Alfred North. 1925. *Science and the Modern World.* New York: Macmillan and Co.

Whyte, William F. 1999. "The Mondragan Cooperatives in 1976 and 1998." *Industrial and Labor Relations Review* 52, no. 3: 478–481.

Whyte, William F., and Kathleen King Whyte. 1988. *Making Mondragan.* Ithaca: Industrial and Labor Relations Press.

Wittrock, Björn. 2000. "Modernity: One, None, or Many? European Origins and Modernity as a Global Condition." *Multiple Modernities,* Dædalus 129, no. 1: 31–60.

World Development Report 2000/2001. 2001. Ed. The World Bank. New York: Oxford.

Worsley, Peter M. 1956. "The Kinship System of the Tallensi: A Revaluation." *Journal of the Royal Anthropological Institute* 86, no. 1: 37–75.

Zaloom, Caitlin. 2003. "Ambiguous Numbers: Trading Technologies and Interpretation in Financial Markets. *American Ethnologist* 30, no. 2: 258–272.

———. 2006. *Out of the Pits.* Chicago: University of Chicago Press.

Zelizer, Viviana A. 1994. *The Social Meaning of Money.* New York: Basic Books.

———. 1999. "Multiple Markets: Multiple Cultures." In *Diversity and Its Discontents,* ed. Neil J. Smelser and Jeffrey C. Alexander, pp. 193–212. Princeton: Princeton University Press.

———. 2005. *The Purchase of Intimacy.* Princeton: Princeton University Press.

Zizek, Slavoj. 2000. "Da Capo Senza Fine." In *Contingency, Hegemony, Universality,* ed. Judith Butler, Ernesto Laclau, and Slavoj Zizek, pp. 213–262. London: Verso.

❧ INDEX